MW01251502

the best of ontario

This book is dedicated to
Ted, Louise, and Audrey Lehman,
The best neighbors I ever had.

"Life's too short to know bad people."
Ted Lehman

The Best of Ontario

BY MARY MACPHERSON

For Sheila

Mary MacPherson

broadview press • 1994

Canadian Cataloguing in Publication Data

MacPherson, Mary
The best of Ontario

Includes index.
ISBN 1-55111-052-0
1. Ontario - Guidebooks. I. Title
FC3057.M33 1994   917.1304'4   C94-931609-1
F1057.M3 1994

©1994 broadview press Ltd.

Broadview Press
Post Office Box 1243, Peterborough, Ontario, Canada, K9J 7H5

in the United States of America
3576 California Road, Orchard Park, NY 14127

in the United Kingdom
c/o Drake Marketing, Saint Fagan's Road, Fairwater, Cardiff, CF53AE

Broadview Press gratefully acknowledges the support of the Canada Council,
the Ontario Arts Council, the Ontario Publishing Centre,
and the Ministry of National Heritage.

Cover photographs by Olga Tracy.

PRINTED IN CANADA
5 4 3 2 1 94 95 96

Contents

Foreword

About ten years ago I read that Vermont makes the best maple syrup in the world. I was sceptical, knowing about the tradition of sugaring in Ontario and Quebec. I wondered if perhaps the author of the book hadn't heard of either province. But then I realized it really didn't matter who made the best maple syrup. Americans believed that they did and were willing to say so. This struck me as one of the fundamental differences between Americans and Canadians and it sewed the seeds for this book. I was curious to find out what it is that we do best in Ontario.

The Best of Ontario is my own discovery of the province. I was the perfect candidate for the job: being a typical Ontarian I was relatively unfamiliar and poorly travelled in my own back yard.

I set out without bias or parameters, which explains the somewhat eclectic collection of "bests" in the book. And I want to apologize right up front for the "bests" that are missing from these pages. But let me tell you, it wasn't easy finding out what's unique or different about this province, for two reasons. Many people don't want to talk about themselves, and those who do have a hard time doing so. But that should come as no surprise given our "no-show in the annals of maple syrup.

This book is a start. It's proof that there are many talented people with ingenuity and an entrepreneurial spirit doing amazing things in this exceptional province. I'm sure this is only the tip of the iceberg.

For those who participated , who put up with my barrage of questions, phone calls, endless correspondence, I say thank you. You are the best!

For those who were skeptical, who didn't answer my phone calls or my letters, who couldn't really get to the meat of the matter, don't worry. There's always the next edition and you can drop me a line care of the publisher.

As the provincial license plate says, Ontario is yours to discover. The Best of Ontario is my invitation to do so. When more of us explore this beautiful land, we will all benefit in some way, grand or small.

Mary MacPherson
Peterborough, 1994

P.S. The Potters of Sandy Flat Bush near Warkworth won the maple syrup World Championship at the Royal Winter Fair in November of 1993. The runner up was the steed family of Indian River's Sugar Valley Farm.

Yes, they are both in Ontario!

Daniel Kramer's Corn Dollies

In the tiny town of St. Jacobs, Daniel Kramer carries on a tradition that began some 5,000 years ago in the countries of Greece, Egypt, and North Africa. He makes corn dollies.

The name is a misnomer. Corn dollies are not made from corn, but from wheat. And they don't resemble dolls. Wheat stocks are braided and woven into decorative ornaments in traditional and original designs that range in size from a few millimeters up to half a meter. The myriad of shapes include fans, lanterns, horseshoes, quilt patches, and baskets. They are extremely popular among collectors who add them to their decor from designer kitchens to cottages.

Corn dollies were originally made by the peasants of agrarian societies. At harvest time, the last standing grain, which was believed to hold the spirit of the field, was formed into a sheaf or a crude figure to offer thanks for the bounty. It was kept in the home over the winter and sewn or mulched back into the fields in spring. Wherever grain was grown the corn dolly became a fetish, an object of ritual. "Corn" became the generic term for the many grains of wheat, barley, oats, rye, and maize from which the dolly was made.

Designs, techniques and customs varied from country to country. For example, spiral plaiting was first done in Greece, then made its way to the British Isles and other areas of Europe. African fringes combine plaiting and weaving; fan shapes are typical of Wales and bordering English counties.

When agriculture became mechanized, the tradition of corn dollies almost died out. A change in wheat varieties was also significant, for most techniques require a long, hollow straw not extensively cultivated. In the late 1950s and early 1960s the Women's Institute in England became aware that the craft was being lost, and set out to catalogue the many techniques and designs. They assigned geographic names like Yorkshire, Essex, and Suffolk to indicate the place of origin of each design. The work of the Institute helped revive the art form.

Corn dollies are a relatively new craft in North America. Doris Johnson, a native of Kansas, is credited with bringing the work to the United States and spreading its popularity in the early 1970s. It was in Kansas that the term "wheat weaving" was coined, although it is not a name used by purists.

Daniel Kramer learned the art of corn dollies from a cousin in Germany who learned it from an Englishman. Prior to harvest time (in Southern Ontario that's about the second or third week of July) he keeps a close watch on the local wheat fields. He cuts his crop when the heads are standing straight and the straw is flexible with a high moisture content. Using a hand sickle, he crops the wheat close to the ground, then gathers it and binds it with twine, in small bundles.

The wheat must be dried in a well-ventilated area and turned inside to out several times a day. Once dry, it is cleaned by making a cut above the first node on the straw and stripping the outer husk. Care is taken to store the wheat away from mice and birds.

Before working the straw, it is soaked in cool to warm water for several hours and kept wrapped in a towel while the design is being made. The finished ornament is then dried for 24 hours.

From one sheaf of wheat, about 30 centimeters (12 inches) in diameter, Kramer will make between 25 and 35 dollies. Depending upon the design, a dolly can take anywhere from 10 minutes to two hours to make.

Kramer's designs and the precision of his work have won him a number of awards at craft and folk art shows. He makes corn dollies on a full-time basis and sells them from his studio-shop.

THE TOP DRAWER
The Village Silos,
10 King St.,
P.O. Box 314,
St. Jacobs, Ont. N0B 2N0
TEL 519-664-2421

Meggan Moriarty's Doll House

In the world of dolls and doll collecting, the most prestigious event is the World Showcase of Dolls, an international convention hosted by Disney World in Orlando. The first of these annual shows was held in 1989. Twenty-five doll artisans from around the world were asked to create a limited edition doll to commemorate the event. The only doll artist selected from Canada was Heather Moriarty, known as Meggan to her friends. She's the creative talent of Meggan's Doll House, Canada's foremost porcelain dollmaker.

Meggan made her first doll in 1971. It was from a reproduction mold called Crying Bye-Lo Baby, from the period circa 1924. For the next fifteen years, she made and sold reproduction antique dolls and taught reproduction dollmaking. Although the dolls were not originals, they helped Meggan develop the distinctive style that would become her trademark. Rather than painting the faces in the traditional way, with strong colors, she worked the faces in softer pastel tones. Today, connoisseurs of porcelain dolls immediately recognize Meggan's work by the quality of her delicate faces.

In 1986 Meggan began to experiment, sculpting original dolls of her own creation. Currently Meggan's Doll House produces more than 40 different porcelain dolls and roughly 25 percent are originals. The 36- to 53-centimeter (14- to 21-inch) dolls have porcelain bodies. Many of the more recent ones have jointed bodies with as many as 16 separate porcelain pieces. All are signed and dated, and bear the Meggan's Doll House hallmark of quality on the back of the head.

The dolls are also protected by a breakage policy, the only one of its kind in the world of collectible dolls. Meggan keeps the molds of each doll, including the limited editions. If a doll is ever broken, it can be replaced for the owner. Each doll has a name, a registration number and a certificate of authenticity.

Meggan makes up to 3,000 dolls a year. The more complex the design, the fewer she makes.

"Meggan's Collectibles" are produced in unlimited quantities, while "Meggan's Classics" are made in limited editions that range from one to 300 depending upon the doll. "Cherish", for example, created in 1991 for Mother's Day, was a limited edition of forty dolls. It sold out in three weeks. There's also a series called the "Especially Yours Collection." Each doll is a Meggan original, created according to the purchaser's specifications for eye color, hair color and length, and the color of trim to complete the white satin dress. The new owner chooses the name which is engraved on the doll's pendant or bracelet. The doll is officially certified with the selected name and assigned an individual registration number. Like all Meggan's creations, each doll has expressive facial features and lifelike skin tones. The costuming is highly detailed with French seamed, single needle tailoring, satin and lace trim, and accessories to match the character. One of Megan's series is a calendar collection, representing the months of the year. Another recreates nursery rhyme characters.

In spite of the popularity and increased demand for Meggan's heirlooms, she makes the original sculpture and paints each doll. She also designs every costume, selecting all the materials and trims, and makes each prototype. She has trained artisans who work at home on the dolls. Her husband, Jim Moriarty, takes care of marketing, sales, and shipping. Their gingerbread-trimmed Victorian house in Smith's Falls is the doll studio as well as their home.

Meggan's Doll House is strictly a wholesale business. The dolls are sold to retailers who attend the major gift shows held in Toronto each year and are carried by more than 250 stores across Canada. They are also sold in the Canadian Pavilion in Disney World's Epcot Center. Meggan's Doll House is happy to advise individuals of the nearest retailer.

MEGGAN'S DOLL HOUSE

50 Main St. East,
Smith Falls, Ont. K7A lA4
TEL 613-283-2225 9:00 to 5:00
800-563-DOLL

MEGGAN'S TIPS FOR BUYING AN HEIRLOOM PORCELAIN DOLL

- Know who created the original sculpture. Many are made from manufacturers' molds. Often the phrase "designed by" is used. Buyer beware.
- The doll should be the creation of one person from start to finish, from sculpting to clothing.
- A limited edition should refer to the number of dolls made. They should not be limited by time, "produced only until 1990" or by "firing days."
- Ask where the doll was made. It may say that it's "imported European quality." The quality may be European but the doll may have been made in Taiwan and shipped by the hundreds of thousands.
- A doll that is fully porcelain is much more unique and is usually only available from an artist's studio. Dolls with stuffed bodies are very common.

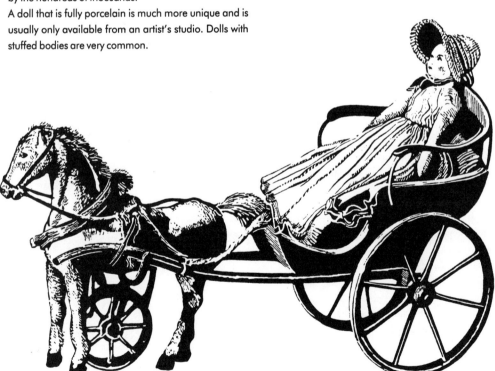

Will Jamieson & the Little Dollhouse Company

Customers of the Little Dollhouse Company run the gamut from Miss Piggy of Muppet fame, who used one of their designs in her Christmas special (the windows had to be made bigger for her!) to TV and print advertisers who photograph models to look life-sized.

Will Jamieson took over the company about 2,000 dollhouses ago, when most dollhouse kits were flimsy imports. This "chief elf and wood-butcher," as he calls himself, invested years of hands-on carpentry to create beautiful, sturdy dollhouses that are a joy to assemble, even for those "who have never built anything more complex than a sandwich." In fact, says Jamieson, "if you can use a hammer you're over-qualified, no nails needed!"

The Little Dollhouse Company makes 12 different designs. They sell directly to the public, with no middlemen to keep the cost down. Among the models are an Ontario house, complete with pine siding and gingerbread trim; Windcrest Manor, a Victorian home that features a mansard roof and French doors to a balcony; and an old-time General Store with plenty of display windows for products.

The Company also supplies miniature furniture and accessories, all on a scale of 2.54 centimeters to .305 meters (one inch to a foot), including wallpapers, flooring, working lights, and oriental carpets, handcrafted figurines, less than 2.54 centimeters (one inch) tall, and complete meals on a plate, smaller than a dime, with knives and forks to suit. For the miniature do-it-yourselfer, they carry miniaturist's tools and supplies.

Those fortunate enough to visit the store, located in Toronto, can browse and smell the sawdust! A very knowledgeable, congenial staff will help with the exact touches to customize a room setting, down to the most minute detail. A special order service searches worldwide to find any item.

Those who can't visit the store will appreciate the illustrated catalog now in its twenty-first edition, the price of which will be deducted from the first order. The Little Dollhouse Company ships worldwide and accepts phone orders with major credit cards.

THE LITTLE DOLLHOUSE COMPANY
617 Mount Pleasant Rd.,
Toronto, Ont. M4S 2M5
TEL 416-489-7180

Timothy Laurin, Glass-blower

There's nothing new about glass-blowing: it's been around for the last 2,000 years. It was the Romans who discovered that a vessel can be formed by inflating a sphere of fluid glass and the Venetians who refined the method. Still, there is something of this ancient magic, captured whenever a glass blower is at work, especially if it's Timothy Laurin, transforming molten glass into elegant pieces of frozen light.

Laurin is a glass-blower, among the best in the field. His perfume bottles, vases, candlesticks, paperweights, lamps, and sculptured pieces have been exhibited across Canada and the United States and are in the prestigious collections of Toronto's Royal Ontario Museum and the Corning Glass Museum in New York. Among the many accolades he has received, he won the top award at the Glass Art Society of America's Conference in 1984 and is often commissioned for his work in addition to selling his pieces in over 70 galleries across the country.

Laurin, a graduate of the Sheridan College School of Crafts and Design where he majored in glass-blowing, taught at the college and received a scholarship to work at the Harbourfront Studios in Toronto. He now resides in his home town of Penetanguishene where he works from a studio he built in 1988. With so few glass-blowers in Canada, there are no suppliers of hot glass equipment so Laurin designed and constructed all his own.

Laurin welcomes visitors to his studio which also functions as a display gallery of his work. Chances are you'll catch the artist in action for a glass-blowers' furnace runs continuously. Set at 315 degrees C (600 F), it takes 24 hours to melt 100 pounds of crushed glass which will keep the artisan busy for three to four days. Laurin uses soda lime glass. It's durable and soft for blowing and takes all colors which are added by melting certain metals. One of Laurin's specialties is adding silver and gold in layers.

TIMOTHY LAURIN
15 Laurier Rd.,
P.O. Box 1593,
Penetanguishene, Ont. L0K 1P0
TEL 705-549-6051

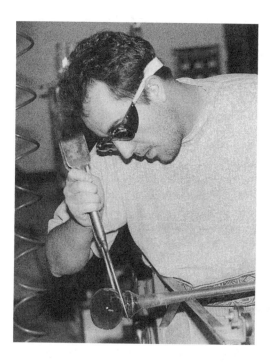

Cliff North's Maple Leaves

The maple leaf has been symbolic of Canada since the 1700s. It was used as the emblem of the first St. Jean Baptiste Society in North America. In 1848 the Toronto literary annual, *The Maple Leaf* called it the chosen emblem of Canada. By 1860 it was incorporated into the badge of the 100th Regiment. Alexander Muir wrote the "Maple Leaf Forever" as the country's Confederation song in 1867 and the coat of arms of both Quebec and Ontario includes a maple leaf. Today it appears on the penny, having appeared on all coins between 1876 and 1901, but it was the proclamation of Canada's new flag in 1965 that established it as Canada's most prominent symbol.

In 1979, Cliff North of Kemptville quit his position in the government computer field to pursue his hobby of one year, on a full time basis. The hobby was sculpting maple leaves. Today these leaves are familiar to tourists and Canadians alike. The leaves are sold in more than 80 shops across Canada, including Eaton's, the Canadiana Shoppe, the CN Tower and Cara Gift Shops.

North's sculptured leaves are patterned after the silver maple with 23 to 27 points. They are cut from solid copper or brass with an oxyacetylene welding torch, and are accurate down to the veining. North has developed his own mix of colors by heating chemicals. Once assembled and colored, the leaves are finished with a tarnish-resistant coating, so their beauty is everlasting. Most artists establish themselves in local and regional craft shows. However North had his own ideas about marketing, staging private displays in shopping malls across Canada. Initially, his two school-age sons helped cut out the leaves and his wife did the packaging.

Since 1986 North has targeted the wholesale market and now has three sales representatives. To keep up with demand, the cutting of the leaves is sub-contracted and an individual from ARC Industries manually lays out the veins. North still does all the assembly welding, coloring, cleaning, and painted finish of each and every leaf.

He also designs sculptures of trees and branches, fashioned after the maple, birch, oak and aspen. Commissions for his work include a piece designed for the Archbishop of Canterbury who visited the Kemptville area, designs for the RCMP Headquarters in Ottawa, Agriculture Canada, and a number of private companies and individuals across Canada.

The leaves are priced between $10 and $50, depending upon the size. A bilingual card is included with the leaves, still gift-boxed by North's wife!

Visitors are welcome at North's shop in his home. He will also mail order the leaves in Canada and the United States by UPS, or be happy to suggest the closest retail store.

HANDCRAFTED METAL SCULPTURES

Cliff North,
278 Gabert Rd.,
R.R. #1, Kemptville, Ont. K0G 1J0
TEL 705-743-9890
FAX 705-743-8353

Mrs. Potter's Wax Works

Ontario possesses a unique collection of wax models of fruits and vegetables that is the envy of museums around the world. Gardeners, artists, historians, anyone who appreciates rare things, and those who enjoy intrigue, will be fascinated by the collection and the story of its creator, Mrs. Elizabeth Potter.

There are 875 replicas formed with the life-like accuracy of a lost art. Among the wax models are 257 varieties of apples, 85 of plums, 43 of pears, 26 of strawberries, 19 of grapes, 16 of raspberries, 11 of currants, 10 of gooseberries and 66 of peaches. Most of these varieties, popular in the early 1900s, are now extinct. This collection represents the only accurate record of these crops, since black-and-white photographs and lithographs are too primitive to convey details.

Furthermore, this is the work of a single individual, of whom very little is known other than that she was an American artist of incredible skill and an expert in the field. In 1893 she placed samples of her work in the Columbian Exposition in Chicago. The official catalogue reads: "Mrs. Stanley Potter, South Haven Michigan, wax models of fruits and vegetables, imitations in wax for nurserymen, seedsmen and museums."

This work attracted the attention of Professor Hutt of the Ontario Agricultural College. He persuaded her to come to Guelph in 1903 where she was given rooms in the old horticultural building, long since demolished. She lived and worked there until 1909, and when she left, she took all her supplies and skills with her. There isn't so much as a scrap of paper that remains to tell of her methods or materials. The College records reveal that the entire cost of the project over six years was $2,893.20, and contain two photographs of the lady. One of these photographs, of Mrs. Potter at work, shows that she used the relatively simple plaster-of-Paris mold technique. It is believed that she brought some molds with her to Guelph, which suggests that

other examples of her work may be found, but as yet nothing has surfaced.

It is Mrs. Potter's skill with color and texture that makes her work museum quality and intriguing. The Canadian Conservation Institute examined a damaged model and revealed that it was made from a blend of beeswax and paraffin finished with a microscopically thin coating. The use of beeswax alone or with other waxes has a long history as a modeling medium. It was used as an aid to sculptors, to make anatomical specimens, and for death masks of important personages. In Victorian times modelling with beeswax was a leisure pastime of middle-class ladies. Examination of Mrs. Potter's peaches reveals she dyed the wax to give them a translucent look. Since oil-based paints do not adhere to wax surfaces, some means of sealing the wax was needed, such as a natural resin like Dammar. It's still unknown how Mrs. Potter combined her colors with the resins to make such an enduring "skin." For more than thirty years, the collection was displayed in the Biology Building at the Ontario Agricultural College and used as a teaching aid there. It was placed in storage in the early 1960s when the College became part of the University of Guelph and remained there for twenty years. In the 1980s, the bulk of the collection, 715 specimens, was placed with the Ontario Agricultural Museum near Milton where a program of cleaning and remounting was started. Only a portion of these models is on display at the museum. Some are made available to those researching the history of fruit and vegetable varieties of North America. The balance of the models, depicting damage by insects and disease, along with the edible fungi group, are still at the University.

ONTARIO AGRICULTURAL MUSEUM
P.O. Box 38,
144 Town Line (Tremaine Road),
Milton, Ont. L9T 2Y3
TEL 905-878-8151 FAX 905-876-4530

Raymond DesChenes' Military Miniatures

Raymond DesChenes of Victoria Harbour is a fine artist and illustrator whose paintings have graced the National Gallery of Canada and galleries in Toronto, Washington, D.C., Philadelphia, and Boston. Yet he has had little time to pursue his art. For the past 47 years, he has devoted most of his days to the field of museology. With a doctorate in fine arts, studies in interior design at New York's Pratt Institute, practical programs in art restoration, and an apprenticeship under the watchful eye of his mentor, John Sloane, DesChenes is a conservator and restorer of original artifacts, par excellence.

DesChenes has clients across Canada, in the States and as far away as Japan. He has worked on the King Tut exhibit which toured North America; restored paintings by Gainsborough, Kreighoff, Forester, and Homer Watson; and helped with the restoration of buildings in Venice. He has refurbished vintage railway locomotives, airplanes, and buildings, and made a pair of gessoed candlesticks for Ontario's first European community, Sainte-Marie Among the Hurons. He feels he contributes more to the world through restoration than creating anew.

However, what DesChenes is best known for is his work in miniatures. He is the only prolific producer of Canadian military miniatures in the world. It's a hobby he began seriously in 1987, a pastime that combines his artistic talent with his great love of history.

The fourth generation of the DesChenes family to live in Victoria Harbour, he comes from a long line of military people, many of whom have served in the British military since 1642. In 1759, one family member served as a captain of militia with Major-General James Wolf in the battle of the Plains of Abraham.

He himself is a member of the world's oldest Order of Chivalry and Knighthood (c 1300), the Descendants of the Knights of the Garter & Friends of St. George's Chapel at Windsor Castle in England. He served under King George VI and Queen Elizabeth II and was presented to both on several occasions. His interest now is strictly in the history as opposed to the practice of war. His outlet — miniature soldiers.

Miniature soldiers presented in scarlet boxes were very much a part of DesChenes' youth, the presents of boyhood Christmases and birthdays. In his youth, he first made miniatures cast from his own plaster molds, filled with lead he melted in the family furnace.

The miniatures he makes today are limited editions, sets of Canadian regiments of many different periods. A basic set consists of 6 figures — an officer and 5 soldiers marching at slope arms. There are also color guards and regimental bands.

Each one is researched down to the most minute detail, then cast in metal in the international scale of 54 millimeters. Painting and detailing a set with special gloss enamels requires an average of 3,800 hand operations. What sets DesChenes' miniatures apart from store models is the accuracy of each piece, complete down to the minutiae of facial expressions and shoelaces. Every set of six is contained in a hand-made, scarlet box with period labels of the Victorian era.

DesChenes' regiments can be found in private collections and regimental museums around the world, including Cairo, Italy, France, Germany, England, Scotland, Canada, and the United States. His work is greatly in demand and collectors must wait patiently

The miniatures are relatively inexpensive — just over $100 a set or $50 individually.

RAYMOND DESCHENES
Balaclava House,
P.O. Box 83,
Victoria Harbour, Ont. L0K 2A0

John Nicholson's Miniature Boats

Greavette, Ditchburn, Duke, Minett-Shields — these are just some of the turn-of-the-century, Muskoka boat builders, whose classic mahogany launches with their streamlined hulls have outlived the companies that made them and still grace the waters of cottage country today.

This era of wooden boating is relived in the hand-crafted, one-of-a-kind, scale model replicas built by John Nicholson in his workshop in Gravenhurst. Among his flotilla are a Greavette Streamliner, a 1937 Minett-Shields, a 24-foot Duke, a Seabird from the Port Carling Boatworks, and the Miss Canada hydroplane.

You might say Nicholson has boat building in his blood. He grew up on the banks of the Muskoka River. His father worked at Minett-Shields in Bracebridge, one uncle at Greavette in Gravenhurst, and another at the Port Carling Boatworks. Nicholson says his work is really a tribute to the artistry of the early boat builders such as they were.

Using a scale of one inch to the foot, he works from pictures, sketches, and actual measurements. He is accurate down to the finest detail of a miniature boat cleat complete with rope. The construction of each craft takes at least a month.

He begins with about 12 board feet of mahogany to create the bottom, the hull and the deck, testing along the way to ensure the craft floats at every stage. It is sanded and varnished to the mirror-like finish that is the trademark of these launches — about ten coats of varnish, the same brand as the original, make the boat waterproof.

Attention to detail comes with the accessories: the cleats, lights, hatch handles, pennant poles, flags, propellers, gear shifts, dashboards, and windshields. Some boats may require as many as 84 pieces. This is not the stuff of local hobby shops. Nicholson constantly creates and improvises, using everything from watch parts to a .410 calibre rifle casing, which with a few alterations, becomes a perfect navigation light for a Ditchburn.

Whatever can't be found or fashioned is carved from soapstone, then cast in lead before being coated with chrome plate or silver solder. Even the flags, often the Union Jack, are painted by hand with a brush that has only four hairs.

What began as a hobby for Nicholson, a carpenter by trade, has become almost a full-time job. Most of the miniatures are commissioned by individuals who want an exact replica of their own boat. Prices are considerably cheaper than the real thing, ranging from $2,000 to $4,000. Nicholson quips, "the only difference between men and boys is the price they pay for their toys."

Commissions may only be made through Michael Cole's Muskoka Tamarack Gallery in Gravenhurst. Some of Nicholson's boats are on display there and he usually has a showing of his antique collection in the month of August.

JOHN NICHOLSON
Muskoka Tamarack Gallery,
155 Church St.,
Gravenhurst, Ont. P1P 1H3
TEL 705-687-3211

Erik Roth, Goldsmith

Ontario might seem like an unlikely place to find a medieval jeweller, but in fact Erik Roth of St. Jacobs is the only medieval jeweller in the western world. He produces the largest selection of Celtic designs of any manufacturer, world-wide, as well as the largest selection of Viking and Heraldic designs, fashioned into pendants, rings, brooches, badges, pins, earrings, or any other item of jewellery that can contain a design.

Roth is as much an historian as he is a goldsmith, for the designs of medieval jewellery are steeped in artistry and symbolism that can be traced back to the Dark Ages, the period between the fall of Rome and the Renaissance. The Celtic cross for example is a Christian cross with a circle superimposed upon it. The circle represents the sun which the Celts worshipped before they accepted Christianity. When they changed religions many of their former symbols remained.

Roth became interested in the Middle Ages when he was a teenager and studied ancient history at university where his passion for Celtic art began. He attended evening classes after graduation, to learn jewellery-making. It was here that he fashioned his first Celtic design.

Roth began his jewellery-making career in New York City, the heart of jewellery manufacturing, but went to Europe for the opportunity to work on hand-made jewellery and to study the ancient designs first-hand. He learned German and Swedish in preparation for his European adventure, then found jobs as a journeyman goldsmith in Sweden, Germany, and Switzerland. He visited national and medieval museums throughout Europe, photographing and sketching historical images.

Back in Canada, Roth worked for large jewellery manufacturers, but on weekends produced his own Celtic designs. Gradually he developed a wholesale clientele and has been self-employed for nine years.

Each design is thoroughly researched and painstakingly crafted in much the same way as the ancient craftsmen worked. Roth designs exclusively in sterling silver and gold; many Celtic shops are gradually replacing poor quality, pewter jewellery with his more authentic designs.

Roth's jewellery is available in stores from Ottawa to Vancouver and in his own St. Jacobs shop where he also stocks items of every sort relating to the Medieval period including musical tapes and CD's, cookbooks, books on military history, brass rubbings, paintings, calligraphy, weapon reproductions, crests, coats of arms, and seals. His expertise in heraldry has recently earned him a commission to craft a baton for the Speaker of the House for the federal parliament in Ottawa.

GOLDEN ARROW GOLDSMITH SHOP

Erik Roth,
The Mill,
10 King St.,
St. Jacobs, Ont. N0B 2N0
TEL 519-664-2722

Edward Fulawka's Steel Guitars

That twangy sound you hear accompanying your favorite country singer is made by a steel guitar. It's often confused with a Hawaiian guitar but differs in that the sound is simply much "twangier." As country singers continue to top the music charts, the people who make their instruments are also making a name for themselves in the country music business.

Edward Fulawka of Penetanguishene makes steel guitars that have attained a level of technical and aesthetic excellence unsurpassed by any others. He makes single-neck and double-neck steel guitars, which resemble a piano in that they have pedals operated by the feet, but also levers controlled by the player's knees.

A double-neck guitar has about 1,250 pieces, each constructed by hand, and requires a high degree of accuracy in its manufacture. Fulawka even winds his own humbuckling pickups which give his guitars their great sound. A double-neck takes about 200 hours to build, a single-neck about 150 hours. Fulawka doesn't have to advertise these instruments which sell for between $1,500 and $3,500. They sell by word of mouth, across Canada and the United States and in countries like Great Britain.

Fulawka didn't always make guitars for a living, but has had a keen interest in music from a young age. His first instrument was a 4-string banjo when he was seven. He played his first wedding at the age of nine in a twelve-hour session that paid him fifty cents. He gave up the banjo to his brother and got a Dobro guitar. Then when he was 19, he left his farm home in the town of Rama, Saskatchewan and found a job in Toronto at Massey Harris.

Fulawka bought a Hawaiian guitar and later a double-neck, 8-string instrument. He was so impressed with the steel guitar player in the Webb Pierce Band that he listened to on the radio, he began to change the strings on his own 8-string to approximate that sound. He began to make custom guitar parts on the kitchen table in his spare time after work. This was the beginning of his custom guitar business.

Fulawka retired in 1978 and moved to Penetanguishene, taking his guitar parts with him. He operates out of his house, repairing guitars and building steel guitars that carry the Fulawka logo.

FULAWKA GUITAR ENTERPRISES
P.O. Box 141,
Penetanguishene, Ont. L0K 1P0
TEL 705-549-3033

Stoermer Bell and Brass Foundry

English writer Thomas Hood said that bells are music's laughter. In Canada, there is one man who knows more about that sound than perhaps any other person: Herwarth Stoermer is the third generation of Stoermers to cast bells, a tradition that began in the family's native Germany more than a thousand years ago.

Nestled in the rural village of Breslau, between Guelph and Kitchener, the Stoermer Bell and Brass Foundry is Canada's only bell foundry. Stoermer bells can be as small as two and a half centimeters (one inch) dinner bell, or as large as the 1,135-kilogram (2,500-pound) church bell in the tower in Dunnville.

The foundry's first bell, made in the 1930s, was for a church in St. Jacobs. The 550-kilogram (1,200-pound) giant at Massey College, in Toronto, is a Stoermer bell. It's run electrically from a clock to strike the hour. Stoermer bells grace the steeples of churches and university towers from Newfoundland to Vancouver. They are used to call meetings to order, are a permanent fixture on fire trucks and locomotives, regulate schools and hotels, and serve on ships that sail around the world. Some bells made in Breslau for Canadian ships during World War II are now lying at the bottom of the Atlantic Ocean.

The foundry also makes a variety of other bells like cowbells, Swiss bells, sleigh bells, and table bells, as well as metal plaques, street signs, and letters. They are all made from a secret alloy used by no other foundry in the world. Brass or bell metal, which is made of copper and tin, is poured when molten into molds made of aluminum and packed with sand. A rough bell is formed when the metal cools, in about 24 hours. It's then finished and polished in the machine shop.

The tone of a bell is determined by its size. The larger a bell, the deeper the tone. Pitch however is a function of the bell's shape or thickness. That means a small bell can sometimes be heard farther away than a large one.

Herwarth Stoermer's grandfather began the business in East Germany in 1886. Carl, Herwarth's father, emigrated to Canada in 1931 and began the business in a basement in Breslau. Herwarth Stoermer learned the craft from his father who died in 1971.

Entire church committees come to the foundry to order church bells. Stoermer welcomes visitors to see all phases of bell making, other than the hazardous area where the casting is done. Bells are for sale at the site.

STOERMER BELL AND BRASS FOUNDRY
285 Woolwich St. South,
P.O. Box 2,
Breslau, Ont. N0B 1M0
TEL 519-648-2281

DRIVE Highway 401 to Road 17, north towards Breslau. The plant and showroom are located on Woolwich Street South.

Keates-Geissler Pipe Organs

Regardless of one's religious affiliation, or lack thereof, it's difficult to enter a church and not be affected by the presence of the church pipe organ. It's not just the music, which some believe is the closest thing to heaven on earth — the distinct melodic voice which soars to the heights of angels and crashes like the crescendos of thunder. It is also the physical presence of the organ that embodies the space of a church the way no other instrument can.

Although we associate organs with churches, they were first used as an instrument of war to lead soldiers into battle. The troops of Alexander the Great marched to the tune of an organ. But the oldest organ in existence, thought to be 2,000 years old, was discovered buried under a church in Budapest. A museum piece, unfortunately it can't be played.

Keates-Geissler Pipe Organs of Guelph builds organs that are meant to be played and that will last for centuries and, one could dare to say, are already museum quality, from the hand-carved console shell to the sterling silver contacting on every key. Owner Dieter Geissler believes that over the centuries the soul of the organ has never changed. He should know: he's been working in this specialized field since he was fourteen, in Germany, where he learned all aspects of the trade from woodworking to voicing.

A voicer has the special skill of matching an organ to the church or cathedral in which it is played, being sure that the tones the instrument creates, by forcing air through the pipes, is acoustically suited to the building. The subtleties of tone are as intricate as shades of color. It's the blending and mixing that gives the organ its voice and its soul, according to Geissler.

Among the company's finest creations is the 8,000 pipe, five keyboard masterpiece, built for the First Baptist Church in Dallas. At the time of its dedication, in 1985, the organ was the fourth largest church organ in North American and now ranks among the top ten in the world. One of the most specialized features in the art of organ building is creating mixture stops—several ranks of pipes per note rather than one pipe per note on the keyboard. The Dallas organ has 22 mixture stops containing 105 ranks of pipes. The 200 draw-knobs and 8,000 pipes which range from 5 millimeters (.18 inches) to 12 meters (39 feet) in length, produce sounds soft enough to accompany a sermon or powerful enough to be heard above a choir of 200 voices. One can scarcely imagine the voicing of an organ of this complexity.

Every organ made by Keates-Geissler is a custom order, whether it's new or a rebuild which incorporates an existing system. The company combines woodworking and electronics skills. Its 18 employees are capable of building an organ with up to five keyboards, fitted with solid state computers, and up to 12,000 pipes ranging from 15 centimeters (6 inches) to 12 meters (39 feet) in sound length. The company also services what they build.

KEATES-GEISSLER PIPE ORGANS LIMITED
40 Regal Rd.,
Guelph, Ont. N1K 1B5
TEL 519-836-5742
FAX 519-836-5747

My Acadian Heritage

Who says you can't re-invent the wheel? Gerald Le-Blanc has done just that, breaking new ground with an old-fashioned product — the spinning wheel. It isn't just any spinning wheel, but an antique replica of his Acadian grandmother's. He calls it the "Rumpelstiltskin," after the fairytale he so often heard as a child while he operated the foot peddle for his *grandmère* who spun flax into yarn that would later be knitted into mitts and socks for loggers near the Nova Scotia town of Corberrie.

Generally, reproduction spinning wheels are decorative or utilitarian, but rarely fulfil both needs. That's what sets LeBlanc's wheel apart: it's a true spinner's wheel, but also a work of art. The Rumpelstiltskin is a Saxony style wheel, also known as the American Colonial wheel. It has a three-legged, slightly sloping saddle; a medium-sized, double-grooved drive wheel; rounded base for the mother-of-all; and a stem and screw tension.

Each wheel is part of a limited edition, made completely by hand. The spokes, maidens, and legs are hand-turned on the lathe and assembled by hand. It takes more than 30 hours of labor and over $200 worth of materials to make one wheel.

Experienced spinners approve of the Rumpelstiltskin's fine 15:1 spinning ratio. LeBlanc consulted with a number of professional spinners to learn the requirements of a good wheel. He was able to retain the old-fashioned appearance while making improvements to the working mechanics. He added bearings and made minor adjustments so the drive wheel runs with increased smoothness. Overall, the wheel is more efficient and easier to operate.

LeBlanc is a cabinet-maker by profession. He learned woodworking skills from his father, Denis LeBlanc, and has done extensive restorations of churches, boardrooms, carriage trade homes, and staircases. He also makes other pieces of fine, replica furniture.

LeBlanc and his partner, Marilyn Carlton, have opened up their Markham workshop for private woodworking workshops for both men and women. There is instruction for both the novice and experienced woodworker. The company is called My Acadian Heritage, a name which recalls LeBlanc's Nova Scotian roots.

MY ACADIAN HERITAGE
27 Wales Ave.,
Markham, Ont. L3P 2C4
TEL 905-472-3952

George Rossiter, Boat Builder

George Rossiter of Ravenna, a community in the highlands of southern Collingwood Township, is trying to save one of the province's endangered species — the rowboat.

This craft had its heyday from the early to mid-1900s. At one time, almost every cottage had a rowboat. It and the canoe were the only means of transportation around the lakes until the invention of the outboard motor when the rowboat all but disappeared.

Lost too is the great rowing tradition this country once knew. Lost to all those but a handful of conditioned athletes who perform at the competitive level. Yet rowing can be a lifelong, family pleasure. Apart from the aesthetic enjoyment one can only derive from negotiating the waterways in a self-propelled craft, rowing provides the body with a balanced exercise, and of course it's high on the list of the environmentally conscious.

George Rossiter is working to revive the spirit of rowing in two ways — in his capacity as a restoration specialist and as a marine architect.

Although Rossiter has the ability to repair any type of wooden craft from sail boats to cabin cruisers, he specializes in rowboat restoration, preferring to work on the crafts made by the old-time boat builders of Peterborough, Lakefield, Port Carling, Gravenhurst, and Midland. He appreciates the craftsmanship of the people who made these boats, men like Walter Dean, in the early 1900s.

Rossiter hand scrapes the old paint and varnish from the cedar-plank masterpieces, uncovering oak keels, ribs, and stem pieces and trim detailed in black walnut. Old copper nails are replaced with new ones. The bow, keel, and stern joints, lifted by years of dirt, are pried open, cleaned, and reseated. For days, Rossiter hand-sands the hull, then re-varnishes it to its former, pristine beauty.

In their day, these rowboats sold for $50, complete with two sets of oars. Today, a 16-foot, wooden rowboat costs about $6,000 with just one set of oars! The restoration alone can be upwards of $3,000.

Recognizing these prohibitive costs, Rossiter has applied his expertise as a marine architect, with a degree in small craft design from the Yacht Design Institute in Maine, and his practical experience working on rowboat restoration since 1974, to come up with an exciting alternative — rowboats designed with the great lines of the classic originals, but constructed with modern materials. The result is an original boat, both affordable and durable.

The "Loudon" is Rossiter's most popular model, named for Professor Loudon, a fellow cottager who rowed until the age of 92. Its design is the culmination of Rossiter's work on roughly 100 rowboat restorations, representing 90 years of rowboat technology by the masters, and 20 years of his own precise scale measurements and flotations testing.

The Loudon is a 5-meter (17-foot) boat, 1 meter (three feet six inches) in beam, and weighs 59 kilograms (130 pounds). The hull is made of fiberglass which is not only light-weight and durable, but comes in a variety of colors, so you can have one made to match your boathouse door, the trim on your cottage, or even your bathing suit for that matter. The Loudon is beautifully appointed with solid teak decks, seats, and gunwales, teak being the most weather resistant, durable wood available. It tracks well and is quite fast. With fully adjustable footstops, it's easily rowed by adults or children (age 8 and up).

The "Whitehall" model, a modified design of a boat traditionally rowed on the eastern seaboard, is larger than the Loudon, built to carry a greater cargo and more people and is excellent in rough, open water. The wineglass transom can be fitted with a small engine. The Loudon retails for about $2,500, the Whitehall for $3,000.

Rossiter also makes two other fiberglass models and has more designs in the works. The Pocket Rowing Skiff is a 4 meter (12-foot) starter boat.

Ideal for young children, it weighs just 30 kilograms (65 pounds). For those keen on competition, he makes a 4 meter (23-foot) training skull.

Rossiter spends roughly a third of his time building his own boats and appreciates a month lead time with each order. He still devotes half his hours to restoring wooden boats and teaches his skills to others. He will also do boat appraisals.

ROSSITER BOATS
R.R. #2,
Ravenna, Ont. N0H 2E0
TEL/FAX 705-445-2908

DRIVE south on Highway 2 from Thornbury, take Grey Road #19 east to the 1st Concession. Drive south to Rossiter Boats on the West Side of the road. Call first.

Walter Walker, Canoe Builder

Walter Walker, last of the master canoe builders, works at his craft in an obscure, crowded workshop in the Otonabee Valley town of Lakefield, the birthplace of the lightweight canoe. When Walker hangs up his varnish-stiff apron for the last time, a unique, century-and-a-half tradition of wooden boat-building will have come full circle, ending where it began.

The cedarstrip canoe, nicknamed the "poor man's yacht" by paddler George Washington Sears in 1885, has always been considered as much a work of art as a boat. Its classic lines and warm-hued natural finish, combined with lightness and water-tight strength make it the Rolls-Royce of canoes.

Walter Walker not only represents the last of a rich, Canadian tradition, but the best. People know his work at forty paces. He surpassed his teachers and his rivals, building what many consider to be the finest canoes known today.

Since 1967, Walker has worked alone. At age 86, he is semi-retired but still capable of building a masterpiece, a task which takes between 120 and 140 hours. This equals the shift of a six-man production crew, back in the days of the Golden Age of the canoe (between 1880 and 1910), when twenty-four companies in and around Peterborough and Lakefield made it the undisputed capital of canoe building.

There are no blueprints for Walker's cedarstrips, or "stripper" canoes, as they're called. They are made from wooden molds and patterns just as the earliest canoes were fashioned.

A mold is the exact replica of a canoe's dimensions, less its "skin." The mold rests upside down on sawhorse supports and must be precisely level, horizontally. The "rib cage" of the craft is built over the mold. No more than a dozen or so molds have survived in the industry, eight of which are in the Peel Marine workshop where Walker worked until recently, before retiring to his home workplace. One such mold, the "Gordon," belonged to Thomas Gordon who established the world's first wooden canoe building shop in the 1850s. Walker also repairs wooden canoes, makes beaver-tail patterned paddles, oars, and rowboats.

An investment in one of Walker's canoes is around $3,500. Expensive, yes, but as affordable a piece of history as one might find. When your child paddles at the regatta, you will be reminded it was a similar craft which so impressed Europeans and Americans at the first, annual American Canoe Association regatta in 1880, when Tom Wallace of Gore's Landing won the one-mile race "while nonchalantly smoking a pipe and pausing to scoop up a drink of water."

When you circle the bay with your spouse, you may recall the bygone era, when many people customized their canoes for water courtship. Designs included a specially molded seat in the stern for the paddling beau, a throne in the bow of the boat which enabled the passenger to face the stern while coyly trailing one hand in the water, and cabinets built beneath the deck for refreshments, with a sliding door that opened to reveal a built-in Victrola.

These were the canoes of the Klondike-bound sourdoughs, the American and Canadian engineers who surveyed the Alaska boundary, a threesome who paddled the Amazon, and one of the greatest canoe trips ever attempted, that of the Tyrell brothers who paddled through thousands of miles of water in the then barren lands west of Hudson Bay.

As you admire your cedarstrip in its berth in the boathouse, you can also take pleasure in the fact that Princess Elizabeth received a Cedar Rib, (made by the Peterborough Canoe Company and worked on by Walter Walker), from Canada, on the occasion of her wedding, as did Prince Charles and Princess Diana from Prime Minister Pierre Trudeau. And Walter Walker made the canoe presented to Prince Andrew in 1978 after his semester at Lakefield College School.

WALTER WALKER
70 Queen St., Lakefield Ont. K0L 2H0

Gerry Cooper, Lure Maker

Harbinger: the name means one who goes before and announces the coming of something; a herald, a forerunner; an avant-courier. It's also the name engraved on one-of-a-kind, hand-made fishing lures. Gerry Cooper of Newmarket is the man behind the name, the Harbinger lure maker, the man with a message of things to come in the world of crackle-backs and wigglers. His plugs are some of the finest action fish catchers to be found anywhere.

"I think that with the enormous growth and interest in bird carving and recently fish carving that it's time for lure making to move forward and produce some really fine lures." And that is exactly what Cooper is doing. About 80 percent of the lures he makes are never used, but mounted on walls like the fishing trophies they are meant to catch. Cooper is flattered, but finds this a real shame. Although lures have historically caught more fishermen than fish, he says Harbinger lures are meant for fishing.

Cooper has been designing and carving artificial bait for more than twenty years. He was hooked on fishing at the age of 10 during a two-week family vacation in Algonquin Park. He recalls his first fishing trip vividly.

"I remember putting on a beetle spinner, casting it out, then watching it vibrate and spin its way back in. This was amazing to me. The whole trip, I became focused on one thing — fishing. The thought of catching a fish on something fake became the world to me. That a piece of metal could fool a living creature, was beyond my comprehension."

All of Cooper's ideas, designs, and methods are completely original, the result of his study of the subject from the first bone hooks to the evolution of wooden lures, plus years of trial and error. When the self-proclaimed "lure fanatic" isn't carving lures or fishing, he's thinking about lures. Each new bait begins with an idea that's been germinating in his mind for some time. As the idea grows, he sketches and refines his vision. The final drawing reflects not only the development of his idea, but what he thinks about the species he's aiming to catch. For muskie, he makes monster lures, 40 to 45 centimeters (15 to 17 inches) long. He also makes bait for pike and bass.

Each lure is made from top-grade basswood or cedar, with strong brass wire. Hand-painted eyes are those taxidermists use and the bodies are painted with an air brush. The finished lure is coated with polymer, not varnish or lacquer. It's a two-part system of epoxy and resin, a curing agent that begins to harden within 10 minutes of use. One coat is equal to 50 coats of varnish. Each lure is numbered and signed by Cooper and the brass lip is engraved, "Harbinger."

Recently Cooper has started to produce a line of identical lures — the Harbinger Pike, a 40 cm (15-inch), deep-diving, trolling lure; the Slim Pike, a 40 cm (15-inch) shallow-diving, trolling lure; a Crank Bait; and a Jerk Bait for casting. Like his one-of-a-kinds, these are Cooper's original designs and completely made by hand.

"I think of my lures, and all lures for that matter, as a sort of folk art. All the different varieties and colors, the ways they are invented, the home-grown feeling they give off, especially antique lures, just amaze me."

HARBINGER LURES
Gerry Cooper,
24 Walter Ave.,
Newmarket, Ont. L3Y 2T3
TEL 905-853-0338

Advanced Taxidermy & Wildlife Design

Taxidermy is an ancient custom that has its origins in the preservation of skins, horns, and skulls as hunting trophies. In the eighteenth century, the introduction of chemical poisons to protect skins and feathers from insects led to the accumulation of large collections of birds and mammals by royalty, and private collectors who used them for parlor ornaments and trophies of the chase.

Today there are laws to prohibit animals from being stuffed, other than by licensed institutions like museums, which preserve them for educational purposes. Only those animals, including birds, which can be legally hunted may be preserved.

Sports fishing remains one of the last areas of taxidermy still available to the average individual. However, as angling increases in popularity, large trophy fish are harder to come by. Current trends in conservation, especially catch-and-release fishing, have created the need for making replica fish mounts. This is an art form new to taxidermy but embraced by anglers. They know large fish are the best genetic source for future generations of large fish. Releasing a fish to go and spawn more fish is good conservation. It also gives someone else the thrill of catching a big one.

Another reason replica fish mounts are gaining in popularity is due to the work of two outstanding artists, James McGregor and Sean Galea of Advanced Taxidermy of Toronto, who are pioneers in this art form. Although these two young men are just in their twenties, they have been masters in their field for more than a decade. They have won more first place awards than any other taxidermy studio in the country, and many believe the quality and realism of their work is unmatched anywhere in the world. They have been the subject of articles in most of the popular game and outdoor magazines and have been featured on numerous fishing programs.

McGregor and Galea specialize in fibreglass fish reproductions as well as conventional skin mounts. Their medium of choice is polyester fibreglass, although they have done all forms of wildlife art in wood, metal, clay, and plaster, and stuff fur-bearing species.

The partners were born in Toronto and have been friends since childhood. Both have backgrounds in fine art and became involved in taxidermy in their teens. To recreate an exact replica, they combine their artistic and scientific skills. The angler must measure the catch from the tip of the tail to the tip of the snout and take a girth measurement before releasing the fish. A photo for color detail is desirable but not absolutely necessary, nor is a weight measurement. The men will be able to figure out the weight of the fish to within a fraction of accuracy with the two measurements. They also rely on a considerable library collection of photographs, books, and other materials, and observe and study sports fish in a 909-liter (200-gallon) aquarium.

Each project begins with long hours at the drafting table. Innumerable sketches, including thumbnail drawings of scales and eye details, are done. The pose and position of the fish is determined from every angle, and if a custom display is required, an artistic diorama is designed to incorporate the fish in a lifelike setting that exudes natural balance and motion.

Reproductions can be much more complex than skin mounts. Galea's replica of a largemouth bass he caught on Stony Lake in the Kawarthas is reproduced in an open-mouth, gill position. There is a high degree of difficulty in such a pose, due to the exposure of gills and mouth parts. This particular model required a throat mold and molds for 21 separate mouth parts which had to be assembled afterwards. Details are exacting down to the transparent tissue between the maxillary and pre-operculum, veining in the skin tissues of the lip areas and inside operculum. Every item is made from scratch, including the eyes, rocks, weeds, and imitation-marble base.

Replicas are so lifelike that you want to reach out and touch them. They have the sheen of a fish that has just been pulled from the water. The scale detail and placement is actually more accurate than on a stretched mount, and there are never any flaws like broken fins. What's more, replicas will last longer than a skin mount, up to 100 years compared to 10. Skin mounts tend to dry out and crack. Some species of fish, like salmon and trout, discolor from oil spots which bead out. The work of Advanced Taxidermy is so spectacular, it's guaranteed for a lifetime.

Clients of the company include such fishing luminaries as Bob Izumi, Darryl Cronzy, Charlie Wray, Henry Waszchuck, Italo Labignan, and Dave Kraisosky. Advanced Taxidermy is the official taxidermist for the Ontario Federation of Anglers and Hunters who register record-breaking catches. Galea and McGregor have also made replicas for several Walt Disney productions and were commissioned by the Royal Ontario Museum to reproduce the world's largest fish, a 5-million-year-old, 97 kilogram (215 pound) coelacanth.

ADVANCED TAXIDERMY & WILDLIFE DESIGN
3588 Eglinton Ave. West,
Toronto, Ont. M6M 1V8
TEL 416-614-7320

Decoys

Steven Lloyd is considered one of North America's foremost authorities on hand-carved decoys. Though only in his mid-thirties, he has spent 16 years cataloguing information on carvers and their work, of his own interest, and says that over 80 percent of Canadian antique decoys and thousands of American decoys can be identified and therefore evaluated. Rare bird that he is, he offers his knowledge to others for the cost of a self-addressed, stamped envelope. His pay is two-fold: through such correspondence he continues to gain information on a subject that is his life's passion. Secondly, he confirms that, in addition to the considerable monetary value of some of these wooden relics, which are often given away at garage sales, they are an art form of significant historical importance that say much about the people who carved them, the people who hunted with them, the waterfowl that were pursued, and the times in which they were made.

Before the birth of Christ, Egyptians used decoys of mud and feathers to hunt on the Nile. North American Indians made decoys from natural materials including grass, bark, mud, and the actual skins of ducks. It was the European settlers who began to carve decoys out of wood, as early as the 1700s.

Decoy collecting has been serious business in the United States since the 1930s. It's only been popular in Canada for about the last ten years. Unfortunately, American collectors have rounded up an amazing number of antique, Canadian decoys and shipped them to the States. One dealer alone collected about 1,200 decoys from boathouses along the St. Lawrence for a mere $6 a piece. By 1980, almost half of Canada's antique decoys had simply disappeared.

Some of the "rarer" birds include mallard decoys made in southern Ontario and northern New York; shorebirds and swans which were rarely used after 1915 when the gunning of these birds was outlawed; mergansers, buffleheads and teals; gulls and herons used as "confidence" decoys, a message to waterfowl that the area was safe; and decoys with difficult poses like a turned head or one in a preening position.

Just how valuable are decoys? The world auction record for a preening pintail drake by A.E. Cromwell brought $319,000. The most money paid for a Canadian decoy is a Canada snow goose by George Warin of Toronto which fetched $21,000 US in 1989. It was once used on Pigeon Lake.

To educate the public about this vanishing heritage, Lloyd lectures, writes articles, and attends national and international outdoor shows at his own expense, all for the love of the "dekes". He has appeared on dozens of television and radio programs and has been the subject of innumerable magazine articles. He grew up in a hunting family and his father and grandfather worked in the shop of Cliff Avann, known as the "10-minute decoy maker" because he turned out so many so fast. The two Lloyd men were sanders, and for every dozen decoys they sanded, they received one finished decoy to take home.

Lloyd purchased his first decoy for a few dollars when he was 20. His personal collection now numbers around 400 and includes some of his favorite Ontario carvers, the work of Ken Anger of Dunnville, D.W. Nichol of Smith's Falls, and Ernie Fox of Brockville. Lloyd has stopped acquiring decoys for his own personal use, because he has simply run out of room!

He suggests the best way for an amateur to learn about decoys is to read books to become familiar with the names and styles of carvers. Value is based on who carved the decoy, the condition it's in and how many were made: a carver had to produce many birds to acquire a reputation. A broken beak, cracks, or a coat of paint over the original surface can lower the price considerably.

Lloyd spends much of his spare time talking to collectors and assisting people who have just discovered a decoy in their garage or attic. He answers every letter personally, and often has as many as 125 requests from all over North America and even a few from overseas.

Interested parties may send Lloyd a photograph and description of their decoy. He will tell you the name of the carver (if known), the type of bird, and its value. He is also pleased to answer any other question on decoys. Be sure to send a dollar or two to defray postage and stationary.

CANADIAN DECOY INFORMATION CENTRE
Stephen E. Lloyd,
R.R. #3,
Athens, Ont. K0E 1B0
TEL 613-924-2774

MacPherson Craft Supplies

ONTARIO TRIVIA

Joan MacPherson started a small craft business when her husband Dick MacPherson bought a variety store, located in one of the old limestone buildings in St. Marys. It soon became evident there was a great demand for yarns and craft supplies. The location and size of Dick's large, 3-storey building seemed ideal for both businesses, so they merged, offering their customers an unusual combination of products.

Twenty years later, the variety store is still in business across the street, and MacPherson Crafts is now one of the largest craft supply stores in Canada, occupying two stores, side by side. That's about 2,500 square meters (about 8,000 square feet) of yarns, beads, ribbons and trim, crewel and needle-point, caning and wicker, wedding supplies, dried flowers, pot-pourri, and Christmas decor, as well as everything for the quilter, dressmaker, dollmaker, rughooker, and much, much more.

The old limestone building, formerly the Royal Edward Hotel, was built about 1854 and is an official historical site. The fireplace also enjoys a heritage designation and the hotel bar now serves up floral supplies instead of libations. There's a staff of 18 friendly, knowledgeable people and the MacPhersons are often on hand. Craft workshops are a regular part of the operation.

Those unable to get to the store can join the 10,000 customers across Canada who regularly shop MacPherson's by mail. There's a 150-page catalog available and a toll free number for orders.

MACPHERSON CRAFT SUPPLIES
83 & 91 Queen St. East,
St. Marys, Ont. N4X 1C2
TEL 519-284-1741 (information)
FAX 519-284-4060
800-265-8518 (order line)

ACTON at one time was the largest tanning centre in the British Empire.

ALLISTON is known as the Potato Capital of Ontario. It's also the birthplace of Sir Frederick Banting, co-discoverer of insulin, and T.P. Loblaw, Canada's pioneer in the food industry.

ALMONTE is the birth place of James Naismith, credited with inventing the game of basketball. While teaching in Springfield, Massachusetts, he placed refuse boxes on the balcony at each end of the gym. He instructed students to throw balls into the boxes. The players tired of going up onto the balcony each time someone scored a goal. The boxes were replaced with peach baskets with the bottoms removed. Thus basketball was invented.
By 1925, the game had become a professional sport, regulated by many rules. Disillusioned, Naismith said "it's an amateur's game, invented by an amateur, and everyone should have a chance to play."

Elmira Stove Works

The cast-iron, woodburning cookstoves first made around 1850 were the focal point of the kitchen. They had two doors, one for the fire and one for the oven; there was always a pot of water brewing on top for tea or washing-up. A warming oven was useful for letting bread rise or drying out mittens. The range was often the only source of heat in the house. Everyone could gather around its pot-bellied shape and the dog could curl up beneath the stove's legs.

Since the 1970s, Elmira Stove Works has been building stoves authentically styled like the 1850s antique, but with modern range features inside. Tom Hendrick, the company's founder, was introduced to the old models by Mennonites and Amish residing near his Elmira store. They would come in search of replacement parts for their cast iron stoves. Hendrick believed that a stove which combined the nostalgic appearance of the woodstove with the convenience of a modern appliance would be perfect for the decor of Early American or Victorian-style kitchens, country and farm homes, cabins and cottages.

He created the "Cook's Delight." "The styling is old, the technology brand new; the design is borrowed, and it even comes in blue." All the castings and decorative trim are made from aluminum and are historically accurate. Great care has been taken to hide modern features from view. For example, the exhaust fan, cooktop light, and electric clock timer are hidden away in the former warming cabinet. Behind the pleasing exterior is a range that can rival today's products for durability, technology and performance. The oven is full-size and self-cleaning. The cooktop is a durable, porcelain surface; elements are available in solid electric or sealed gas burners. The 76 centimeter (30-inch) version offers four range top burners, the 112 centimeter (44-inch) version features six.

There is an all electric model or a gas cooktop/electric oven combination. Gloss white and almond colors are the most popular but the Cook's Delight is also offered in Country Blue and Black. Options include a warming shelf and pancake griddle and a country motif design on the backsplash and cabinet doors. Prices are thoroughly modern, starting at $2,995. There will soon be a matching wall oven for less money.

ELMIRA STOVE WORKS
145 Northfield Dr.,
Waterloo, Ont. N2L 5J3
TEL 519-725-5500
FAX 519-725-5503

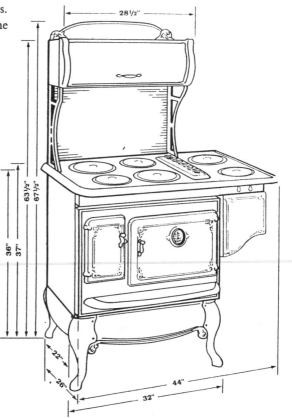

Woodbridge Advertiser

For those who don't know the Woodbridge *Advertiser*, the name is deceiving. This is an auction sale newspaper, the only one of its kind in Ontario, dedicated to auction-goers and antique collectors alike. It was founded in 1935 and has enjoyed continuous publication under the direction of three owners. The current publishers, Karl and Beverly Mallette bring their own personality to a publication that's already unique.

While the 16-page paper is chock full of province-wide auctions, from antiques in Grimsby to cattle sales in Barrie, to household goods in Lemonville, the *Advertiser* has a small-town, family flavor. Most subscribers probably first turn to page two for "The Week That Was...", Beverley's 7-day summary of life among kin and folk. It reads more like a note from a sister than the column of a journalist, and includes anecdotes of trips, weddings, lunches, and dinners. There are congratulations sent to the Woodbridge *Advertiser* Ball Team, belated birthday wishes and references to characters like Bren-Da which border on T.V. soap opera fare. The *Advertiser* is also the outlet for Beverly's other writing career. She's the author of *Jessica*, and *Letitia* both serialized in the paper before publication, and she has several other books in the works.

The *Advertiser* is a source of rural fairs and festivities with its calendar of events, farm news, and features from two regular columnists with a range of views on topics like collecting ephemera and retirement.

The history of the paper documents a slice of rural Ontario life. Founder Roy Lavery of Palgrave named the paper after Woodbridge, the closest large town at the time. He printed it on a hand-fed, 1908 Lee flatbed press, from the confines of an addition behind his general store. When he died, his home cum store cum press was willed to Howard Walton, a man Lavery had hired as a boy out of high school to operate the linotype.

Discouraged by the longest postal strike in history, Walton put the *Advertiser* up for sale in 1982.

The Mallettes purchased it on April Fool's Day in a deal that was agreed by a handshake. For Karl it marked the end of two years of looking for a job. Two days later he received two job offers.

Walton continues to run the general store. It hasn't changed much since his predecesor ran it in the 1930s. Karl took one of the two positions he was offered and Beverly became publisher of the paper for the first nine years. Karl has since retired from his city job, preferring to walk 65 feet from his bedroom to the office rather than the 65-mile commute he made to Toronto.

The paper continues as a cottage industry. Each week it comes off the press in the Mallette's home among the cedars on Nottawasaga River in picturesque Hockley Valley. It's a bargain at under $32 for a year's subscription.

THE WOODBRIDGE ADVERTISER
Box 9,
Loretto, Ont. L0G 1L0
TEL 905-729-4501
FAX 905-729-3961

Ephemera

The collecting of "ephemera" has been referred to as "waste basket archaeology." Ephemera include a wide range of printed and handwritten material, including trade catalogs, tickets, maps, atlases, magazines, diaries, greeting cards and posters: things that are vital when needed and afterwards become waste material, "the minor transient documents of everyday life."

The collecting of ephemera has a long and interesting history. For example, fourteenth-century diarist Samuel Pepys collected the street literature of his day, refering to it as "vulgaria." His vast collection is now housed in Magdalene College in Cambridge. There are wonderful collections of Canadian ephemera preserved in the Archives of Ontario in Toronto, the National Archives in Ottawa, and the Metropolitan Toronto Reference Library.

The first ephemera society was formed in Britain in 1975. They are now popular throughout the world, including Canada. The Ephemera Society of Canada meets regularly in Toronto. It publishes a newsletter, arranges lectures, and notifies members of upcoming shows and society events. Archives, museums, schools, colleges, and universities as well as individuals belong and are dedicated to the "preservation, study and display of printed and handwritten memorabilia."

While ephemera is significant as a social barometer of the times, providing researchers and historians with a candid view of our culture, it can be a fascinating and relatively inexpensive hobby for the rest of us. There are any number of items to collect, the older the better—bus tickets, envelopes with printed corners, bill heads, tourist guides, diaries, candy wrappers, or post cards. A good place to start is to attend "paper" shows. Toronto hosts the Old Paper Show & Sale, the largest of its kind in Canada, held every Spring and Fall at the North St.Lawrence Market. The show is a nostalgic trip back in time, and attracts many celebrities. Tom Kneebone browses the paper shows on a regular basis, looking for sheet music and Dan Ackroyd collects RCMP memorabilia.

EPHEMERA SOCIETY OF CANADA
36 Macauley Dr.,
Thornhill, Ont.
L3T 5S5

THE OLD PAPER SHOW & SALE
St. Lawrence North Market,
92 Front St. East,
Toronto, Ont.
TEL 416-366-1310

ONTARIO TRIVIA

BATCHAWANA BAY has a cairn at Chippewa Falls to mark the centre point of the Trans-Canada Highway.

BRAMPTON is known as the Flower City due to the number of nurseries there.

BRANTFORD is the location of Ontario's oldest Protestant church, Her Majesty's Chapel of the Mohawks, which is the world's only Royal Native Chapel.

BRANTFORD is the home of Alexander Graham Bell who invented the telephone in 1874. Two years later the world's first long distance telephone call was made from his home to the town of Paris, Ontario.

BROCKVILLE has the oldest railway tunnel in Canada.

Denise Kenny

Postcards

Denise Kenny fell into the ephemera business when her husband, Neil Hayne, gave up stamp collecting for postcards. Together, they're the only fulltime ephemera dealers in Canada, with one of the largest collections. Kenny handles all the non-postcard material that the couple buy and sell. They are noted for both the quality and condition of their stock.

She began her collection with early women's magazines, *Ladies Home Journal* (1915-1925), *Vogue Magazine* (1920), *Chatelaine*, and the now defunct *Canadian Home Journal* and the *Delineator*.

Her interest in history led her to collect road maps, county atlases, souvenir books of towns and cities, brochures, pamphlets and timetables for the Canadian Pacific, Grand Trunk, and Canadian National railways. Over the years she's added calendar art, advertising items, trade cards, needlework, cookbooks, and labels.

The next time you're cleaning out the attic or poking about at an auction sale, keep in mind what Kenny outlines as some of the "hot" ephemera in the market place today: any material on the Titanic; any embossed paper from the Victorian era; old road maps, especially the official ones or those issued by oil companies; trade catalogs, in particular those dealing with agricultural equipment and early oil lighting; early diaries, 1920s *Vogue Magazines*, 1940s pinup calendars and art poster ads of beer or coke. Among the pricier items Kenny has sold are two trade catalogs: one depicts early carriages; the other is from the California perfumer, 60, the forerunner of Avon. The selling price was $250 each.

Kenny and Hayne go to the major paper and nostalgia shows in the province. They buy, sell, and do appraisals, by appointment, from their home office in Bath.

DENISE KENNY
147 Church St.,
P.O. Box 220,
Bath, Ont. K0H 1G0
TEL 613-352-7456

Postcards originated in Austria in 1869. A year later, Great Britain issued them at a cost of 6d. a dozen. They became so popular in Europe that by 1871, one and a half million cards were passing through the mail each week. In the days preceeding Ma Bell, they were the primary form of communication between people.

The Germans flooded the English market with chromolithographed cards. Soon artists, photographers, and printers jumped on the bandwagon of this craze which spread to the United States and the British colonies. Every home had a postcard album. Many collected cards in their "mint" state.

The Golden Age of postcards was from 1905 to 1920. The fad began to die out during World War I. Today, they are still widely used by vacationers, and nostalgia buffs have rekindled an interest in vintage items. There are only a handful of postcard clubs in Canada, but the hobby has taken off in the United States where there are more than 100 organizations. The late Barbara Frum was a postcard collector. Diane Keaton is often seen making purchases at New York shows and Whoopi Goldberg is said to have a collection.

N.A. Hayne Postcards

The tiny Ontario town of Bath is home to one of Canada's largest postcard collections, owned by postcard dealer, Neil Hayne. The collection has more than 200,000 cards that can sell for as little as a quarter, or more than $200 a piece. The subject matter is just as varied as the cost. There are postcards for every season and occasion, including Halloween, Christmas, Easter and Valentine's Day. Cityscapes and views of small, fourcorner towns and country scenes are just as likely as exotic vacation spots. The faces of movie stars and sports figures adorn postcards, as do airplanes, dogs, and cats.

Hayne, a retired civil servant, took a serious interest in postcards in 1980 after selling off his mail order stamp business of 20 years. He now services customers across Canada, the United States and overseas.

Most collectors seem to specialize, choosing for example a particular subject matter, time period, geographic area or perhaps artist. Hayne says there isn't a topic that postcards don't cover, and the cost of the hobby is less expensive than most.

One of the more intriguing varieties of postcards from his collection is the "hold-to-lights." They are made with a colored backing. When held to a light source they project a different picture. One such black-and-white postcard of the Chateau Laurier Hotel in Ottawa, will show colored light in the windows as if the lamps inside the hotel have been turned on.

Among the choice and most expensive are Christmas ones on which St. Nicholas or Father Christmas is featured in a robe other than red and without the portly figure of our modern St. Nick. Also significant are real photo views of railway stations or small town main streets, and sports cards featuring golf, baseball, and hockey. The most expensive postcard Hayne has sold to date is one of a horsedrawn hearse which fetched $150.

Working from his home office, Hayne buys, sells and appraises postcards by appointment. He also goes to a number of nostalgia and collectable shows throughout the province, including Toronto's Old Paper Show & Sale.

N.A. HAYNE POSTCARDS
147 Church St.,
P.O. Box 220,
Bath, Ont. K0H IG0
TEL 613-352-7456

ONTARIO TRIVIA

CARLETON PLACE was home to Arthur Roy Brown, the man credited with shooting down the Red Baron.

CARLETON PLACE is the location of Canada's oldest canoe club.

CLINTON is the "home of radar" where the first radar training school in North America was located.

COBALT is where the world's richest silver vein was discovered in 1903 when a blacksmith threw his hammer at a fox and missed, chipping a piece of rock. The town is now home to the world's finest display of native silver.

COBOURG'S Henry Ruttan introduced air conditioning to train travel in 1858. His system channelled a flow of air through a ventilating cap and over a shallow, cold-water tank placed atop the rail car.

COBOURG is the birthplace of 1930s Hollywood actress Marie Dressler. The house, at 212 King Street West, is now a museum.

Concord Candles

Throughout time, the small flickering flame of a candle has been a symbol of hope, virtue, truth, fire, and light. Candles were once the principal source of light. Now their mellow glow is used to create atmosphere and set a mood of romance, and it is always reassuring to have a candle on hand in a power failure! Regardless of the economy, candles remain one of life's affordable luxuries.

Apart from color and scent, consumers want a candle that is well behaved and won't drip on an expensive tablecloth and that will last the length of a dinner party or the stay of company. Robinson Products of Barrie, makers of Concord Candles, produce a full range of dinner and scented candles with just these qualities in mind. That's why they have become the leading candlemaker in Canada.

To them candlemaking is still a craft, not just an industrial process. They use non-toxic materials in a non-polluting environment. Their candle boxes are made from recycled fibre and they use a minimum of packaging.

Until paraffin was created in the last century, candles were made with tallow (animal fat) which had an unpleasant odor, or beeswax which only churches and the wealthy could afford.

Candles made by Concord contain no animal fat. They are produced from "food grade" paraffin, refined from mineral oil, the type of paraffin used, for example, to coat apples. Concord also make 100 percent beeswax candles. They caution consumers to beware — candles may be termed beeswax with up to a 60 percent paraffin content.

Concord candles are not "overdips." That is, they are solid colors which gives them rich color depth. They are relatively dripless and smokeless (all candles will drip or smoke in a draft) because of the high quality of paraffin, and dyes and wicks, designed to burn cleanly. They are also long-burning. A 25 centimeter (10-inch) dinner column averages 9.5 hours and a 19 centimeter (7.5-inch) pillar about 100 hours.

Traditionally, candles were made by dipping a wick into liquid tallow or beeswax until a taper formed. Concord makes some of its candles in this manner but the process has been updated with computerized, hydraulic dipping equipment.

Hand-poured votive candles were used in the first Christian churches for votive offerings — hence their name. Concord's votive candles are made in 1,000-mold machines that recycle every half-hour. Some of the scented varieties are still poured.

Concord distributes candles in Canada and the United States; their products are priced below American competitors. They are sold in quality gift shops and at Eaton's department stores. There is a retail outlet at the Concord Candle factory in Barrie and tours are available to see candlemaking first hand.

ROBINSON PRODUCTS LIMITED
116 Saunders Road
Barrie, Ont. L4M 6E7
TEL 705-725-1248
FAX 705-725-1247

CANDLE BURNING TIPS

- Place candles in still air, away from drafts, fans, and open windows.
- Candles are best used at room temperature. Use a "contained" candle in a setting which will become warm with activity.
- Before lighting, trim the wick to 1/4 inch. Light candles and burn a few minutes before extinguishing. Candles will now relight easily.
- Place a teaspoon of water in a votive holder before lighting to allow easier cleaning of residue.
- Store candles in a cool dark place in a closed box.
- Polish marred candles gently with a nylon stocking to restore the finish.
- To clean a spill: allow wax to solidify. Remove pieces, then cover remaining traces with brown paper and press out wax with a warm iron. Spills on wood can be removed by lifting hardened wax, then rubbing any traces with a cloth and liquid furniture polish.

COLOR CANDLE LORE

- Burning a new, white candle on your wedding day will bring true happiness.
- Candles of silver and gold, when lit together, bring fortune and fair weather.
- Light a pink candle for love,
  Light a green one for money,
  Two burning red candles mean lust,
  Try them all if you must.
- Burning a black candle will banish evil spirits.
- Burning a purple candle will bring power. Burning two will bring success.
- A red candle burned on the Eve of Yule ensures prosperity for the new year.
- Candles on a Christmas tree ensure a year of light, warmth and plenty for the family.
- Lighting candles on a birthday cake is a symbol of good luck and health for the coming year.
- If a candle falls and breaks in two,
  Double trouble will come to you.

Beam Bedding

You inherit a sleigh bed or perhaps pick up a Jenny Lind at an auction sale. To bring the bed back to its original, natural buff is a labor of love. Unfortunately, the mattress is as much an antique as the bed itself. It may even be the original! You measure the frame and realize no new standard mattress will fit.

Fortunately the Beam Bedding Company in Waterloo can help. For three generations they've been making custom mattresses that range from crib size to exceptionally large ones, bigger than a king. They also do many antique configurations, base and matt, or posture-board and matt. One of the most famous beds they worked on was the childhood bed of William Lyon Mackenzie King. Located at Woodside Historic Site, the bed required a mattress and feather-tick, both of which the company supplied.

The company was founded in 1932 by Gideon Beam who learned the mattress trade at Waterloo Bedding before setting up on his own. Present owner, Ralph Beam, took the business over from his father, Oscar Beam, who ran the business from the early 1940s to 1970.

Early mattresses were made of latex foam rubber. Today they are a polyfoam construction that is lightweight and affordable. Beam also gets requests for non-allergenic spring mattresses filled with all natural cotton.

The company caters primarily to a local market due to the awkwardness of shipping. However they have sent their mattresses out of the Waterloo region and the province. They also do a variety of other custom work like making souvenir seat cushions for ball clubs and theatre-goers and sewing re-useable grocery bags.

BEAM BEDDING COMPANY
48 William St. West,
Waterloo, Ont. N2L 1J5
TEL 519-743-3219
FAX 519-745-6234

The Blackwood Chair Company

In 1982, Carl Krempien returned to his native Stratford from Toronto, and began making what no-one else in Canada was making, at the time, the Windsor continuous armchair, a design popular in America between 1730 and 1830. Today, there are a handful of people making the Windsor, but only the Blackwood design is being crafted the way it was in the eighteenth century — completely by hand, without the use of nails.

What's particularly appealing about this chair is its classic good looks. It's also surprisingly comfortable for a wooden chair, and incredibly durable. One in the Krempien workshop is more than 200 years old!

What makes the chair so strong is the way in which it is crafted. Green ash, because it bends easily, is used for the back hoop. When wet, the ash is pounded down over the spindles; when it dries, the wood tightens. Maple is utilized for the spindles and legs because it's a wood that gives good definition. The soft pine of the seat lends itself to easy carving. It's the ability to hand-carve the seat, deep at the back, that makes it so comfortable. There is a great deal of hand-sanding resulting in a smooth finish which can't be achieved by machine. In total, there are about 16 hours of labor in each chair.

Krempien has been joined in the business by his brothers Paul and Mark who share his sense of doing things the old-fashioned way. In spite of the fact that they have never advertised, they turn out about 1,200 pieces a year.

Blackwood chairs are distributed across Canada by several wholesalers who finish them with stain or paint. They're available in stores like Nitty Gritty in Toronto and a Touch of Country in Shakespeare.

The product lines have been expanded to include a two-seater settee, a three-seater bench, a rocker, and a highback chair. All are the Windsor continuous design. Most recently, the Blackwood Chair Company has turned out a few birthing stools for local midwives.

THE BLACKWOOD CHAIR COMPANY
167 Frederick St.,
Stratford, Ont. N5A 3V6
TEL 519-271-6032

The Designworks Gallery

Doug Byers combines his childhood love of scavenging for treasures in places like the woods and the local dump, with his adult abilities in furniture design, honed at the School of Design and Crafts at Sheridan College. The result is the Designworks Gallery, a unique furniture and accessories business in Jordan. Located in wine country, it's not surprising that featured items in the Gallery include one-of-a-kind, rustic grape-twig furniture, as well as nature crafts.

The Designworks Gallery is a family business with a very 1990's philosophy. Byers and his wife Una successfully mesh creativity and ingenuity with their strong appreciation for the environment. They utilize what they call "taken for granted materials," including twigs, vines, and rough lumber. Virtually all of the materials come from local development sites (the future homes of plazas, industrial malls, and housing projects) and from local fruit farms and domestic cuttings. The Designworks Gallery even offers the unique service of making personalized, heirloom furniture from your own favorite backyard tree.

The Designworks Gallery gives one-day workshops for those who want to stimulate their own creativity by making a twig furniture. All materials are supplied along with a gourmet lunch that features local Cave Spring wine.

THE DESIGNWORKS GALLERY
Doug and Una Byers,
3836 Main St.,
P.O. Box 88,
Jordan, Ont. L0R 1S0
TEL/FAX 905-562-4772

Caners Corners

When Theresa and John Prentice married in 1975, they had a home but no furniture and little money. They picked up and refinished flea-market finds. One of these items was a caned chair which needed repairs. John Prentice taught himself to cane from a book and successfully repaired it. Gradually friends and neighbors brought their pieces to him. This led to a mail-order business which has become Canada's widest selection of products for chair seat weaving and basket-making.

The Prentices have become experts on fibres and grasses, like wicker, rattan, willow, seagrass, and hemp. Many of these products come from Hong Kong, the tropics, Italy, and Denmark. Rattan, for example, is a vine which grows in tropical countries like Borneo and Sumatra. About two and a half centimeters (one inch) in diameter, rattan can grow to 400 meters (1,300 feet) in length. It's jointed like bamboo, but isn't hollow. Each joint is believed to represent a single day's growth growth.

Prentice offers tips for people buying wicker or rattan furniture. The support pieces and uprights should be of solid rattan, not hollow bamboo. Sit in the furniture and move around in the seat: if it creeks and complains, it's not solid rattan. Quality pieces should last a lifetime.

Caners Corners publishes a catalog and they offer next day shipping within Canada. All supplies are guaranteed. The Prentices cater to a wide variety of home hobbyists, antique dealers, furniture refinishers, and craft people. Since many of their customers are first time do-it-yourselfers, instructions are supplied with most supplies. The Prentices are pleased to make themselves available for problem-solving. They're currently working on a video on seat caning.

CANERS CORNERS
John and Theresa Prentice,
4413 John St.,
Niagara Falls, Ont. L2E 1A4
TEL 905-374-2632

Stanley Knight Limited

Hardwood flooring as we know it today (kiln dried, tongue-and-grooved, matched and end-matched) originated in the United States around the turn of the century. About that same time, two enterprising men in Ontario, William Seaman and Frank Kent, saw the potential for this popular new product in Canada. In 1901 they formed the Seaman-Kent Company and became the first company in the British Empire to manufacture hardwood flooring.

The company was located in Meaford, heart of the finest hard maple stands in the world. Here, the limestone beds lend a uniqueness to the maple, unequalled anywhere else: the wood is free of mineral stains and has the whiteness preferred in the flooring market.

The two men formed an ideal business partnership. They were the exact opposites in temperament. Seaman was a cautious, conservative man while his partner was a flamboyant extrovert. Together, they built up a company that within a few years was shipping "Beaver Brand" hardwood flooring of maple, oak, beech and birch across Canada, to the United States, and the United Kingdom. By 1920 they had manufacturing facilities and warehouses from Quebec City to Edmonton with a head office in Toronto. The principal manufacturing plant however remained at its birthplace, in Meaford.

With the stock-market crash and Great Depression of the 1930s, the Seamen-Kent Company was over-extended. One by one their plants and warehouses were closed, auctioned off, or left idle. By 1931, the sole activity of the company was from the Meaford plant. Finally, it closed its doors that same year. The property and premises reverted to the town for back-taxes and the factory was deserted.

In 1937, at the height of the Depression, F. Stanley Knight, a local woodworker, acquired the abandoned plant from the town of Meaford. He purchased the "Beaver Brand" name, refurbished the plant, and once again hardwood flooring was made in Meaford.

Today, fifty-six years later, the Stanley Knight plant, situated on the original Seaman-Kent premises, produces some of the finest quality flooring available. They supply markets worldwide, shipping native woods across Canada, to the United States, the United Kingdom, Germany, Spain, Japan, Taiwan, and Korea.

Beaver Brand flooring is seen in squash courts, gymnasiums, industrial and commercial sites, as well as in fine residences. Even some of the facilities at the 1993 Olympic Games in Barcelona, Spain were made by this Meaford company.

STANLEY KNIGHT LIMITED
226 Boucher Street E.,
P.O. Box 1150,
Meaford, Ont. N0H 1Y0
TEL 519-538-3300
FAX 519-538-5020

Secret Gardens Willow Works

Twig or rustic furniture is enjoying a renaissance among collectors and decorators. It seems our high-tech, urban environment has sparked a trend back to basics. The choice is traditional, nostalgic furniture for the home, cottage, and garden, in contrast to the impersonal styles of the workplace. The origin of twig furniture is rooted in the same rustic sensibilities, prevalent in eighteenth-century England and France. As families retreated to the country from a world turned upside down by progress and the industrial revolution, they celebrated nature with landscape gardens and rustic furniture made from the unfinished parts of trees, including roots and stumps, as well as other materials like hides, animal horns, and shells.

American twig and rustic furniture was rough-hewn, made in the earliest colonial times. It wasn't until the establishment of professional landscaping in the mid–1800s, that rustic garden houses and furniture appeared in any abundance. The famous Adirondack furniture arrived later, at the end of the nineteenth century, the choice of people escaping city life and seeking the comfort and tranquillity of hunting, fishing, and camping. Now this style of furniture shows up on the best verandahs and gardens of America.

It wasn't trained carpenters with their planes and squares who made twig furniture. Tree art was the work of artists and country craftspeople.

Among today's artisans is Dale Mullins of the Secret Gardens Willow Works in Warkworth. She creates one of the most popular styles of rustic furniture, bent willow, a whimsical style with free flowing, graceful, romantic lines. Mullins discovered the art of willow bending while working in the landscape design business in Toronto. It was furniture that harmonized well with the English perennial gardens she created.

There are some 250 species of willow which grow abundantly throughout the world. The majority of willow is a "bush-type" known as the sallow, the most often used in willow construction.

Sallows thrive in moist, loose soil in flood plains, on river banks, near ponds, lakes, culverts, and drainage ditches. The species is often considered a nuisance because of its weed-like, rapid growth.

Mullins harvests most of her willow from a large beaver swamp. It's difficult, physical work that requires tools like pruning saws and loopers; frequently she competes for the wood with the local beavers. Depending on heat and humidity, the green willow is workable for roughly two weeks. The design for a chair, bench, sofa, or even a bed frame follows the natural shape of the wood. Knots, bark, and disfigurations add to the rustic, one-of-a-kind appearance. Raw ends are sealed to prevent the bark from peeling. Completed pieces are then treated to preserve their natural color and flexibility.

Mullins makes a large assortment of twig items, including baskets, Victorian planters, arbors and trellises, bird feeders, coffee and end tables, loveseats, chaise lounges, étagères, footstools and chairs.

She teaches the art of willow working at two weekend workshops in April and May and in September and October. The first weekend of June she hosts a garden show and sale at Secret Gardens along with other artists and crafts people who feature garden-related items. Secret Gardens is also part of the Warkworth and Coldcreek Studio Tour held annually the weekend after Thanksgiving.

Mullins' work is available at Country Accents, Port Hope; Northumberland Trading Co., Warkworth, Down the Garden Path, Peterborough; and at her studio by appointment or chance, year-round.

SECRET GARDENS WILLOW WORKS
R.R. #1, Warkworth, Ont. K0K 3K0
TEL 705-924-2856

DRIVE west from Warkworth on Highway 29 to the top of the hill and turn right (north) on Concession 2. Travel approximately 2.4 kilometers (1.5 miles) to the yellow house with the blue shutters and the "Secret Garden" sign.

Sitting Pretty

Justin Starkweather has been a dancer, an actor, a film editor and a Montessori teacher and has tried communal living at Twin Oaks, in Louisa, Virginia. It was here that he learned the art of hammock making, one of the main cottage industries of the commune. When Starkweather found himself in Canada without a job, he began applying the skills he had learned at Twin Oaks.

He now owns and operates a business he calls Sitting Pretty. From his workshop in Lanark, he makes and sells two sizes of hammocks and has expanded the business to include a line of unique chairs and swings that combine old-fashioned principles with new methods and materials. The result is a modern version of the traditional porch swing, a rope rocker, and two comfortable types of suspended chairs. The clean lines of the furniture which incorporate naturally finished hardwood and cedar are appropriate for cottage or home.

The hammocks are woven with soft, synthetic rope which doesn't get hot the way cloth does. The mesh effect lets the air circulate for added summer coolness. A patented knotting method which holds the hammock to the hardwood spreaders is superior to traditional methods, in which the rope can rub in the hole and wear out so that the knots hang unevenly. Not only is the Starkweather version more durable than other rope versions, it's prettier.

The hammock can be hung between two trees or a custom stand. Starkweather supplies two. One is metal, can be assembled in minutes, and is compact and lightweight for shipping or storage. Yet at 18 kilograms (40 pounds), it's substantial enough to take the weight of two people.

The cedar stand can be adjusted for tension or size. It too folds up for compact storage and at 30 kilograms (65 pounds) can be moved from sun to shade by one person.

The Curvilinear Porch Swing is a suspended model made of cedar slats joined on rope. There are no metal fasteners so the wood creaks like an old-fashioned swing. The Breezy Chair is suspended from macrame-style hanging ropes with a wooden frame that holds a woven seat. At Twin Oaks Starkweather designed a speed-weaving jig for quicker assembly and production.

Sitting Pretty also makes a Hammock Chair, a Suspended Chair that looks somewhat like a hammock, a Rope Rocker that folds up easily to be taken to the beach or the cottage, the traditional yard swing, and a toddlers' swing. The company also makes a very innovative version of the picnic table that can be stored flat against a wall with collapsible legs and seats. It comes ready-made or in kit form.

Sitting Pretty for Birds incorporates a variety of cedar birdhouses and birdfeeder styles.

SITTING PRETTY
R.R. # 4,
Lanark, Ont. K0G IK0
TEL 613-259-3033
FAX 613-259-2525

The Bug Protector Jacket

Andy and Fergie wore one in the Yukon. Linemen for Hydro, Bell Canada, and the Ministry of Natural Resources wear them. It's perfect for bird watchers, fishermen and women, sports enthusiasts, gardeners, joggers, and cottagers — virtually anyone venturing into bug country. But don't be fooled by look-alikes. There is only one Bug Protector Jacket, the invention of Meneatha Dawe of Peterborough.

What sets the Bug Protector Jacket apart from its competition is its fabric — rip-stop nylon, the same fabric used for hot air balloons and some tents. Mosquitoes can't penetrate it and bees just slide off. It won't rip or tear and is both water- and wind-resistant, so it doubles as a windbreaker. There is no need to soak it or spray it with insect repellent or wear it in combination with a bee keeper's hat.

Dawe first got the idea for the Bug Protector Jacket in 1985 when her son, Ministry of Natural Resources lineman, Michael Dawe, experienced insect bites much worse than usual. A background in tailoring and drafting helped her design a good-looking, full-cut jacket that could be worn comfortably over other clothes. The unique hood design protects the face with mesh that's fine enough to keep out the smallest insects, including "no-seeums." It doesn't restrict vision and there's room inside for a peak cap or a hard hat. What's really amazing is the jacket's light weight — an adult size weighs only 198 grams (7 ounces).

Battling the bugs was the easy part. It took Dawe 18 months to go from prototype to a marketable product. Along the way, this seamstress-turned-entrepreneur became an expert in insect behavior, assembly-line production, quality control, industrial design patent law, and salesmanship.

Today the Bug Protector Jacket also comes with pants and in sizes for men, women, and children and there's a new version with a detachable hood. The colors (banana yellow, grey and camouflage), are those that Dawe learned are least attractive to insects. In the works is an alternative fabric of 100 percent cotton.

The Bug Protector Jacket is manufactured by Prosafety Accessories and can also be purchased directly from Dawe. If you're lucky enough to catch her vacationing with her husband in their mobile home, you can be sure she'll have a few on hand.

PROSAFETY ACCESSORIES INC.
181 Rutherford Rd. South,
Unit #9,
Brampton, Ont. L6W 3P4
TEL 905-456-1090

MENEATHA DAWE
1889 Stewartcroft Cresc.,
Peterborough, Ont. K9K 1G7
TEL 705-742-4724

Pelican Bay Needle Art

At one time, if you wanted to design your own cottage logo and have it embroidered on t-shirts for a few weekend guests, or personalize a special gift for a friend, the cost would have been prohibitive for such a small order. Custom embroidery such as you find on monogrammed towels, sports uniforms, and school blazers, has long been confined to the wholesale market. But now Pelican Bay Needle Art in Bracebridge, one of only a handful of storefront, computerized embroiderers, has eliminated the middleman, making single orders affordable and the design possibilities only as limited as the customer's imagination.

Store-owner Elizabeth Mitchell opened Pelican Bay in May 1992. A casualty of the recession, her unemployed status gave her the opportunity to initiate a career change. She had seen computerized embroidery equipment in the United States and researched the possibilities. She combined state-of-the-art equipment with the perfect location — on the main street of Bracebridge, a town where the influx of tourists triples the area's population in the summer months.

Needle art was immediately popular with local cottagers wishing to embroider the name of their summer home on clothing for family and friends. Mitchell also popularized her own Muskoka themes of moose and loons for the resort and campground trade.

She stocks her store with 100 percent cotton clothing, including hats, t-shirts, sweatshirts, casual shirts, jackets, and two-piece outfits for women. And she has taken baseball caps to new heights with original Muskoka designs. All are quality items that take the colorful designs well, and will not fade with washing.

A good deal of thought goes into each design: creating a logo, placing lettering in relation to the logo, developing an overall balance, and selecting the color threads. Frequently more time is spent in the creative stage than the actual needle work. However the computerized design function of the equipment allows customers to view the work and change it immediately.

Mitchell has come a long way since buying her equipment after a one-day training session. The store is now open seven days a week with a night shift in the busy months to keep on top of orders. A design specialist has been hired and Mitchell is looking to expand her clothing line.

Pelican Bay accepts phone orders and will ship anywhere. Most mail order is from people who have visited the store previously.

PELICAN BAY NEEDLE ART
Elizabeth Mitchell,
12 Manitoba St.,
P.O. Box 458,
Bracebridge, Ont. PIL IR9
TEL/FAX 705-646-2142

Sassafras

Sassafras is a type of southern, deciduous tree. It's also the name of an exciting clothing and jewellery venture, the brain-child of Lynne Taylor of Sault Ste. Marie.

Try to imagine your favorite Harris tweed jacket (the one you can't bring yourself to part with, although it's seen better days) transformed by a wonderful, hand-painted design along the lapels and pockets. The resulting "funwear" will take you to the opening of an art gallery or a cocktail party at Christmas.

Former landscape designer, Lynne Taylor, combines her passion for the environment, especially new ways of recycling, with her creative talents, and breathes new life into used clothing with fabric paints, some of which have an additional textile medium.

To create the design, Taylor responds to the shape and color of the garment. She works entirely freehand, with no preconceived ideas until she actually begins to work the piece. She starts with line-work, applied with a "fineline" nozzle, and brushes in patches of color. Designs vary from abstracts to florals, and may include animals or cartoon figures, architectural motifs, populations of stick people, recreational motifs, and even symbols. The design may completely cover the piece or be confined to painted, rolled-up cuffs.

The color scheme of the design is chosen to compliment, not compete, with the original clothing. Taylor works from a large library of spectacular colors including the most popular contemporary shades. Some of the paints are "slicks" (paints with a smooth, glossy appearance) and others are pearlized. Glitter paints sparkle in the light; metallic glitter paints have inset stones. Some dimensional paints puff up when ironed. All have been tested and may be dry-cleaned. Each design seldom contains fewer than eight colors, effecting one-of-a-kind looks that are extremely versatile.

Taylor is very particular about the recycled clothing she chooses to paint. They must be free of stains and wear on both surface and interior and must be particularly well-constructed. She limits her clothing to men's suit and sports jackets and vests. The over-sized, boxy styles give her both the casual and formal looks she wants to create. She also paints on blue jeans, blue jean jackets, vests, and skirts. She avoids personal commissions, but offers discounts to those with acceptable trade-ins.

Sassafras clothing is available at The Green Room, Stratford, and G & C Casuals, Lions Head. The jewellery is sold at the General Hospital Gift Shop, Stratford; Village Studios, Stratford; G & C Casuals, Lions Head. All items are also available direct from the artist.

SASSAFRAS

Lynne Taylor,
113 Kohler St.,
Sault Ste. Marie, Ont. P6A 3V2
TEL 705-949-0806

Philosopher's Wool Company

Tucked away in the tiny, rural community of Inverhuron, about 20 kilometers (12 miles) north of Kincardine, Ann and Eugene Bourgeois are single-handedly revolutionizing the wool industry.

On their small, 4.2 hectare (10.5 acre) farm, they essentially became wool manufacturers in order to earn a reasonable price for their own, raw fleece and to produce a quality of wool that is superior to anything in the marketplace. Not only is Philosopher's wool not itchy or scratchy against the skin, but it's durable and strong and even smells good! In addition, Ann Bourgeois creates wonderful patterns for the knitter.

The Bourgeois left the rat race of city living for "the good life in the country" in 1976. Eugene Bourgeois had been working on a doctorate in philosophy (thus the name Philosopher's Wool) which he abandoned for the simplicity of a rural life-style. He built his own house and barn and, with 50 ewes, was able to cover his family's basic living costs.

On one occasion, while taking lambs to market in Toronto, he picked up some wool for his wife, an avid knitter. During the three-hour drive home, he figured out that the wool cost $22 for half a kilogram (per pound). Yet he received just 32 cents for half a kilogram (a pound) for his fleece, a price that didn't cover the cost of shearing. He also wondered why woollen goods are so uncomfortable to wear next to the skin when his experience in handling sheep confirmed their wool was never itchy, only soft to the touch.

Over the course of the following year, Eugene Bourgeois made phone calls and wrote letters, determined to find a mill that would process his own fleece into yarn. He finally contracted an American company that washed fleece without all the chemicals, acids, and bleach that rob it of lanolin and leave the wool uncomfortable to wear.

Eugene tried washing fleece in the family washing machine which resulted in a clogged drain but nonetheless proved his principle in theory. He concluded that farmers could be enticed to produce cleaner fleece if they were paid more, and if the fleece could be washed as little as possible. Cleaner fleece would also weigh more after washing, contain less dirt and moisture. The return to the farmers would also be substantially greater. Thus the seeds for the Philosopher's Wool Company were sewn.

The Philosopher's Wool Company now buys approximately 7 percent of the Ontario fleece available from between 200 and 250 farmers that live throughout the province from Gananoque to Ottawa, from Sault Ste. Marie to Windsor. Eugene drives the fleece to Adamstown, Pennsylvania, where it is washed, picking up a clean order when he drops a load off. The fleece is then spun by a variety of companies throughout the country, who have been selected for their individual milling strengths.

The company inventories about 13,620 kilograms (30,000 pounds) of fleece, about 20,430 kilograms (45,000 pounds) of washed wool, and between 2,951 kilograms (6,500 pounds) and 3,178 kilograms (7,000 pounds) of yarn. Most of the wool comes from the "down" breeds, like those on the Bourgeois farm. The wool is characterised by an 8-centimeter (three-inch) staple (length) and high crimp. This is a relatively coarse wool suitable for the bulky sweaters Philosopher's Wool designs and sells. Ann Bourgeois oversees the designing of new sweaters and patterns. A good deal of input comes from customers who use the yarn and visit the farm's shop.

All the patterns are written for circular needles and there are never more than two colors per row. These are features which bring complex looking patterns within the reach and capability of ordinary knitters. This is in contrast to designers like England's Kaffe Fassett whose complex patterns are beyond all but accomplished knitters, and can require as many as forty different colors.

The Bourgeois are very responsive to customers' needs and look for new ways to improve and expand their product. They have begun to develop an inventory of breed wools: Lincoln, Romney, and Dorset yarns. They have experimented with dying these yarns using a gas barbecue to simmer pots of wool in, of all things, Kool-Aid. The Kool-Aid colors the yarn as an acid-based dye would. Various effects are created by tying and untying the wool and adding more color to the dyed wool.

The Philosopher's Wool Company sells yarns wholesale and retail from their farm shop and by mail order via UPS and Canada Post, throughout North America. Yarn is available open-stock or in kits. They also sell completed sweaters, employing a number of local knitters.

The Philosopher's Wool Company is between Kincardine and Port Elgin, on Lake Huron, opposite Inverhuron Provincial Park.

THE PHILOSOPHER'S WOOL COMPANY
Inverhuron, Ont. N0G 2T0
TEL 519-368-5354

South Mountain Mohair

Among the world's most luxurious fibres is mohair. It comes from the fleece of the angora goat, an animal that is small in stature and at first glance looks more like a sheep than its relatives which are raised for milk and meat.

Mohair has been admired since biblical times for its exceptional qualities. No other fibre combines such great durability with soft lustre. Although angora goats are thought to have originated in the Himalayan Mountains of Asia, they made their way to Turkey and flourished in the Province of Ankara, from which the name angora is derived. The Turks guarded their flocks jealously. Interest in the fibre prompted the Sultan to forbid the export of raw mohair until 1838. The animals themselves were not exported until 1849. From a small flock of seven does and two bucks, the United States has become the second largest producer of angora in the world, South Africa being the largest.

Mohair is usually identified with expensive sweaters, suits, and rich velours. But now it is also the main ingredient in Canada's warmest socks, called Thermohair. They are the creation of Theresa van Grunsven, who raises a herd of 60 angora goats on her South Mountain farm.

This University of Guelph graduate, mother of four, and partner in her husband's steel business, became interested in goats through her enjoyment of spinning. In 1983, she started her hobby with four animals. When the price of raw fleece in the marketplace dropped drastically, van Grunsven decided to produce a finished product she could make and sell herself. Rather than expensive items like blankets, she came up with the idea of mohair socks which would be warm, soft and wear well. The fibres wouldn't mat, pill, or crush and would be a wonderful alternative for those allergic to wool. Another advantage over wool, mohair can be machine washed and dried if kept at the same temperature during washing and drying — hot or cold.

She had difficulty finding a mill that could spin the mohair to a precision that could be handled by a commercial hosiery machine. Also, the mohair had to be blended with another fibre to hold its shape. It took a year to come up with the correct combination of mohair and nylon; the first pairs of socks were test-worn by her husband and the local postmaster. In 1992 she went into full production.

In spite of the spinners and knitters who discouraged van Grunsven from using such a wonderful fibre for socks, and the business minds who suggested North America is a throw-away society and doesn't want a durable sock, sales of Thermohair doubled after one year. She can no longer get enough quality mohair in Canada and has had to purchase some supplies from the United States.

She still oversees the production from raw mohair to finished socks and sorts and labels them with the help of her two younger children. Her son keeps track of the business on his computer and she employs sales agents for distribution across Canada.

Van Grunsven is dedicated to the angora goat breed. She shows her goats at the Royal Agricultural Winter Fair and won the Premier Breeder and Exhibitor awards in 1990 and 1993. She also judges goats and is an elected director of the Canadian Goat Society and the Ontario Goat Breeders' Association. She lobbied the provincial government to recognize goats as livestock and to get them on the red meat plan, like sheep and cattle.

Thermohair socks are available at more than 100 retailers across Canada. They can be ordered from the Canadian Goat Society (proceeds going towards the organization).

SOUTH MOUNTAIN MOHAIR
P.O. Box 213,
South Mountain, Ont. K0E 1W0
TEL 613-989-2017
FAX 613-989-3328

THE CANADIAN GOAT SOCIETY
P.O. Box 357,
Fergus, Ont. N1M 3E2

Biltmore Corporation

The Biltmore Corporation has been manufacturing men's hats in Guelph since 1917. Through two world wars, the governments of thirteen prime ministers, a depression, a bankruptcy, and a recession, the name Biltmore has always stood for style and quality in the better hat circles of North America.

The broad range of Biltmore styles over the decades (felt hats of wool and rabbit, caps of wool and cotton, and straw hats) reveals the changes in fashion, as hat brims varied to balance with the lapels on suits and hatbands were selected to work with the latest trend in ties. Whatever the fashion, Biltmore's hats have been compared to the finest in the industry including British and Italian hats. Even Canada's most outstanding hatter, the late Sammy Taft, was quoted as saying Biltmore makes as good a hat as any in the world.

A history of the Biltmore company provides a microcosm of the world at large. Those in the industry will tell you that fashion goes in thirty-year cycles. Hats were in their heyday during the 1930s. The business suffered a huge setback in the 1960s when John F. Kennedy didn't wear a hat to his inauguration. People on the move and much more active found hats awkward to carry on airplanes and to wear in cars. Men were paying higher prices for styling longer hair; the fifty-cent haircut was a thing of the past. Men didn't want to hide their professionally coiffed heads under hats or get "hathead."

Biltmore managed to stay in business during the lean years with hat sales to orthodox Jewish men, Mennonites, senior citizens, and western music

fans. John Travolta's 1979 movie, *Urban Cowboy*, created a hat craze that launched an added night shift at Biltmore to keep up with orders. The company went from producing hats on a custom-order basis to making them on spec. As quickly as the fad caught on, it died. In fact some agents for Biltmore say it happened in a single weekend. The company went bankrupt and was bought out by the American Stetson Hat Co. Inc. Continued decline put Stetson into receivership and subsequent purchase by a West Virginia company which then decided to unload the Biltmore operation. It was then rescued by two anonymous Guelph natives.

The 1990s seems to be bringing the hat business out of its thirty-year slump. Short hair on men is back in vogue, women are wearing men's hats. There's also the new desire to seek protection from the suns' rays and the depleted ozone layer. Biltmore hats now carry the tag "Sun Busters."

Biltmore's current inventory consists of more than 100 styles of hats for every season, including a line for women. They have outlets in Guelph, Cambridge and Mississauga with plans for more across the country.

BILTMORE CORPORATION
139 Morris St.,
P.O. Box 690,
Guelph, Ont. N1H 6L7
TEL 519-836-2770
FAX 519-836-2774
800-265-8382 (order desk)

Apples

Apples were one of the first fruits in the world to be cultivated. In the Caucasus, the region between the Black and Caspian Seas, evidence has been found that apples were eaten there some 8,000 years ago.

There were no apples in the Americas before Columbus. Settlers brought seeds and grafts with them in an effort to establish their old way of life in a new land. Through trial and error, they found that the seedlings survived much better than the grafts of European varieties. This gave rise to a great number of new varieties, very distinct from European ones, because an apple tree grown from seed is, technically speaking, a new variety, whereas a graft gives rise to a clone of the parent tree.

There are between seven and eight thousand named varieties of apples world-wide, some best for apple sauce or cider, others for baking or eating. Regrettably, many of the old favorites have disappeared over the years. Fortunately, some continue to survive in the private collections of Ontario apple epicures like Emile Janssens and Fred Janson.

Campina Orchard

Retired white bean farmer Emile Janssens and his wife Mary now devote all their time to their 4-hectare (10-acre) historic orchard in Parkhill, northwest of London. There, they grow apples as big as melons and others as small as cherries; apples that are red, green, yellow and brown; apples that are round and even some shaped like lemons. The 460 varieties of apples planted in alphabetical order, beginning with Astracan and ending with Zoete Aaeht make this the largest collection of apple varieties in Canada.

All 460 varieties have been grafted onto M9 or B9 rootstock. Janssens learned the art of T-bud grafting in his native Belgium where he was a peach and tomato farmer before moving his family to Canada in 1950. Grafting shortens the fruit bearing time and ensures the final product will be that of the parent.

Each tree and variety is tagged with the name given by the original grower. There are those named for women, like Maidenblush, Marie D'Othee, Sweet Rosy. The Ribston Pippin, an old English apple, was brought to southern Canada because the growing climate was more suitable. It was then shipped back to Britain up until World War I. Lady Apis was popular in France before the Revolution; ladies carried this exquisitely scented apple in their drawstring bags for perfume. Lady Apis was also used as a mouth wash and a Christmas ornament. The Newtown Pippin originated on Long Island about 1700. It produced a heavy crop of yellowish-green apples which ripened in midwinter. Towards the end of the nineteenth century, many people gave up growing this variety because the trees were difficult to manage.

Janssens has collected scions (grafts) from temperate climates throughout the world, including his native Belgium. His collection ranges from common commercial apples like Empire and Jonagold to species that date back to the Middle Ages.

He reads and collects as much information on apples as he can and has accumulated an impressive library with titles in several languages. He has become an expert in grafting techniques, including triangular grafting and green grafting. Most recently he was asked to graft 19 pre-1850s varieties of apples onto two dozen McIntosh trees at the John R. Park Homestead in Essex County.

In addition to apples, Janssens has 80 varieties of pears and 30 crab apples. He is eager to share information and scions with other fruit enthusiasts and welcomes visitors to his farm year-round. Look for Janssens at local fairs, including the Parkhill Fair where no-one else bothers to enter the raw fruit competition because Janssens always wins. His apples are available at local markets.

EMILE JANSSENS

Campina,
R.R. #4,
Parkhill, Ont. N0M 2K0
TEL 519-294-6535

DRIVE Highway 401 west to Highway 402 at Westminster. Drive north on Highway 81 at Strathroy to Highway 7. Campina farm is southwest of Parkhill on the 18th Concession, Lots 7 & 8, two rows of apple trees just west of the high school.

Janssens' Favourite Apple Recipe

175 ml (3/4 cup) apples
50 ml (1/4 cup) prunes
unbaked pie shell

- Cook apples and prunes separately in enough water to cover until soft. Mix together and spread thin on a pie shell. Bake at 180 C (350 F) until pie shell is cooked.

Pomona Orchard

The sign in the apple shed of Pomona Orchard reads "taste before beauty." It's the credo of Fred Janson, a connoisseur of the fruit, who has grown and tasted more than 800 varieties of apples, an incredible feat given the limited number of apple varieties available in today's grocery stores.

Janson, in his early seventies, and wife Walda, currently raise around 240 varieties of heritage and gourmet apples on their 10-hectare (26-acre) farm along Highway 522 near Rockton, 30 kilometers (18 miles) southeast of Kitchener. He is known as a world authority on apples, and Canada's expert in pomology. He planted his first apple orchard when he came to Canada from Germany in 1955, and since retiring from the food industry, his hobby has become a full-time passion.

Janson has developed his own varieties. Perfecting an apple with pink or red flesh for apple cider is his goal. For apple-growing enthusiasts he has a list of a dozen varieties to help individuals break the "McIntosh-Delicious-Granny barrier": Manet, James Grieve, Kidd's Orange Red, Kandil Sinap, Priscilla, Tumanga, Mutsu, Ashmeads Kernel, Sandow, Melrose, and Freyberg. The Pomona Orchard is planted with the earliest ripening trees closest to the house. It's divided into two sections: the production orchard has many trees of the same variety; the museum collection is worthy of preservation, with trees from around the world, centuries old or modern, discovered in exotic locales or in the backyards of Ontario.

The Ontario Apple Marketing Commission recognizes the Jansons' work and has declared Pomona Orchard a private-testing facility. Among the objectives are to select highly flavored and aromatic cultivars with a high vitamin C content, to test and develop environment-friendly pest controls, to test methods of controlling weeds by mulching without fostering orchard mice, and to evaluate the symbiosis of apple trees and orchard stationed geese.

The Jansons have also pursued their hobby from the theoretical side. In 1967, Janson founded NAFEX, a network of Canadians and Americans dedicated to sharing and furthering their knowledge of fruits and nuts. The first issue of the organizations publication, *Pomona*, was produced in the Jansons' home.

NAFEX now has more than 3,000 members and operates as a nonprofit corporation out of Illinois state. It runs the R.W. Daniels Library, a large collection of old and out-of-print materials, available to members by mail.

In winter months, when the trees lie dormant, the Jansons are engaged in the literary side of the apple business. Both are published writers, and Fred Janson is busy with research on pre-1825 pomology. They also operate the Pomona Book Exchange. They are the only book sellers in Canada specializing in horticulture, agriculture, and food (no cookbooks). Many of their books, periodicals, and prints are rare and out-of-print. The Jansons produce a free catalog of roughly 500 titles three times a year, and get requests from around the world.

Those fortunate enough to live in the vicinity of Pomona Orchard may purchase apples from the Janson's farm, although they "don't grow apples to sell, they sell apples to grow others," which allows them to scout for grafts and continue their experiments.

The surplus of 220 varieties is for sale at different times of the apple season, varying according to ripening times. Janson believes in picking apples late, when they are at their peak of sweetness. He encourages visitors to taste first and buy according to personal preference. Common varieties may include McIntosh, Courtland, Snow, Mutsu, and Wolf River. Some of the best quality, uncommon species are Cox Orange, Pippin, Ontario, Marigold, and Ribston Pippin. Janson also presses his own cider, a fabulous blend of 12 or more varieties. Only hand-picked, not windfall apples are pressed, to avoid contamination by soil-borne bacteria.

In spring and summer, home gardeners may select graft sticks and buds for budding from those available. Janson also ships them throughout Canada.

FRED JANSON or THE POMONA BOOK EXCHANGE

Pomona Orchard,
953 Hwy. 522,
Rockton, Ont. L0R 1X0
TEL 519-621-8897

NAFEX,
Route I,
Box 94,
Chapin, Illinois 62628

WALDA JANSON'S APPLE TIPS

- Save top quality apples for eating, and cook with the others.
- Quarter apples, cut out bad parts, then peel.
- Apple sauce and strudel are best made with more than one variety of apple.
- Only 1/3 cup of sugar is necessary to make an apple pie if the correct blend of apples is used.
- The best apples for hollowing and filling with nuts, raisins, sugar and butter, before cooking, are Mutsu.

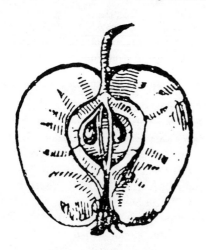

Walda's Vienna Apple Strudel

Dough:
375 ml (1 1/2 cups) flour
dash salt
1 egg
15 ml (1 Tbsp) cooking oil
90 ml (6 Tbsp) warm water
Filling:
30 ml (2 Tbsp) butter, melted
30 ml (2 Tbsp) fine bread crumbs
8-10 apples (mixture of tart and sweet)
30-60 ml (2-4 Tbsp) sugar
Optional: cinnamon, a few raisins, and/or a few chopped nuts
250 ml (1 cup) hot milk

- In a mixing bowl, sift flour, and make a hollow in center. Add salt, egg and oil. Using some of the flour, make into a paste. Gradually add water and continue to mix. Form into smooth ball (if too moist use a little more flour) and let rest one hour in a warm covered bowl.
- Roll out dough and transfer to floured cloth and stretch by hand to form rectangle about 30 cm X 5 cm (12" X 2"). (Dough should be stretched thin, almost transparent, but no holes should develop). Brush with some melted butter and sprinkle with bread crumbs (to absorb some of the juice). Spread apples (peeled, cored and thinly sliced) evenly on dough, leaving free about 2.54 cm (1") on long edges and about 8 cm (3") on one narrow edge. Sprinkle with sugar (and cinnamon, raisins, nuts if desired). Starting on one narrow edge, roll up with help of the cloth, ending with the free edge. Press edges slightly and transfer into buttered baking dish (2.5 L; 12" X 8" X 2"). Brush with rest of melted butter. Bake in 160 C (325 F) oven 10 minutes. Remove and pour 250 ml (1 cup) of very hot milk over strudel. Return to oven and bake another 25 to 30 minutes or until golden. Serve warm.

The Original McIntosh Apple

The apple is the most widely grown and eaten fruit in the world today. One of Ontario's greatest contributions to pomology (the science of fruit and fruit culture) is the McIntosh red apple, the most popular variety grown in Canada.

The McIntosh apple is named for John McIntosh, a United Empire Loyalist who left his farm in the Mohawk Valley of New York State and settled at Dundela, between Brockville and Cornwall, in Dundas County.

In 1796, he discovered some apple seedlings on his property while clearing brush. He transplanted the young trees to a fenced plot, close to his house. It isn't known how the seedlings came to be on the property in the first place but it is thought they had been sown by some early French settlers because the apples were similar to the Fameuse trees brought to Quebec from Normandy in the seventeenth century.

Only a few of the young trees survived and one tree in particular produced exceptional fruit. McIntosh planted more trees from seed, but none equalled the tree he had found in the bush. The ability to propagate his outstanding species remained an unsolved problem until 1835, when he hired an itinerant American farmhand who knew how to graft apple trees. Before leaving the farm later that year, he taught McIntosh's son, Allen, the art of grafting. The boy and his father took scions from their prized tree and grafted them onto three-year-old crab apple seedlings. They packed them in sawdust and stored them in the cellar until spring planting. The McIntoshes continued this successful practice each fall and spring and eventually began selling their seedlings to other farmers and teaching the art of grafting.

The McIntosh apples gained a local reputation for excellence. The trees were hardy and produced large yields. Word spread throughout Canada and by 1900 the McIntosh tree was well established in Eastern Canada. It went on to become the leading variety in North America.

The original McIntosh tree survived almost 100 years, outliving John McIntosh who died in 1845 and son Allen, who died in 1899. The tree, located about 15 feet from the farmhouse, was partially damaged by a fire that levelled the building in 1893. However, branches farthest from the blaze continued to bear fruit until 1908. Two years later the tree fell over from old age. Today there are thousands of its offspring throughout North America.

In 1912, a granite monument was erected on the property to commemorate John McIntosh and his famous McIntosh red apple tree.

DRIVE Highway 401 to Highway 35, north at Morrisburg. Take Highway 18 west to Dundela.

ONTARIO TRIVIA

DELHI is the Tobacco Capital of Ontario and home to the province's only tobacco museum, the Ontario Tobacco Museum and Heritage Centre.

DRYDEN greets visitors with Maximillian Moose, a statue of a bull moose, located on Highway 17, next to the Tourist Bureau. Maximillian stands 6 meters (18 feet) high.

DUNDAS is the location of the world's tallest white elm. The tree is 30 meters (97 feet) high with a crown of 34 meters (112 feet), a 152 centimeter (60 inch) trunk and a circumference of 4.5 meters (15 feet), 20 centimeters (8 inches). It is located at 25 Parks Street.

Chudleigh's Apple Farm

For anyone growing up in and around Toronto in the past twenty years — from the Beaches to Richmond Hill, from Willowdale to Hamilton and Burlington — Chudleigh's apple pies have been part of that experience and possibly one's entrée to Chudleigh's Apple Farm, located north of Milton.

These wonderful apple pies which come with a pastry crust or crumble pie top, have been a feature of specialty food stores since the early 1970s. They continue the Chudleigh family tradition of introducing new ways to grow and market the fruit. A tradition began with Eric and Marion Chudleigh, who resided on the apple farm of Eric's father in Dixie, Ontario (now the corner of Tomken Road and Bloor Street in Mississauga). Eric was particularly interested in dwarfing rootstock fruit trees and in 1939 was the first grower in Canada to import dwarf rootstock from England.

When the Chudleighs' son Tom was fifteen, the Dixie farm was sold for future development. The Chudleighs purchased 40 hectares (100 acres) north of Milton, and in 1956 began planting a dwarf orchard on the property.

Unfortunately, Eric and Marion were killed in an accident. Tom and brother Ted were raised by an aunt until they finished university. In 1962, Tom and his wife Carol moved to the Milton property. Now they have over 24,000 apple trees: 8 kilometers (5 miles) of continuous rows of apples! Each year, 2 hectares (5 acres) are re-planted.

The Chudleighs opened their orchard to friends and neighbors around 1967 and were among the forerunners of the "pick-your-own" concept. As business grew, they looked for better ways to accommodate their customers, becoming leaders in what is now known as "entertainment farming." They began baking and selling their famous apple pies in 1973. Two years later they added sweet Silver Queen corn to the "pick-your-own" list and in 1977 expanded the barn to include a cider press and cold storage area. The cider, is a blend of three or more varieties of apples producing a mixture that balances sweetness and tartness with good body.

Cross-country skiing began in 1981 and that winter the bake shop and gift shop were open all year. By 1987 there were over 200 employees helping to harvest and market Chudleigh's products at the peak of the season.

Today Chudleigh's Apple Farm continues to be a great outdoor facility that is open year-round. Guided school tours to the mixed forest and the apple orchard are conducted in December, March, May and the fall with lessons in fruit growing, maple syrup, and honey bees. Children are treated to apple cider, a wagon ride, a tour of the cider mill, and apples for the classroom. In May there are also farm animals on view. The orchard provides an enchanting cross-country ski trail in winter and an exquisite place to jog or walk the dog when the blossoms are in full bloom in spring. In December, there's an opportunity to select a Christmas tree from Chudleigh's man-made forest.

Baking, cider, apples, and gift boxes are available year-round and country lunches are served from May to October. From November to April there is take-out soup, pies, chili, and beverages. On weekends there are horse, pony, and wagon rides, weather permitting, and Chudleigh's also accommodate birthday parties and weddings with parking space for 1,000 cars.

Chudleigh's baked goods continue to be sold at a number of Ontario specialty stores and events like the Royal Agricultural Winter Fair. The bakery is now located minutes from the farm in Milton and they have an outlet at the St. Lawrence Market on the lower level.

APPLES AVAILABLE AT CHUDLEIGH'S

- Tydeman's Red
- Wealthy
- Spartan
- McIntosh
- Cortland
- Empire
- Red Delicious
- Russet
- Golden Delicious
- Northern Spy
- Ida Red

CHUDLEIGH'S APPLE TIPS

- Handle apples with care as if they were eggs, for even squeezing will produce bruising.
- Take the field heat out of your apples as soon as possible by refrigerating them.
- Store apples in a cool, humid temperature. Golden Delicious and Russets will shrivel unless stored in high humidity, so keep in a plastic bag for added moisture.
- Remove spoiled apples so they don't contaminate the others.

BEST APPLES FOR EATING

- Spartan, McIntosh, Cortland, Empire, Red Delicious

BEST APPLES FOR BAKING

- McIntosh, Cortland

BEST APPLES FOR PIES

- Wealthy, Northern Spy

BEST APPLES FOR SAUCE

- Wealthy, McIntosh, Cortland

CHUDLEIGH'S APPLE FARM

9528 Hwy 25,
P.O. Box 176,
Milton, Ont. L9T 4N9
TEL 905-826-1252; 905-878-2725
FAX 905-878-6979

OPEN year-round Wednesday through Sunday 10 a.m. to 5 p.m.

DRIVE Highway 401, take exit 320 north on Highway 25. Drive 2 miles north on Highway 25, located on the west side of the highway.

CHUDLEIGH'S
St. Lawrence Market
TEL 416-366-7957

Chudleigh's Mulled Cider

1 L (4 1/2 cups) Chudleigh's Apple Cider
2 cinnamon sticks
30 ml (2 Tbsp) honey
6-8 whole cloves

- Combine all ingredients. Heat to boiling point, but do not boil. Simmer 20 minutes. Remove spices.
- For a clear drink, strain through cheese cloth. Serve hot with a lemon twist and a cinnamon stick to stir.

Joywind Farm Rare Breeds Conservancy

Jy and Gail Chiperzak manage a working farm that few city folk have heard of, yet the Chiperzaks' work is an amazing link with our cultural past and may well be the key to preserving our future.

Chiperzak is a modern-day Noah. His ark, the Joywind Farm Rare Breeds Conservancy, is the only organization in Canada dedicated to the conservation, study, and evaluation of rare and minor breeds of farm animals as a genetic resource. It is Canada's most diverse collection of endangered farm animals, with Irish Kerry cattle, Dorset Horn sheep, Karakul sheep, Cotswold sheep, a Newfoundland pony, Barred Plymouth Rock chickens, and Newfoundland sheep, the first of their kind to leave the island. When Chiperzak realized that domestic breeds of livestock were declining in appalling numbers, in some cases even becoming extinct, he took up the cause of saving them.

The livestock industry has tended over the past couple of decades to specialize in only a few breeds, based primarily on productivity and breeding management. For example, approximately 90 percent of all cows milked in Canada are Holsteins. Roughly three-quarters of Canadian Holsteins are artificially inseminated by only 12 bulls. This results in what Chiperzak refers to as a "narrow, fragile gene pool."

In 1985, salmonella invaded the American poultry industry. Many states were forced to close their borders and slaughter their chickens. "Those chickens were so nearly identical that when one bird got sick, they all got sick. The fear is that in 10 or 20 years we might have nothing left but a few highly productive breeds that are terribly susceptible to disease. A whole industry could collapse in one season because of some sickness."

The rare breeds nurtured at Joywind are an insurance policy for the future. Many of these breeds have the ability to survive on poor land and resist drought, while some are known for their low cholesterol and fat levels. Others have greater longevity, easy and multiple births, and are disease resistant. With changing world climatic conditions, changing consumer preferences, and the evolution of new strains of disease, the importance of maintaining access to the genetic traits of rare and minor breeds becomes essential to our own survival.

Aside from the scientific and agricultural significance of the rare breeds, Chiperzak views them in much the same way that an historian sees an old building, as part of our cultural heritage. Many livestock breeds represent over 7,000 years of domestication and selection by man. The "Canadienne" cow, for example, an ancient dairy breed, originated from stock imported to Canada by Jacques Cartier in the late 1500s. There were more than one million of these hardy dairy cows when the population of Upper and Lower Canada was 900,000 people. Now there are scarcely over 1,000 pure Canadienne.

Today, Joywind is a federally incorporated body with charitable-organization tax status and an advisory board that includes scientists from Agricultural Canada, the Ontario Ministry of Agriculture and Food, and the Department of Animal and Poultry Science at the University of Guelph. In 1992, it was chosen as the charity of choice by *Harrowsmith* magazine.

Anyone can join this non-profit, charitable organization. Membership in the Rare Breeds Conservancy includes a variety of individuals and groups from a number of countries including Canada, the US, New Zealand, Holland, England, and Brazil.

Some of the Conservancy's programs include the Host Farm Program which places animals at members' farms for breeding; a Student Internship Program at Joywind; the Canadian Gene Resource Collection, a frozen semen collection for cattle breeding which now represents 13 breeds; the Hart

Poultry Barn Breeding Project for rare lines of poultry stock; the publishing of the *Genesis* newsletter, Canada's first directory of minority livestock breeds; and a number of research projects including the Kerry Milk Protein Study, White Park Sire Cattle Embryo Transfer Project, the Eastern Canadian Native Indian Horse, the Arapawa Goat Study, the Heritage Hatchery Network Program, the Cotswold Gene Bank Breeding Program, and the Newfoundland Sheep Study.

Visitors and school children are welcome to visit Joywind Farm; however, it is best to make an appointment. Joywind Farm is approximately 30 miles north of Belleville.

JOYWIND FARMS RARE BREEDS CONSERVANCY INC.

General Delivery,
Marmora, Ont. K0K 2M0
TEL 613-472-6160
FAX 613-472-5565

DRIVE south on Highway 1, in Marmora, past the sign that says "Bonarlaw." Turn right on Rawdon Concession Road. Drive approximately 3 kilometers (2 miles) and take the left-hand turn (the only road that turns left). Joywind is the first farm on the left. Look for the Black Kerry Cow.

Egli's Sheep Farm

In 1952, Robert and Margarit Egli emigrated from Switzerland to Canada with a dream — to own their own sheep farm. They began their new life just a few miles west of Dryden with some bush-covered acreage and a handful of sheep. They cleared most of the land themselves as the flock expanded. Today, their 405-hectare (1,000-acre) farm competes in the world market for meat, wool, and sheepskin products, and their farmstead store is known as Canada's largest specialized wool and sheepskin shop.

The flock now numbers in excess of 1,000 head, with almost twice as many lambs as ewes. Two breeds are prominent: Suffolks, which are first and foremost a meat breed of sheep, produce lean, fast-growing lambs, usually born as twins. The lambs are black, and turn white as they mature, with the exception of their legs and head. The Suffolks produce a short, medium wool, often with black fiber, between 2 and 4 kilograms' (5 and 8 pounds') worth. The Dorsets are also popular for their meat, producing prime, light-weight lambs. This breed has white legs and faces with pink noses and is noted for producing lambs in any season, and 3 to 4 kilograms (6 to 8 pounds) of wool.

There is also a small flock of Corriedales on the farm, a breed of sheep developed in Australia and New Zealand. Corriedales are known as a dual-purpose breed for both wool and meat production.

The Eglis grow all their own feed right on the farm to ensure their animals are free of growth hormones and antibiotics. The lamb meat is cut and wrapped on the premises. In addition, about 8 crafts-people work in the atelier, making sheepskin products, while the woollen goods are very much a cottage industry, employing local knitters who work at home.

In 1987, the Eglis expanded their market-place with a mail-order business and catalog sales. They now bring in a good deal of additional wool and sheepskin, processing about 4,000 skins annually to keep up with the demand for a range of products — everything from slippers to steeringwheel covers.

Visitors to Egli's Sheep Farm will be treated to a view of the barns, fields, and the artisans at work in the atelier. During July and August, there's a daily one-hour show of sheep shearing, dog trials, and display of the various breeds.

EGLI'S SHEEP FARM

P.O. Box 10,
Minnitaki, Ont. P0V 2E0
TEL 807-755-5231
FAX 807-755-5246
800-465-2966 (Mon-Sat 8 a.m.-6 p.m.)

VISIT: Egli's Sheep Farm is located on Highway 17, 20 kilometers (12 miles) west of Dryden.

STORE HOURS: May 15-Aug 31, Mon-Fri 8 a.m.-8 p.m.
Sat, Sun 9 a.m.-5 p.m.
Sept 1-Dec 31, Daily 8 a.m.-6 p.m.
Jan 2-May 14, Mon-Sat 9 a.m.-5 p.m. Sun- closed

Ontario Agricultural Museum

Absolutely one of the best places in Ontario to take children is the Ontario Agricultural Museum in Milton, just 30 minutes west of Toronto. But that's not to say that adults won't be equally delighted, entertained, and amazed at this project of the Ontario Ministry of Agriculture and Food.

Never heard of it, you may say? Then you will be surprised to learn it's visited by 70,000 people annually, during the four months of the year it's open. Nearly half the visitors are school children, participating in structured, hands-on, educational programs designed to complement the Ontario School curriculum, making it a teacher's utopia.

Not confined to a museum building, the Ontario Agricultural Museum is a 32-hectare (80-acre) parcel of land with more than 30 buildings and display areas, with plenty of green space, gardens, crops and animals. There are three aspects to the site: a series of farmsteads trace the development of domestic and agricultural life in rural Ontario; the services of the crossroad communities, available to rural people, are featured; and there are exhibits which comprise one of the largest agricultural equipment collections in North America. Historical interpreters perform the daily activities of farm families and rural business people from the nineteenth and twentieth centuries.

The buildings have been moved from across the province and are unique and interesting examples of local, rural architecture. Among the rarities is the Troyer-Fraser barn, an unusual eight-sided structure with no internal framing and a cupola on top. It was built in the days when superstitious farmers eliminated corners in their barns where "gremlins" might hide out. The Lucas House is a classic example of Ontario Vernacular Style, constructed in a fashion to escape the tax man.

Among the crossroad services are the carriage works, a portrayal of a fanning mill, and wagon manufacturing by a Fergus, Ontario firm, circa 1910, that features a wheelwright shop. There's a 1928 Ford Automobile and Tractor Dealership,

with Ford products from 1919 to 1953; an Imperial Esso Gas Station; and a one-room school house built in 1886.

There are more than 15,000 artifacts representing the evolution of rural life and agriculture from earliest times to the present. There are tools and equipment used in a steam-powered shingle mill, elements of an ever-evolving dairy business, and the apple industry, a slaughter and smoke house, and different modes of transportation including carriages, sleighs and buggies.

The Museum is also home to a number of outstanding collections. It houses the world's largest display of Massey Harris Ferguson equipment and the company's archives. Many of the international visitors to the Museum only know Canada through their use of "Harris" equipment. There is also an amazing collection of more than 700 wax models of fruits and vegetables, created at the turn of the century, by Mrs. Elizabeth Potter for the Ontario Agricultural College. This collection is described in this book in a separate essay.

A recent acquisition is the Quilt Collection, a permanent exhibit which displays Ontario's best quilts from rural fairs. There's an annual quilting event to compliment the collection, considered one of North America's best competitions. The Zurbrig Collection of rural folk art is also not to be missed.

Second only to the Canadian Agricultural Library in Ottawa, the Museum has the best reference library specializing in agriculture, horticulture, and rural life in Ontario.

In addition to daily demonstrations in the historic buildings, there are special events scheduled every month. They are designed to address contemporary issues in food and agriculture, in addition to giving historic perspective. "Dairy Days," billed as an "udderly awesome" event, attracted people in droves to see inside a cow's stomach and operate a cream separator. There was plenty of opportunity to sample milk products, feed and milk cows, make butter, see cheese being made, and examine the components of "nature's perfect food," — butter fat, protein, and milk solids.

There are events for seniors, a Christmas Craft Fair in September which gives shoppers an early opportunity to patronize local artisans, and the Museum is host of the Great Canadian Antique Tractor Field Day, the only show of its kind which annually features Canadian-made farm machinery. A list of special events is well worth writing for in advance.

Come equipped with comfortable shoes and clothing to get around in. You can walk the paved paths or ride the tractor or horse-drawn wagons that circulate the grounds regularly. Picnic grounds and snack bars provide places to eat.

Group visits are welcomed and must be booked in advance. Educational programs for elementary and secondary school curricula can be pre-arranged for half and full days through the Tour Co-ordinator.

ONTARIO AGRICULTURAL MUSEUM

144 Town Line (Tremaine Road),
P.O. Box 38,
Milton, Ont. L9T 2Y3
TEL 905-878-8151
FAX 905-876-4530

DRIVE Highway 401 to Exit 320 (Highway 25) at Milton. Go north on Highway 25 about 2 km (1.2 miles) to the first traffic lights (Campbellville Road). Turn left at the lights and drive west 2.2 km (2.3 miles) to the second road, Townline Road. Turn left, following the Museum signs, cross over Highway 401 on the overpass to the museum entrance on the right.

OPEN May 29 to September 25 10 a.m. to 5 p.m. daily
MODEST admission fee
EVENTS take place, rain or shine

Maple Syrup

Perhaps nothing is more Canadian than maple syrup. What can be more reassuring that spring is just around the corner than the tradition of tapping maple trees?

Maple syrup is, in fact, a distinctly North American product. The Sugar Maple (*Acer saccharum*), found only in northeastern North America, is the tree primarily used for syrup production. Most of the world's supply of maple syrup is produced almost exclusively in the Great Lakes region. Only four Canadian provinces and about a dozen American states produce commercial maple syrup.

Maple syrup and maple sugar were among the earliest agricultural crops produced in Ontario which is the second largest maple syrup producer in the world, following Quebec. In 1992 Ontario's maple syrup crop had a farmgate value of about 20.9 million dollars. It's estimated that there are approximately 70 million tappable maples trees in Ontario, but surprisingly only about 1.5 million are currently under production.

Perhaps what's more significant than the commercial value of the sugar bush is the opportunity it gives people to commune with nature and participate in a ritual that's deeply rooted in our past.

Native people were tapping the maple when the pioneers arrived in Eastern Canada, some 300 years ago. They made spiles or taps from reeds or pieces of bark and buckets from birch bark to collect the sap. They added red-hot stones to clay evaporating vessels to heat the sap. This first method of evaporation was replaced by boiling in iron kettles, and today has evolved to the sophistication of the evaporator.

In some sugar camps, sap pails or buckets are still used while other producers have developed a system of plastic tubing to carry the sap directly to the sugar shack. Whatever the method, the principle remains unchanged from early days. It still takes 130 to 180 liters (30 to 40 gallons) of maple sap to make 4.5 liters (1 gallon) of maple syrup.

The reason why sap flows remains a mystery. Most tree species contain sap which does not flow in the spring, and none is as sweet as the sugar maple. Maple sap normally runs some time during March and April. It takes a cold night, with temperatures below freezing, followed by a warm day when the thermometer climbs to between 5 and 8 Celsius (42 and 48 F) for the sap to flow. Towards the end of the season the sugar concentration of the sap almost doubles. Sap flow ends by the time the trees bud and the leaves open. Strangely enough, a maple that has snapped off in a winter storm will still produce sap during its first dead spring.

All maple syrup sold in Ontario is required by law to have a sugar content of 66 percent, and no additives are allowed. It is also divided into two grades and four color classes. Canada #1 maple syrup is intended for table use and is classed according to color — extra light, light, and medium. The lighter the color, the milder the flavor. Canada #2, amber, is a stronger flavored syrup considered best for cooking. For genuine, 100 percent pure product, consumers should look for "Maple Syrup" or "Pure Maple Syrup" on the label. The container will also give the name and address of the producer or packer as well as the volume, grade, and class of syrup.

Unopened maple syrup is best stored in a cool, dry place like the refrigerator, or it can be frozen for long-term storage. Once opened, return to either the refrigerator or the freezer. Syrup will not freeze solid, and can be brought to room temperature in about one hour.

To substitute maple syrup for sugar use 175 ml (3/4 cup) syrup for each cup of sugar called for in the recipe. Reduce other liquids by 45 ml (3 tbsp) for every cup of syrup substituted.

Refrigerate maple butter in a tightly covered container to prevent drying, or cover with a layer of water. It may also be frozen.

Maple sugar was the first kind of sugar made in North America and was the standard sweetener until 1875. It's still a popular treat today. Soft maple sugar will not keep longer than one week unless crystal coated. Then it will store for two months in a cool, dry place. Hard maple sugar may be refrigerated or frozen.

Ontario's maple industry provides the public with a unique recreational and educational opportunity. There are nearly 50 maple syrup producers open to visitors and almost as many Maple Syrup Festivals. Many of the producers are open year-round and will ship their product mail order. A list of producers and festivals may be obtained from the Ontario Maple Syrup Producers Association. It's best to call ahead to the sugar bush of your choice to make sure that Mother Nature is co-operating.

The Maple Syrup Museum of Ontario, located in the village of St. Jacobs, is preserving the heritage of maple syrup making in the province. The museum collects the artifacts of the industry, and offers displays on the history and production of local maple syrup.

THE MAPLE SYRUP MUSEUM OF ONTARIO

Spring St. South
St. Jacobs, Ont. N0B 2N0

OPEN year-round.

DRIVE Highway 401 to Highway 8. Take Regional Road 17 to St. Jacobs Village.

ONTARIO MAPLE SYRUP PRODUCERS ASSOCIATION

R.R. #6,
Strathroy, Ont. N7G 3H7
TEL 519-232-4596
FAX 519-232-9166

Maple Baked Beans

500 g (1 lb or about 2 cups) dry white pean beans
250 ml (1 cup) Ontario maple syrup
125 ml (1/2 cup) chili sauce
1 small onion, chopped
10 ml (2 tsp) salt
5 ml (1 tsp) dry mustard
3 slices bacon, cut in 2.54 cm (1") pieces
500 ml (2 cups) boiling water

- Place beans in large saucepan, cover with water and bring to a boil. Simmer 2 minutes and remove from heat. Cover and let stand 1 hour, then drain. In a small bowl combine syrup, chili sauce, onion, salt, and mustard. Place half the beans in a 2-liter (2-quart) casserole, top with bacon and remaining beans. Pour syrup mixture over beans. Add boiling water. Cover and bake 6 to 7 minutes at 150 C (300 F). Add more water if beans seem dry.

Maple Syrup Cake

125 ml (1/2 cup) butter
50 ml (1/4 cup) sugar
2 eggs
250 ml (1 cup) maple syrup
1 ml (1/4 tsp) ginger
125 ml (1/2 cup) hot water
550 ml (2 1/4 cups) all-purpose flour
15 ml (1 tbsp) baking powder
3 ml (3/4 tsp) soda
2 ml (1/2 tsp) salt

- In a mixing bowl, cream butter and sugar until light. Add eggs, one at a time beating well after each. Blend in maple syrup gradually. Add sifted, dry ingredients alternately with hot water (3 dry and 2 water). Blend well and spread evenly into a 4-liter (13" X 9") pan or two 2-liter (8") layer pans. Bake 45 minutes at 180 C (350 F); 25 to 30 minutes for layer pans. Cool on wire rack. Frost with icing using maple syrup as the liquid.

Christmas Trees

One of the great family traditions in this country centers around the Christmas tree — scotch pine, white spruce, balsam fir, fraser fir, white fir and douglas fir, depending upon where you live and your family's long-standing tradition. In a world of arch-consumerism, perhaps at its height during the Christmas season, the "natural" Christmas tree, in all its fragrant glory, stands as one of the last bastions of the true spirit of Christmas. At least this is the case for three million Canadians who annually celebrate the festive season with a natural tree. About one million of these families reside in Ontario, and according to the Christmas Tree Growers' Association of Ontario, the number of people going back to natural trees is growing.

Ontario is one of the major Christmas-tree-producing provinces; the others are British Columbia, Quebec, Nova Scotia, and New Brunswick. Canadian grown trees are a significant export commodity and the industry employs thousands of people.

Historians trace the roots of this custom to many parts of the ancient world. The Egyptians brought green palm branches into their homes in late December, symbolic of growing things. The Romans were the first to trim evergreen trees with trinkets and top them with an image of their sun god, in honor of Saturnalia. The winter solstice was celebrated by the Druids who decorated oak trees with golden apples and lit candles. During the Middle Ages, the feast of Adam and Eve was held December 24. The symbol, a fir tree hung with red apples, was called a Paradise Tree. The use of an evergreen tree in the Christian celebration of Christmas began in Germany some 400 years ago. The tradition spread to most of northern Europe by the nineteenth century.

Baron Friederick von Riedesel introduced the custom to Canada in Sorel, Quebec, in 1781. After the War of Independence, Mennonites and other German-speaking settlers who fled the United States to Canada, brought the custom to the area settled around Kitchener. Toronto adopted the custom in the late 1790s with the arrival of Lutherans, Pennsylvania "Deutsch," and Mennonites in the communities of Markham, Unionville, and Stouffville. Eventually the twinkling of white candles on yuletide trees spread throughout the country.

While the first trees came from the provinces' dense forests, today most are grown on Christmas tree farms or plantations. Life for a tree begins in a nursery where superior strains of seed are planted. Two-year-old seedlings are then transplanted on farms.

Environmentalists tell us Christmas tree farming is good for the planet. Besides being a renewable resource, and biodegradable (most Ontario municipalities recycle them, chipping the trees into mulch for use in parks) half a hectare (1 acre) of Christmas trees produces enough oxygen to support 18 people in a year. During the 7 to 15 years it takes to grow a 2- to 3-meter (6- to 8-foot) tree (more exotic species take longer), the trees increase soil stability and provide habitats for wildlife, not to mention their aesthetically pleasing appearance. Many plantations are deliberately planted on marginal land where little else will grow.

At harvest time, selected trees are tagged for cutting. An entire field is never ready for sale in the same year. For every tree that is cut, two or three new seedlings will be planted.

For anyone who has ever seen the prize-winning trees at Toronto's Royal Agricultural Winter Fair, trees so perfectly shaped and packed with thick, vibrant branches they could well be ornamental, it becomes obvious there is an art to growing a Christmas tree that these growers have perfected.

A grower faces many obstacles over the lifespan of a tree: too little sun or rain, attack by rodents, insects, disease, hail, and fire. Each year they must nurture each tree and prune it carefully to achieve the fullness of shape desired by consumers. The trees are pruned to hold back upward growth and to stimulate branching. For those who prefer to choose their own tree, the Christmas Tree Grower's Association of Ontario prints an annual directory of "Choose-and-Cut" growers, organized by geographical location in the province. They make the following recommendations for selecting, caring for, and recycling your tree:

SELECTING A TREE

- Many people tend to buy a tree that's too tall. Be sure you know the dimensions of the area where you will display it.
- Test for freshness. Take hold of a branch about 15 centimeters (6") from the tip, between the thumb and forefinger. Pull your hand toward you, allowing the branch to slip through your fingers. Needles should adhere to the branch and not fall off. Bend a needle between your forefinger and thumb. The needle should form a "U" without breaking, unless the tree is frozen. Lift the tree a couple of inches off the ground, bring it down abruptly on the stump end. Older, outside needles should not fall off. Inside needles shed naturally every year.
- The tree should be fragrant and a good green color.

CARING FOR A CUT TREE

If you buy the tree several days before setting up:

- Store the tree outdoors until you plan to set it up. Keep it protected from the wind to retain moisture.
- Make a straight cut across the butt end of the tree about one inch from the end and place in a container of water.

Bringing the tree indoors:

- Make another one inch cut on the butt end of the tree.
- Place in a stand that holds plenty of water, about 7 liters (1 1/2 gallons).
- Trees may drink up to 18 liters (4 gallons) of water per day, so add water daily. Don't let water get below the cut or it will seal over. A tree kept immersed in water will remain safe from ignition for at least three weeks.
- Keep the tree away from heat sources like televisions, fireplaces, radiators, etc.
- Never use lighted candles on a Christmas tree or lights with warm or frayed cords. Turn the light off when you leave or at night.
- Avoid combustible decorations.

CHRISTMAS TREE GROWERS' ASSOCIATION OF ONTARIO INC.

R.R. #1,
Lynden, Ont. L0R 1T0
TEL 519-647-3530
FAX 519-647-3515

Cranberry Marshes

As spectacular as the changing fall leaves, but far more unique to the Ontario landscape, is the spectacle of a cranberry bog, a giant, red lake, the color of the crimson jelly that accompanies the holiday turkey. Experience this photographer's dream, a sea of glistening, red berries floating against a backdrop of autumn foliage, and you'll be tempted to re-read Henry David Thoreau, who described in 1854, the fields of "red gold" on the Cape Cod landscape in his book, *Walden*, "small waxen gems, pendants of the meadow grass."

Cranberries are uniquely North American. These low, dense shrubs are indigenous to areas of Newfoundland and New England, so profuse, in fact, the Norsemen named the area Vineland. Cranberries have been cultivated in North America since the 1800s, and now they are grown in Ontario.

The original cranberry marsh in the province belonged to George Mollard and was located in the town of Mactier. Today, there are two independently owned working marshes near Bala.

The Iroquois Cranberry Growers is the largest bog, with 17 hectares (43 acres) planted and a further 8 (20) under construction. It's entirely owned and operated by the Wahta Mohawks who started it in 1968 to provide employment for reserve members and an economic base for the community. In a good year, it produces 454,000 kilograms (a million pounds) of berries that are shipped to local producers as well as those in the United States and Europe.

Native peoples mixed cranberries with venison and fat to make pemmican. They used cranberries for poultices, as a natural dye, a preservative in food preparation, and as a general source of nutrition, for cranberries are high in Vitamins A, B, and C. They introduced the fruit to the pilgrims who ate them with maple syrup during their first, hungry winter. Today, cranberries are usually made into sauce or jelly. They are also used in beverages, soups, salads, breads, desserts and conserves.

The second cranberry marsh is a family business started in 1952 by brothers Orville and Melville Johnston. It's now operated by Orville's two sons, but at harvest time, usually the first three weeks of October, family and friends pitch in.

Cranberry growing is a four-season operation. Commercial cranberries require a rather bizarre tango, danced between Mother Nature and mankind. What begins as a natural marsh is drained, stripped of any vegetation, and bulldozed into dykes that run between the beds. The dykes allow for vehicle access and flooding of individual beds which are levelled, ditched and installed with sprinkler irrigation prior to planting.

Perhaps no other crop is so intricately tied to irrigation as cranberry cultivation. In the growing season, excessive moisture is required to re-establish the wetland habitat. Flooding is used to control pest and insect infestation; closer to harvest, low lying bogs are susceptible to frost, and must be flooded to protect the vines. Thousands of gallons of water are sprayed on the berries to provide a protective coating of ice.

The water system also plays an important part in the harvest. One bed at a time is flooded until the plump, red berries float to the surface, enabling a mechanical picker to comb them off the vines. Rectangular flat boats float alongside the pickers and receive the berries by conveyer belt.

In winter the beds are filled with water to form a sheet of ice to protect the vines. Once the ice sheet has formed, the water is drained and the vines breathe again. Should the ice not form quickly, the water must be drained or the vines will be damaged. The process is repeated until the ice sheet is in place.

In summer the bogs are a breathtaking vision of pink flowers shaped like the profile of a sand crane. Thus the name from the German, "kranbeere," which means crane's bill. The fruit appears as white berries and begins to turn crimson in late September with the first chill of fall. The later the harvest, the darker the berry.

A perfect cranberry has a good bounce. During sorting they are given a bounce test and must make the grade, jumping a series of wooden hurdles.

Most of Bala's best berries are packed for shipping to processors of juice, jam, sauce and baked goods. Fortunately for Ontarians, both operations sell fresh cranberries and their own brand of juice, sauces jellies and related items on site. For those who make the harvest pilgrimage to the marshes for an annual supply of cranberries (they freeze well) and cranberry products, there is no returning to the stuff of supermarkets. Johnston's also sell their goods at the Royal Agricultural Winter Fair.

Visitors are welcome at both cranberry marshes during harvest, usually between September 15 and October 31. Those planning a trip to the bogs are advised to wear flat shoes for walking the farms and warm clothes for unpredictable, fall weather.

IROQUOIS CRANBERRY GROWERS ASSOCIATION

Wahta Mohawks,
P.O. Box 327,
Bala, Ont. P0C IA0
TEL 705-762-3343 (Office); 705-375-5275 (Plant)
FAX 705-762-5744

DRIVE from Barrie north on Highway 69, north of Muskoka Road 38. The marsh is located on the east side of Highway 69.

THE JOHNSTON FAMILY CRANBERRY PRODUCTS OF CANADA LTD.

Medora Lake Rd.,
P.O. Box 24,
Bala, Ont. P0C IA0
TEL 705-762-3203

DRIVE from Barrie north on Highway 11 to Gravenhurst and Highway 169 north to Bala. Continue north on Highway 169 for about 3 kilometers (1.8 miles). Follow signs turning west off the highway onto Medora Lake Road.

OPEN September 15 to October 31.

Bala Cranberry Festival

Bala celebrates the cranberry season the weekend after Thanksgiving. There are events in the town and regular transportation to and from the marshes.

FOR BEST RESULTS WITH CRANBERRIES

- Use fresh and frozen cranberries interchangeably in recipes.
- Benzoic acid, a natural preservative in cranberries enables them to store well.
- Refrigerated cranberries keep several weeks.
- Frozen cranberries keep up to a year. They are free-flowing. That is, they won't stick together, so can be removed from the freezer by the cup-full. Freezing actually improves color.
- Cranberries are high in pectin so sauces and jellies thicken naturally with very little sugar.

JOHNSTON'S CRANBERRY SAUCE

750 ml (3 cups) fresh or frozen cranberries
250 ml (1 cup) sugar
250 ml (1 cup) water

- Wash cranberries. In a saucepan, mix sugar and water. Bring to a boil and boil 5 minutes. Add cranberries, return to a boil, gently boil until the skins pop off, about 5 minutes. Remove from heat. Refrigerate. Makes about 625 ml (2 1/2 cups).
- VARIATIONS: For a thicker sauce, decrease water by one third. For a tarter sauce, decrease sugar by one third. Apples, raisins, lemon, or orange peel may be added before cooking, as well as spices such as cinnamon, cloves, or ginger.

Ontario's Golden Treasure

There is no other crop with such a curious and romantic character as ginseng. It has been the foundation of Chinese medicine for over 5,000 years and is still the most widely used medicinal herb in the Orient. Although we tend to think of the plant in an Asian context, one ginseng species is native to North America. Native peoples valued it as part of their diet long before the arrival of Asian and European immigrants, primarily in the fight against disease.

Historical evidence shows that the trade in local ginseng, at one time, was second only to that of the fur trade. It was first discovered by Europeans in Quebec in 1704. In 1720, a company was formed to gather and ship to China wild ginseng in the form of dried root.

Roughly 60 years ago, a Waterford family began to grow ginseng commercially in Ontario. They planted seeds from the wild Canadian ginseng plant and created a woods-like habitat with straw mulch and a framework of wooden laths to provide shade. Today Waterford is the ginseng capital of Canada with approximately 150 growers in the Haldimand-Norfolk region producing 400,000 kilograms (900,000 pounds) of Canada's total production of roughly 700,000 kilograms (1.5 million pounds).

Ontario-grown ginseng has the reputation of being the highest premium quality root available in the world. *Panax quinquefolium* differs from its Asian cousin, *Panax ginseng* in its effect. While the Asian plant is used to stimulate and warm the body, Ontario ginseng has a cooling effect, which is thought to calm, soothe, and relax the body systems. It is useful in relieving stress, reducing fatigue, increasing endurance, and helping the immune system.

Proof of the quality of Ontario ginseng, which contains high concentrations of the 29 active ingredients in the plant, lies in its demand in Asian markets. Ninety percent of Canadian ginseng is exported to Hong Kong; the remaining 10 percent is marketed in Canada and the United States. Since World War II, the total harvest is sold in three to four months. The average price range in 1993 was $45 per pound which makes North American ginseng the most valuable legal crop in the world today.

Ginseng is a stocky, perennial plant that grows between 18 and 53 centimeters (7 and 21 inches). Each stock has five distinctive, jagged leaves and the seed head features a cluster of crimson berries. It grows naturally on the slopes of ravines and in shady, mountainous hardwood areas. Ginseng will not grow in many soils or climates, but parts of southern Ontario are ideal.

Commercially, ginseng is planted in the fall from seed. Shade must be provided, and the plants must be carefully nurtured for a minimum of four years. The root of ginseng is harvested in October. Creamy white or yellow in color and somewhat resembling a parsnip, it has rootlets off the main branch. These can resemble a human body and so the plant has been called the "root of man." Each root is meticulously washed and dried and the best are selected by hand, meeting stringent specifications.

A highly knowledgeable team of doctors, professors, and researchers have formed the Canadian Ginseng Research Foundation. There is ongoing research at the University of Toronto, McMaster University and the University of Edmonton. Promising evidence suggests that the Rbl ginsenoside contributes to memory retention. Dr. Lawrence Wang of Alberta has patented and registered Rbl with the US Food and Drug Administration for the treatment of Alzheimer's disease. There is also research underway to examine ginseng's potential in treating heart disease, stress, diabetes, aging, short term memory loss, PMS, and high blood pressure.

Asian ginseng is on the government pharmaceutical list of medicines in Japan. In North America, both types can be purchased at health food stores and Asian markets, usually in gelatin capsule or root form. It is also used in tea, gums, candies, jellies, and colognes.

GINSENG GROWERS ASSOCIATION OF CANADA

P.O. Box 87,
Waterford, Ont. N0E 1Y0
TEL/FAX 519-446-3544

CANADIAN GINSENG RESEARCH FOUNDATION

C/O Dr. Tom Francis,
150 College St.,
Toronto, Ont. M5S 1A8
TEL 416-978-3616
FAX 416-978-5882

ONTARIO TRIVIA

EARLTON is known as the Dairy Centre of the North.

ELMIRA'S Kissing Bridge, which connects the town to West Montrose, is the only covered bridge of its vintage left in Ontario. It was built in 1881 and gave shelter to courting couples.

ELDORADO is the site of Ontario's first gold strike in 1866.

ELORA is home to John Cannon, who patented the world's first panoramic camera in 1888. It photographed 360 degrees in one exposure by advancing the film at the same speed as the lens moved.

EMO has one of the smallest churches in the world which can only accommodate eight people at a time. It was built in 1973 from the spire of St. Patrick's Catholic church which had burned the previous year. It is located on Highway 11.

Heritage Seed Program

Heather Apple is the chief bean counter, both figuratively and literally speaking, for the Heritage Seed Program (HSP), a national organization that networks among backyard gardeners, farmers, horticulturalists, scientists, museums, historical sites, and government bodies. HSP searches out, preserves, and exchanges heirloom and endangered seed species of fruits, vegetables, grains, herbs, and flowers.

Co-ordinating 1,800 members and keeping track of nearly 800 varieties of heritage seeds is more than a full-time effort for its president and sole employee. Heather Apple operates the living gene bank from her home near Uxbridge, where her own garden and greenhouse display her commitment to the crops of our ancestors.

Each variety is unique, not only genetically, but for its tale of survival. "Jacob's Cattle Bean," for example, was given to Apple by a neighbor. Thought to date back to AD 1200, the seed was discovered in Native American ruins in the southwestern United States. The "Cherokee Trail of Tears" is a bean raised by Cherokee Indians, seeds of survival they took with them when they were uprooted in the 1800s.

One of the most precious plants in Apple's collection is the Mostoller Wild Goose Bean. According to story, in 1865 the sons of Joseph Mostoller, a Pennsylvania miller, shot a goose in the millrace. While cleaning the bird, their mother noticed that its crop was full of unusual white beans with pink and reddish markings. She dried the beans on the window sill and planted them the following season. These beans were handed down in the Mostoller family for successive generations. Custodian of the Mostoller Wild Goose Beans is 81-year-old Ralph Mostoller who answered Apple's appeal for unusual seed varieties.

Saving these rare varieties is important not only for their historical interest, but also as a great investment in our agricultural future. The HSP was founded after a Canadian organic conference was held in 1984. HSP's goals are to preserve a broad and diverse genetic gene pool, necessary to breed plants that are resistant to disease and insects, and to keep pace with a changing environment that's subject to a thinning ozone layer, acid rain, the greenhouse effect, and other unforseen planetary influences.

With the Green Revolution of the 1950s and 1960s, hybrids began to replace the crops farmers had grown for centuries. High production yields and the ability to withstand mechanized harvesting and long distance shipping took priority over taste. Between 1984 and 1987, 940 strains of open, pollinated vegetables were discontinued by North American seed companies. Roughly 74 percent of commercially available varieties, about 4,000 in all, are in danger of becoming extinct. This is the challenge the HSP hopes to meet.

The organization publishes a tri-annual magazine and a December seed catalog. Seeds are not for sale. Those who take seeds from the program learn the proper seed saving techniques, grow the seeds, and are asked to make seeds available to other members. Anyone is welcome to join the HSP, even if they do not wish to become a grower. Apple would also be pleased to hear from anyone with unusual seeds.

HERITAGE SEED PROGRAM
R.R. #3,
Uxbridge, Ont. L9P IR3

ONTARIO TRIVIA

GEORGETOWN is the site of the first papermill in the world to be run by hydroelectric power. The small turbine generated 100 horsepower, built in 1888 by John R. Barber.

Central Experimental Farm

The food we eat, the flowers we enjoy, the crops Canada exports, all owe a great deal to the Central Experimental Farm. But for most individuals, Ottawa's "farm in the city" is just a great place for a family outing or to take relatives visiting the area. It's even been used as a back-drop for wedding pictures! Just minutes from the downtown core, this 500-hectare (1,252-acre) research station was established by an Act of parliament in 1886. Two one-tonne Clydesdales pull a red sleigh across the snow-covered fields in winter and in summer, they pull a wagon past tree-lined lanes where fields are thick with cereal crops, hay, soybeans, and the like. (Between two-thirds and three-quarters of the acreage is under cultivation). Among the 140 buildings are barns where children can delight in the activities of farm life, seeing cows milked, piglets being born or week-old lambs gambolling about.

The barns and grounds elicit the saying "neat as a pin." They are framed by ornamental perennial gardens, including beds of roses, hedges, shrubs, and rockeries, and an arboretum of 2,000 species of trees that grace the hillside down to the Rideau Canal.

What's not so obvious to the tens of thousands of tourists who visit the farm each year is that this is the workplace of more than 200 highly specialized scientists. They conduct research in every facet of agriculture that includes animals, field crops, food, and soils. This is the home of the country's national seed bank, Plant Gene Resources of Canada, with over 100,000 samples of seeds from around the world. As well, the Farm maintains national collections of insects and plants for systematic research trials.

Many Canadians enjoy the benefits of the agri-food research that takes place here without realizing the months and years of experimentation that has gone on. The Central Experimental Farm has been home to a number of "firsts" that have influenced the food on our tables and the plants we put in our gardens.

At the turn of the century, Sir Charles Saunders, son of William Saunders whose report to Parliament prompted the creation of the Farm, performed much of the work to develop Marquis wheat. This variety, the first, short-season variety for the Prairies climate, made Canada a major exporter of wheat.

The first frozen food research was undertaken at the Farm in 1928. A fore-runner of today's freeze-dried foods, this method was developed for soldiers in World War II. The Farm was also responsible for instant potatoes, an early-maturing variety of seed corn, and soybeans, dwarf breeding hens, and a method of quick-freezing berries. Early research into artificial insemination in cattle and later embryo transplants and cloning were performed by the Animal Research Centre. Recently, three new breeds of sheep called Arcotts, have been developed.

At the Farm, Canada's "Lady of the Lilies", Isabella Preston, spent 26 years breeding plants. She's best known for her work with lilies, but also made significant contributions in the cultivation of roses, lilacs, Siberian irises, columbines, and flowering crabs. She successfully crossed two species of lilies to create a tall, strong-stemmed lily, described as the finest trumpet lily in cultivation. She transformed this rather delicate flower, once only grown by experts, into a hardy plant that could be enjoyed by all gardeners. Of the 22 varieties she introduced, 11 received awards.

Today the focus at the Farm is on food quality and food safety, and better ways to manage soil.

CEF 2000

Building 86, Central Experimental Farm
Ottawa, Ont. K1A 0C6
TEL 613-993-4802 (toll free: 800-538-9110)
FAX 613-954-8577
DRIVE Highway 16 to Ottawa. The highway becomes Prince of Wales Drive. Follow it to the traffic circle at the Farm.

Organic Farming

Certified Organic produce is turning up in sections of our supermarkets and at farmers' markets. For people on restricted diets and those concerned about food safety, it's a welcome alternative. Others view organic foods as expensive with less eye appeal, and the Certified Organic trademark is a bit of an anomaly.

The Ontario Ministry of Agriculture and Food defines organic farming as "a method of crop and livestock production...based on sound ecological principles that create ecosystems with a diverse mix of mutually dependent life forms." This type of farming advocates practices like crop rotation, cover crops, the recycling of organic residues and nutrients, preventive insect and disease control, use of improved genetics and resistant varieties, integrated weed management, and the use of natural or non-synthetic pesticides, to name a few. What is prohibited is highly soluble or synthetically compounded mineral fertilizers, pesticides, growth regulators, antibiotics, hormones, coloring, artificial additives, ionizing radiation, and genetic manipulation of plants and animals.

Before a farm may be certified as organic, the strict guidelines of the government must be adhered to for at least three years. Certified Organic is a registered trademark of the Organic Crop Improvement Association (Ontario), OCIA. Farms are inspected to validate their certification.

This type of farming is a real challenge to farmers. Some crops present more difficulties than others, especially in the area of disease and pest control. Yields are usually below non-organic yields, resulting in higher prices, but farmers are motivated to choose organic production methods for the health of their own families and because it is better for the soil.

In Ontario, the number of Certified Organic farmers and products is increasing every year. They are located in almost every county of the province, where they are supported by local organic organizations.

McSmith's Farm Produce

When Cathy McGregor Smith worked for Agriculture Canada, she was referred to as Mrs. McSmith by the receptionist who found her double name a mouthful. Later "McSmith's" became the name of choice for the family's organic vegetable farm. Today it's a name synonymous with organic farming in the St. Thomas area.

Gary Smith and Cathy McGregor Smith are founding members of their local Organic Farmers Association. With the help of an Environment Canada grant, they converted their 40-hectare (100-acre), Yarmouth Township farm into a Certified Organic operation, replacing pesticides and herbicides with organic practices like composting, the use of green manure, and row covers. They followed strict government regulations, taking their farm through a three-year transition period before it could be inspected and certified as organic.

McSmith's is a tribute to the merits of organic farming and the development of a family business. In May of 1993, Gary quit his off-farm job to work full time with Cathy and their pre-teen daughters Janis and Lisa. Is such a return to the farm a contradiction to current agricultural trends, or is it a sign of things to come in the world of organic growing?

McSmith's began as a home delivery service of eggs and vegetables whose customers placed orders once a week. In 1991 they opened their own on-farm market with an ever-expanding product line.

They grow vegetables from a to z — asparagus to zucchini. Vegetarian customers were so pleased with the first crop of dried, colored beans that McSmith's now provides a plethora of varieties like yellow eye, kidney, pinto, Jacob's cattle, navy, and even black soybeans which they export to Japan. Samples of home-grown popcorn were so popular that there's an acre under cultivation. Bagging of spinach and mixed lettuces with their own logo led to the opening of an additional greenhouse.

What isn't sold is pickled, preserved, or dried. The success of salsa kits, jams, jellies, chili sauce, and herbal tea has prompted the building of an on-site cannery. Chickens are butchered at a local abattoir and a small goat herd has been started.

The McSmiths make presentations on the merits of organic farming. They hosted a tour of Japanese organic farmers in the Summer of 1993 and speak at conferences like the National Organic Conference at the University of Guelph.

MCSMITH'S FARM PRODUCE

R.R. #6,
St. Thomas, Ont. N5P 3TI
TEL 519-631-0279

OPEN Friday 3 p.m. to 7 p.m.
Saturday 8 a.m. to 4 p.m.

DRIVE Highway 401 to Wellington Road. Go south on Wellington Road to Concession 11. East on Concession 11 to the turn in the road.

ONTARIO TRIVIA

HALDIMAND-NORFOLK'S rich gypsum veins contain as much as 625 million tons of the mineral. More than 85 per cent of the province's gypsum is mined in its north-central area.

HAMILTON sold the first frozen fish, called Ice Fillets, in January 1929. The process of freezing fish was created by Dr. Archibald Huntsman, a professor of Marine Biology at the University of Toronto.

HAMILTON'S Canadian Warplane Heritage Museum of World War II aircraft maintains the planes in flying condition.

Farmers' Markets

Before feudal times, the first markets were founded on the barter system. In Canada, they were an outgrowth of country fairs, where farmers would show and then sell their cattle in order to avoid feeding them all winter long. Less than a generation ago in Ontario, there were only a handful of farmer's markets. The supermarkets of the 1950s all but wiped them out. But in spite of the advances of trade and commerce, slick packaging and imported food, there has been a renaissance in the Farmers' Markets, led by the province of Ontario.

In 1988 there were 60 local markets in the province. Today there are more than double the number with new ones forming every year. There's even a Farmers' Markets Ontario with a board of directors that encourages towns and villages to recognize the potential of their own marketplace. There are many success stories. All new markets double their sales in just two summers. Gross sales have jumped from the hundreds of thousands of dollars to the millions.

It's more than the price tag that makes public markets viable. This is a forum where urban and farm life comes together. More is exchanged than fresh produce, home baked goods, local delicacies of mushrooms, cheese, honey and maple syrup, arts and crafts, and animals. This is where the social fabric of the community is at its best, where neighbors chat and politicians meet their public, and where charitable organizations publicize their services.

The flavor of each community's market is different, from Toronto's Kensington Market where the ethnic specialties of half the world come together in a few city blocks, to the Waterloo Farmers' Market which features the quilts and preserves of the Mennonites. For those touring the province there's a directory of Ontario Farmers' Markets, available for a fee from Farmers' Markets Ontario.

FARMERS' MARKETS ONTARIO
75 Bayshore Rd.,
R.R. #4,
Brighton, Ont. K0K 1H0
TEL 613-475-GROW
FAX 613-475-2913
800-387-FARM

ONTARIO TRIVIA

IGNACE's Highway 599, known as "The Road North", goes farther north than any other road in Ontario. It ends at Pickle Lake.

INGERSOLL built Ontario's first cheese factory. The town was named for Major Thomas Ingersoll, the father of Laura Secord.

IROQUOIS is the largest town which had to be relocated when the St. Lawrence Seaway flooded the area.

IROQUOIS FALLS is considered the Garden Town of the North with its many planned parks, avenues, and model homes.

St. Lawrence Market

There are pretty much two types of committed shoppers who frequent the St. Lawrence Market. Those who arrive before day-light as the vendors unload to ensure the first choice of quality goods, and those who wait until late afternoon, when the crowds have thinned, to bargain-hunt at a time when the vendors are pleased to sell-off after a long day and pack up for destinations as far away as Holland Marsh, Niagara, and Bowmanville.

Buyers and sellers have been coming to the St. Lawrence Market for almost 200 years, making it Ontario's oldest and largest farmers' market. It was in 1803, when the city was known as Muddy York, that Governor Peter Hunter issued a proclamation recommending the site on Front Street East be made available "...for the purpose of exposing for sale, cattle, sheep, poultry and other provisions, goods and merchandize..."

St. Lawrence is a large, noisy family: vendors yell salutations to one another over the noise of rattling carts as they fill their tables with Yukon Gold and Acadian White potatoes, dumpling squash and bunches of fresh herbs. Many vendors are selling the same products (butter and eggs or fresh sausages), as their great-grandparents sold back in the 1890s. In fact some of the stalls have been in the same family for three generations. It's not unusual to see mothers, fathers, daughters, and sons working alongside grandparents. These are the sellers who know their customers by name, and usually sell out first.

Amid the noise of strolling musicians, people selling lottery tickets, the squeals of delighted children and those who have been misplaced, regular customers line up at their favorite stalls to savor samples and buy rounds of fresh chèvre, buckwheat honey, free range chickens and unusual game birds, tiny, mottled quail eggs, shitake mushrooms, and homemade purées.

It can take the better part of a day to negotiate the crowds and cover both the North and South markets. For those seeking the "real" farmers, they're located in the newer North Market building where they rent space on Saturdays. The restored South Market where the atmosphere is trendier is open Tuesday through Saturday.

ST. LAWRENCE MARKET
92 Front St. East,
Toronto, Ont. M5E IC4
TEL 416-392-7120
FAX 416-392-0120

Poplar Lane Farm

Don Blakney and John Camilleri, partners in Poplar Lane Farm, are among the new-comers at the St. Lawrence Market. They were four years on the waiting list before securing a year-round stall inside, but were pleased to start outside on Jarvis St. Already they have regular customers, but don't yet know them by name, so nicknames have developed — "the artist, the comfrey lady, the English lady and her daughter, pocket, the dentist" and so on. Already their own tradition is starting to build.

From their licensed organic farm in Alliston, Blakney and Camilleri treat customers to designer greens, like arugula, red lettuce, kale, radicchio, endive, escarole, cress, and mustard cress. They sell root crops, tomatoes, sweet and hot peppers, and have a wonderful selection of kitchen herbs including four kinds of basil, thyme, sage, dill, oregano, and chamomile. (They are the only licensed organic growers of such a wide range of potted herbs.) Add to the list homemade items like tomato sauce, herb vinegars, and pickled beets (made from the recipes of a former neighbor, Kate Atkin), free-range brown eggs and naturally raised rabbit and lamb that grace the tables of chef notables Jamie Kennedy and Michael Stadtlander. Not bad for two former civil servants who took over an existing organic farm just four years ago.

Blakney and Camilleri pour through seed catalogues in February and start about 100 different kinds of herbs and vegetables in their greenhouses. That translates into about 40,000 seedlings that are nurtured inside until they can be planted by hand in the spring.

These "nouveau farmers" are dedicated to the European-style farming typical of small farms on the outskirts of Paris. It's market garden farming where vegetables are harvested one day and sold the next, and the small flocks of sheep, hens, and rabbits produce manure that's rich for composting.

A quarterly newsletter keeps customers current with what's happening on Poplar Lane Farm. Look for them at the St. Lawrence Market, indoors, year-round and at the outside stall on Jarvis from May 1 to October 31. Both stalls are open Saturdays from 4 a.m. to 2 p.m.

POPLAR LANE FARM
R.R. #4,
Alliston, Ont. L9R IV4
TEL 705-435-5610

Stratford Chefs School

Canada's Stratford upon the Avon, like its namesake, is noted for its prestigious Shakespearean theatre. From May to mid-November, the tourist town of 27,000 swells by half a million visitors, who come for a "Shakespearean season" of classic and contemporary drama and musicals.

But the town is also famous for its Stratford Chefs School (SCS), acclaimed in Europe and North America as an outstanding culinary training center. Cornell University named the school as one of the top three programs in North America. Culinary writer, Marcella Hazen, goes as far as to say it's the best of its kind in the world.

The SCS was founded to solve a problem common among the town's restaurateurs. Due to the theatre season, Stratford experiences a boom-or-bust cycle. Some restaurants even closed in the off-season. It was very difficult to find competent, well-trained staff for the busy months of the year.

Restaurant owners Eleanor Kane (The Old Prune), Jim Morris (Rundles), and Joe Mandel (The Church) began the school to solve their staffing problems. SCS offers aspiring Canadian chefs two four-month classroom sessions from November to February, alternating with apprenticeships served at the leading establishments in town. It is the only institute outside the community college system that is authorized by the Ontario Training Adjustment Board. The program is much more enriched than at other schools. The academic term is six weeks longer than the provincial standards, and apprentices receive 222 more hours of in-school training.

At SCS there is 100 percent placement of its graduates who are making a name for themselves from New York to San Francisco and throughout the Golden Horseshoe of Ontario.

Much of the school's success is due to the mandate of its founders and the fact that they are successful restaurant owners, not educators. They designed a program that would be different from the generalist training at community colleges. Their focus is the smaller, upscale restaurant with a cuisine that combines classic and contemporary cooking in a way that appeals to Canadian appetites. There is hands-on instruction in the classic techniques of French, Italian, Chinese, and Japanese cooking with visiting chefs like Serge Bruyère of Quebec, Jacques Chibois of Cannes, and Italian Marcella Hazen. Practical courses focus on developing a restaurant concept, marketing strategies, applying for startup loans, and handling staff.

In its inaugural year there were 12 students. The School now selects some 30-35 individuals from more than 200 applications. Typical candidates are in their mid-20s and more than half have university degrees. Most have been in the restaurant business before applying. What Morris and Kane, the school's co-directors, look for in an applicant is a "compulsiveness," people who know what they want and are willing to go for it.

Begun with funding from the Ontario Ministry of Education and Training, the SCS has become more autonomous and self-supporting over the years. The school holds a major annual fund-raiser, a gala dinner held in Toronto that is prepared and served by the students.

To celebrate ten years of culinary excellence, the school also hosted Northern Bounty, a four-day conference on Canadian cuisine. It attracted the who's who of "foodies" from across the country: professional chefs, food writers, critics, academics, food growers, marketers, and vintners. In many ways the conference set new standards of excellence in conference-going, with abundant food well-prepared by the students, and in defining and understanding the heritage of Canada's rich, national cuisine.

The SCS has an impressive board of advisors; Jamie Kennedy of The Palmerston, Franco Prevedelo of Centro, and Donald Ziraldo, President of Inniskillin Wines and executives from major corporations. Co-directors Jim Morris and

Eleanor Kane continue to guide the School at the forefront of the industry.

STRATFORD CHEFS SCHOOL

150 Huron St.,
Stratford, Ont. N5A 5S8
TEL 519-271-1414
FAX 519-271-5679

Soup au Pistou

SOUP

45 ml (3 Tbsp) extra virgin olive oil
250 ml (1 cup) finely chopped onion
3 sprigs fresh thyme
2 bay leaves
1250 ml (9 cups) light chicken stock
125 ml (1/2 cup) paysanne each of carrot, celery, leek, potato, zucchini, and green beans
salt and pepper

PESTO

250 ml (1 cup) fresh basil leaves
50 ml (1/4 cup) extra virgin olive oil
50 ml (1/4 cup) grated Parmesan cheese
1 clove of finely chopped garlic
salt and pepper

GARNISH

125 ml (1/2 cup) tomatoe concassé (tomatoes which have been peeled, seeded, and cut into 6 millimeter (1/4 inch) dice)
250 ml (1 cup) fresh peas
Pesto

PREPARING THE SOUP

- A paysanne is a vegetable cut. The size of the paysanne should be the thickness of a dime and the diameter of half a dime.
- Heat the oil in the pot and gently sweat the onion, thyme, and bay leaves until the onions are soft but not brown. Add the light chicken stock and bring to a boil. Reduce the heat to a simmer and add the paysanne of carrots, celery, and leek, and lightly season. Allow to cook for 10 minutes and then add the paysanne of potato and con-

tinue to cook for 5 minutes. Check the seasoning to ensure it is correct. Add the zucchini and green beans, and continue to cook for another 5 minutes, or until the vegetables are soft.

PREPARING THE PESTO

- Put the basil into a blender, add the olive oil, and process. The pesto should be more of a liquid than a paste, and if necessary more oil can be added. Place this mixture in a bowl. Add Parmesan cheese and garlic and season with salt and pepper.

SERVING THE SOUP

- Just prior to serving, add the tomato concassé and fresh peas to the soup and return to a boil. Reduce the heat, stir in the pesto, check the seasoning, and serve in warmed deep soup bowls.

Lobster & White Corn Chowder

LOBSTER FUMET

one lobster
30 ml (2 Tbsp) unsalted butter
125 ml (1/2 cup) diced onion
50 ml (1/4 cup) diced carrot
30 ml (2 Tbsp) diced celery
50 ml (1/4 cup) diced sweet red pepper
2 sprigs thyme
1 sprig parsley
2 bay leaves
1.5 L (6 cups) water

CORN SOUP

30 ml (2 Tbsp) unsalted butter
175 ml (3/4 cup) finely chopped onion
50 ml (1/4 cup) water
7 ears of corn, shucked, and kernels cut free from the cob
250 ml (1 cup) peeled, seeded, and diced tomatoes
salt and pepper
pinch of cayenne
45 ml (3 Tbsp) chopped fresh chervil

PREPARING THE LOBSTER FUMET

- Kill the lobster by placing the tip of a knife at the base of the head and quickly piercing completely through it. Remove the tail by twisting and pulling it away from the head of the lobster. Remove the claws in the same manner. Reserve the tails and claws. Split the head section in two and discard the green tomalley, the gill tissues, and the digestive tract. Rinse the head sections and cut them into small pieces.

- Melt the butter in a large pot and add the onion, carrot, celery, and pepper. Stew the vegetables over low heat for 15 minutes, stirring occasionally. Raise the heat, add the thyme, parsley, bay leaves, and lobster head pieces. Sauté them, turning often, until their shells redden all over. Pour the 6 cups water over the shells and vegetables and bring it to a boil. Reduce the heat, and simmer for 30 minutes. When finished strain and reserve the lobster fumet, discarding the shells, vegetables and herbs.

- Put a gallon of water on to boil with 30 ml (2 Tbsp) of salt for cooking the tail and claws. Plunge the lobster tail and claws into the salted boiling water for 2 minutes. Remove and let cool on a plate. Remove the meat from the shell, devein the tail, and cut the meat into a small dice. Set aside until needed.

PREPARING THE CORN CHOWDER

- Melt the butter in a large pot. Add the onion and water, cover the pot, and sweat the onion for 10 minutes over low heat. Set aside 250 ml (1 cup) corn kernels, then add the rest to the pot. Add the lobster fumet, bring it to a simmer, and cook for 5 minutes. The lobster fumet should just barely cover the corn; if too much liquid is added the finished chowder will be too thin. Purée the corn and lobster fumet in batches in the blender for a full 2 minutes, then pass the liquid through a fine sieve into another pot. Return this to the boil, checking the consistency, and season with salt, pepper, and cayenne. Once again put this mixture into the blender and purée until smooth. Set aside until needed.

SERVING THE LOBSTER CHOWDER

- Gently warm the soup, adding the tomatoes and reserved corn. When hot, serve in warm bowls and garnish with the chervil leaves and freshly ground pepper.

ONTARIO TRIVIA

KAPUSKASING is the Model Town of the North. The town was designed in the early 1900s like a wheel with spokes.

KEENE boasts the oldest curling club in Ontario, possibly in Canada.

KENORA is the site of an enormous statue of a muskellunge. Made of wood, fibreglass, and steel, the fish is 13 meters (40 feet) high and weighs close to 2.5 tons. It is located in the town's McLeod Park, a symbol of the great sports fishing of Lake of the Woods.

KINGSTON was Canada's first capital city; it's also the oldest city in Ontario.

KINGSTON'S Royal Military College is the oldest military college in the Commonwealth, outside of Great Britain.

KIRKLAND LAKE produces more than one-fifth of Canada's gold. It was home to the millionaire founder of the Lake Shore Gold Mine, Sir Harry Oakes, who was mysteriously murdered in the Bahamas in 1943.

KINGSTON. On Christmas Day, 1855, soldiers in the Royal Canadian Rifles, stationed at Tête du Pont Barracks, cleared the snow from their harbour and slipped their skates on their boots to play the first game of ice hockey with a lacrosse ball and field hockey sticks. The birthplace of organized hockey, the first league game was played here in 1885.

KINGSVILLE is Canada's most southerly town, 56 kilometers (35 miles) south of Detroit.

Algonquin Brewing Company Limited

On April 6, 1988, a group of businessmen held a press conference at the Hotel Admiral in downtown Toronto. They announced the formation of a partnership between Evan Hayter, Drew Knox, Allen Sneath, and Robert Knox (general partners) and Ignat Kaneff and Eric McKnight (limited partners) called the Northern Algonquin Brewing Company Limited. Their plan was to purchase and renovate one of Ontario's oldest brewing companies, the original Formosa Spring Brewery.

Located in picturesque Bruce County, the brewery dates back to 1869. The early settlers of the area were immigrants from Alsace-Lorraine and for them, a German community wasn't complete without a brewery. The plant was built over an underground water source called the Detroit Aquifer, a body of water larger than Lake Huron. It remains one of the purest sources of water in the world.

The original brewery changed hands several times, but by the turn of the century, brewmaster Lorenz Heisz had a reputation for excellence. However, business suffered during Prohibition in the 1920s, the Great Depression in the 1930s, and during World War II.

When the large union breweries in Ontario went on strike during several summers in the 1950s and 1960s, beer drinkers rediscovered the Formosa brewery. Formosa had always maintained a staunch non-union status. At times, it was the only brewery and retail store operating in southern Ontario. Formosa supplied Kitchener's first Octoberfest with all the beer around the clock, doubling its sales. By 1970, Formosa enjoyed a 1 1/2 percent share of the Ontario beer market. But operating to capacity was to be its downfall: on December 31, 1971, all production stopped at the historic old site in favor of a new plant outside Barrie.

Sixteen years later, members of the Northern Algonquin Brewing Company learned that the original facility was for sale. Although the equipment and building seemed beyond repair, the legendary water source and the historic site were attractive.

Two years of hard work and millions of dollars later, a modernized brewing and bottling system emerged. The envy of every small brewery in North America, it uses state of the art equipment while maintaining the brewmaster's craft.

Today, the Algonquin Brewing Company is ranked as the top micro-brewery in the province, doing a volume of more than 100,000 hectoliters. (A hectoliter is the equivalent of 24 cases of 24 bottles.) It employs about 70 people, including many whose fathers or relatives worked at the original brewery.

Two of the top selling brands, Formosa Springs Original Cold Filtered Draft and Algonquin Special Reserve Ale have won a gold medal and a grand gold medal respectively at the Monde Selection in Brussels, Belgium.

To commemorate the 100th anniversary of Algonquin Park, the brewery launched a new beer, Algonquin's Country Lager, in the first party keg to be sold in Ontario. The five-liter container is available at LCBO stores since beer stores aren't equipped to handle the packaging. Sales of the beer will be donated to a charitable organization, Friends of Algonquin Park; between $35,000 and $50,000 is expected to be raised during the year.

Tours of the brewery must be arranged in advance and should include 15 or more people. A brew is included! The original brewmaster's house has been restored as a museum and meeting area. There's also a retail store that sells beer, and a number of logo items including glasses, t-shirts and caps.

The Algonquin Brewery sells Algonquin brand and Formosa Springs products available through the Brewers Retail, selected LCBO stores, and a number of bars and restaurants.

SERVING SUGGESTION: The Algonquin Brewing Company's beers contain no additives or preservatives. To prolong the shelf life, be sure to store in a cool, dark area. For best results, keep refrigerated.

ALGONQUIN BREWING COMPANY LIMITED

Number One Brewery Lane,
Formosa, Ont. N0G IWO
TEL 519-367-2995 (Tours)
FAX 519-367-5414

HEAD OFFICE: 1270 Central Parkway West,
Suite 301,
Mississauga, Ont. L5C 4P4
TEL 905-949-0790
FAX 905-949-1076

Formosa Draft & Cheddar Muffins

375 ml (1 1/2 cups) all purpose flour
125 ml (1/2 cup) cornmeal
30 ml (2 Tbsp) sugar
1 ml (1/4 tsp) salt
2 ml (1/2 tsp) mustard powder
15 ml (1 Tbsp) baking powder
2 ml (1/2 tsp) black pepper
1 egg
50 ml (1/4 cup) vegetable oil
250 ml (1 cup) Formosa Draft
250 ml (1 cup) old Cheddar cheese, grated
30 ml (2 Tbsp) parsley, chopped
30 ml (2 Tbsp) chives (scallions), chopped

- In a mixing bowl, combine dry ingredients. In a separate bowl, beat egg and add remaining ingredients, combining well. Add wet ingredients to dry, stirring just to combine. Spoon into greased muffin tins. Bake at 200 C (400 F) for 20-25 minutes or until golden. Cool 5 minutes before removing from tins. Makes 8 large muffins.

Brewmaster's Chili

50 ml (1/4 cup) olive oil
1 kg (2 1/2 lbs) stewing beef, cut into 12 mm (1/2") cubes
500 ml (2 cups) onions, chopped
4 cloves garlic, chopped
15 ml (1 Tbsp) chili powder
3 ml (3/4 tsp) crushed chilies
12 ml (2 1/2 tsp) black pepper
15 ml (1 Tbsp) dry oregano
12 ml (2 1/2 tsp) cumin
5 ml (1 tsp) salt
1 bay leaf
796 g (28 oz) plum tomatoes, crushed
30 ml (2 Tbsp) tomato paste
2-540 ml (2-19 oz) kidney beans, drained

- In a Dutch oven, heat olive oil over medium high heat and brown meat in two or three batches, adding oil each time. Set beef aside and reduce heat to medium. In the Dutch oven, fry onion and garlic until lightly colored. Add spices and combine thoroughly, for 30 seconds. Add tomatoes, tomato paste and beef. Stir well. Bring to a full boil, place cover on pot. Bake 1 hour at 180 C (350 F). Remove lid and add beer. Stir. Continue to cook 1 hour. Add kidney beans and cook another 20 minutes or until meat is tender. 6-8 servings.

ONTARIO TRIVIA

LAKE SUPERIOR is the world's largest freshwater lake.

LAKE OF THE WOODS is Ontario's second largest inland lake.

LATCHFORD has the world's shortest covered bridge.

WINE COUNTRY

These days there are plenty of good reasons to get excited about Ontario wines. At the top of the list is their excellence: in competition with European products, they have won gold, silver, and bronze medals at world class events like Vin Expo, VinItaly, and Intervin, establishing themselves as premium wines with international profiles. In fact Ontario wines finished second in the overall number of medals for the second year in a row at VinItaly (1993 and 1994). Consumers are happily switching from many of the imported wines to those produced right here in their own backyard.

One reason for the success of Ontario wines is the type of grapes being grown. Since 1988, the government has banned the use in table wine of labrusca grapes: North American varieties like Concord, Catawba, and Niagara. Ontario growers have been successfully cultivating hybrids, the crossbred grapes of American and European species, and *Vitis viniferas*, of European origin. But the growers have also reached a new level of sophistication. They have discovered the best varieties of grapes to grow in the particular subzones of their appellation which will ultimately deliver a consistent quality and style to the wine. For example, the rieslings from the "bench" area tend to show a more intense aroma than rieslings from other zones.

A wonderful way to discover and enjoy these local wines is to tour Ontario's wine country. There are three designated viticultural areas of the province: the Niagara Peninsula; the north shore of Lake Erie; and Pelee Island. Geographers will note they are on the same latitude as three notable European wine districts: Italy's Chianti Classico area, the Rioja region of Spain, and Languedoc-Roussillon in southern France. Ontario's vineyards lie at the center of the world's northern wine-growing belt. Winter cold and summer heat are tempered by Lake Ontario and Lake Erie, and the Niagara Escarpment gives further frost protection to the Niagara Peninsula.

The Wine Route, marked with the distinctive grape logo, covers the Niagara Peninsula from Stoney Creek to Niagara Falls. The countryside is dotted with vineyards, farms, and orchards with pockets of cultural and tourist attractions like the Shaw Festival and Niagara Falls, fine restaurants, antique shops, and craft boutiques.

The new breed of entrepreneurial winemakers have opened up their estate and farm gate wineries, large and small, to share their passion for the grape. As one of their advertisement slogans reads, "We're ready when you are." And ready they are, with tours of state-of-the-art crushing facilities, hayrides through the vineyards, tastings in wine boutiques and wine gardens, the marrying of wine and food in bistros and dining rooms, and the hosting of seminars and barrel tastings. Some combine their operations with bed and breakfast facilities and art galleries, and encourage lunches vineyardside with order-ahead picnic baskets.

From humble beginnings in 1811, when Johann Schiller made wine from domesticated wild grapes growing along the Credit River near Toronto, Ontario's wine producers now number nearly thirty. Each has a story to tell, a unique philosophy of pressing the grape, and a variety of wines to titillate every palate, even the most discerning ones. While the area is best known for its whites (especially Pinot Blancs, Vidals, Rieslings, Chardonnays, and Ice wines), the Merlots, Cabernets, Gamay Noirs, and blends are beginning to bring home the medals.

To select the best wine, the best vintner, the best vineyard, is a subjective task best left to one's personal adventure through Ontario's wine cellars. There truly is something for everyone as each cellar has its own style and approach to wine-making, many bringing generations of expertise from their European ancestors. These are very much family businesses, with spouses and children working alongside the wine-makers and the growers.

Château des Charmes has invested millions of dollars building state-of-the-art cellars and a European-style chateau that befits the opulence of corporate dining and wine-tasting events. After six generations, the Bosc family is reaping the rewards of international gold for wines like their Estate Chardonnay.

Konzelmann brings the know-how of four generations of German wine-making to the shores of Lake Ontario. Among their accolades is the much coveted Grand Gold medal at VinItaly for their 1991 Icewine.

Marynissen has made the leap from grower of fine grapes to a wine-maker of celebrated status. Red wine drinkers will be impressed with their Cuvée winning Cabernet Sauvignon, as well as their Merlot blends and Gamay Noir.

Every establishment has scored firsts and bests, contributing to the enviable position of today's local wine industry as a whole. The wine-making in Ontario is fraternal, a commitment of the parts pulling for the whole. For example, the VQA (Vintners Quality Alliance) was implemented in 1988 at the urging of the vintners themselves.

VQA is to Canada what AOC is to France, DOC is to Italy, QMP is to Germany, and the wine laws are to the United States. VQA assures quality control from the vineyard to the glass. It's Ontario's appellation system that helps consumers identify wines based on the origins of the grapes. A VQA medallion on a bottle identifies a product of the highest distinction as judged by a panel of experts.

One thing is for certain. There is no shortage of entrepreneurs and risk takers among Ontario wineries. A sampling follows to whet the appetite!

Cave Spring Cellars Ltd.

Since 1988 the wines of Cave Spring Cellars have been winning gold, silver, and bronze medals from Intervin to Vin Expo. Among the accolades, their 1990 Chardonnay Reserve ($17.95) edged out the 1989 Marquis de Laguiche (Montrachet) priced at $243 at Cuvée '92, and was judged Best White Wine of the year.

Cave Spring Cellars was established in 1986 by the Pennachetti family. The 14-hectare (33-acre) vineyard is located in the historic town of Jordan, at the heart of the so-called "Beamsville Bench" of the Niagara Escarpment. The estate nestled along the picturesque valley of Twenty Mile Creek, was a crown grant to United Empire Loyalists who settled the area in the nineteenth century and was an abandoned orchard when the Pennachettis purchased the property in the early 1970s.

They systematically cleared, re-contoured and underdrained the land, and planted some of the first *vitis vinifera* grapes in Canada. This they did, in spite of all the nay-sayers, from government officials to old-time farmers and winery field men, who said these temperamental European grape varieties would never grow, ripen, or survive the winters. But the Pennachettis believed in the Bench because of its hillside location, proximity to Lake Ontario's moderating effect, and its unique soils.

The first vines were mainly Chardonnay and Riesling. The plantings were increased to include Gamay Noir, Pinot Noir, Cabernet Sauvignon, Cabernet Franc and Merlot. Today, Cave Spring Cellars continues to use only *vitis vinifera* grape varieties, grown on the Beamsville Bench. Among the oldest vinifera plantings in Ontario, the vineyard is the most densely planted in the province with between 1,400 and 1,600 vines per acre, rather than the provincial average of 800 vines per acre. This is significant because higher density plantings yield better quality grapes.

While the Pennachettis have converted the sceptics with their award-winning whites, they are taking up the challenge of making great reds from classic varieties of Bordeaux grapes; their Gamay Noir and Merlot have both won medals.

Cave Spring Cellars is situated in the old Jordan Winery building which dates back to 1871. They opened Ontario's first, on-site winery restaurant in 1993, for lunch and dinner. It's named On the Twenty, for its spectacular, panoramic view of Twenty Mile Creek. Chef Michael Olson is committed to creating menus that take advantage of fresh local foods and that heighten and complement the distinctive flavors of Cave Spring wines.

The old Jordan winery building also houses an interesting antique market and is home to the local historical museum and the Twenty's new gallery and gift shop. There is a private tasting room with catering available for any occasion or celebration; the Winemaker's Dinner and Tasting Series is an annual event, available by reservation only. Tours of the winery may be arranged by appointment.

The wines are available at Caves Spring Cellars, Vintages, and LCBO outlets.

CAVE SPRING CELLARS LTD.
3836 Main St.,
P.O. Box 53,
Jordan, Ont. LOR ISO
TEL 905-562-3581
FAX 905-562-3232

DRIVE from Toronto, following the QEW west toward Niagara. Take the Vineland exit off the QEW and follow Victoria Avenue south to the first stoplight, at Regional Road 81 (Highway 8). Turn left and proceed east on Highway 8 through the Jordan Valley to the Jordan Hotel. Turn left just before the hotel and follow Main Street.

RETAIL STORE OPEN Monday through Saturday 10 a.m. to 5 p.m.; Sunday 11 a.m. to 5 p.m.

Linguini with Forest Mushrooms & Apples in Romano Cream

Per Person:

125 g (4 oz) mushrooms (shitake, oyster, crimini, button)
olive oil
salt, pepper, garlic, thyme to taste
55 g (2 oz) wine
175 g (6 oz) chicken or vegetable stock
55 g (2 oz) diced Ida Red or Golden Delicious apples
45 g (1 1/2 oz) 35% cream
125 g (1/4 lb) cooked pasta
Romano cheese

- Sauté mushrooms in olive oil for 90 seconds and season with salt, pepper, garlic, and fresh thyme. Deglaze pan with wine; add chicken stock and apples. Reduce to 55 grams (2 ounces). Add cream and cooked pasta. Bind with Romano cheese and serve.
- Serve with Cave Spring Cellars Chardonnay, 1992

Warm Salad of Duck Livers on Field Greens with Rosemary Sweet Cherry Vinaigrette

Per Person

45 ml (1 1/2 oz) olive oil
1 sprig fresh rosemary
85 g (3 oz) duck livers
salt, pepper to taste
55 g (2 oz) cherries
30 ml (1 oz) balsamic vinegar
sweet and bitter lettuce leaves

- In a frying pan, heat olive oil with rosemary. Remove rosemary and sauté duck livers seasoned with salt and pepper at medium and remove from pan. Add cherries and vinegar. Return livers to pan and pour onto a selection of lettuce leaves.
- Serve with Cave Spring Cellars Gamay Noir, 1992

ONTARIO TRIVIA

MERRICKVILLE, built in 1793 on the banks of the Rideau Canal, is one of Ontario's best preserved, nineteenth century villages.

MOOSONEE is the end of the line, the last stop on the Polar Bear Express. Any further travel must be done on foot, by air, or by water.

MOSPORT is Canada's major road-racing track. International races attract crowds of 50,000 people annually.

Stoney Ridge Cellars

Jim Warren, co-owner of Stoney Ridge Cellars is a wine-making success story. He's an amateur turned pro. The former high school teacher was a legend in Ontario and Canadian amateur wine-making circles, winning numerous awards in the 1970s including four home wine-making championships in Ontario and three first place awards in the American Wine Society's 1989 National Amateur Wine Competition. Now he's collecting medals at international events.

Stoney Ridge began when Warren and partner Brian Alexander teamed up with grape-grower Bryce Weylie who owned a farm in Vinemount near the top of the escarpment. In 1985 they produced their first 4,500 liters (1,000 gallons) of wine, increasing production to 36,000 liters (8,000 gallons) by 1988. With Free Trade, Weylie decided he could no longer make a living growing grapes. Consequently Stoney Ridge-2 began when grape-grower Murray Puddicombe bought out Warren's other two partners.

Puddicombe owned an 80-hectare (200-acre) property on Highway 8 in Verona. The farm was acquired as a crown grant by his United Empire Loyalist ancestors, and was already producing fruit, including some excellent Chardonnay vines. In 1989 the partners removed the old barn and built a modern winery with a store, fruit market and a balcony restaurant. The following year they made 91,000 liters (20,000 gallons) of wine.

Their boutique operation now produces 136,000 liters (30,000 gallons) a year with grapes from their own farm as well as other growers. While Puddicombe manages the quality of the grapes, Warren applies his unique style of wine-making to the production. He's committed to small-lot crushing, cold-settling his juice, and aging in French and American oak casks. While his Chardonnay has won gold at VinItaly, his reds are considered among the best in Canada.

This small vineyard boasts the most wines listed with VQA in Ontario. Despite its size it makes the greatest number of wines from the most varieties of grapes.

Visitors will enjoy a visit to their market for fresh breads, cheeses and pâtés and lunch overlooking the vineyard from the balcony. Tours can be arranged by appointment.

STONEY RIDGE CELLARS

1468 Highway 8,
Winona, Ont. L8E 5K9
TEL 905-643-4508
FAX 905-643-0933

DRIVE the QEW to exit 78 and go south of Fifty Road, then east on Highway 8.

A Word About Icewine

Sunday, June 16, 1991, history was made in Bordeaux France at Vinexpo. (The world's largest trade fair is held every other year and attracts over 50,000 people, including vintners, wine professionals, buyers, media, and wine buffs.) More than 4,100 wines from around the world were judged. 109 were selected as gold medallists, and of that group, 19 wines were awarded the prestigious "Grand Prix d'Honneur" by the Oenological Institute of Bordeaux. Inniskillin's 1989 Icewine was among the select 19. The recognition brought world-wide attention not only to Inniskillin, but to Ontario as a wine-producing region. It also peaked the curiosity of wine drinkers, establishing icewine as a cult wine.

One sip of this fragrant, concentrated nectar explains why individuals pay a premium price for it, and why vintners go to so much trouble to make it.

The aroma of icewine is reminiscent of lychee nuts, followed by a taste of tropical fruits, with mango and peach overtones. It is the true essence of the grape.

There is considerable risk for growers and winemakers to produce icewine. It can only be made from thick-skinned, late-maturing varieties like Vidal and Riesling. At their peak of ripeness in October, they are left on the vine, waiting for temperatures to drop to between -8 and -10 C (17 and 14 F). In the meantime, the entire area is netted to protect the sacred crop from feathered predators. It could be mid-November, Christmas Eve, or well into January before the mercury dips to the magic number. And when it does, the call goes out to staff, friends and neighbours, regardless of the day or hour, and the grapes are painstakingly picked by hand. They will be frozen solid, the size of marbles or reduced to raisins, depending on the type of grape and just how long they've been on the vines. Through a repeated process of freezing and thawing the berries are dehydrated. This concentrates the sugar, acids and extracts. A relatively small volume of juice is extracted given the large number of

grapes, generally only between 5 and 10 percent of a normal yield.

Ontario is now the most prolific source of icewine with roughly 20 vineyards producing it. Its limited quantities are in high demand especially out of country. To guarantee your pleasure, wineries will sell you icewine futures.

ONTARIO WINE FACTS

- Ontario produces 80 percent of Canadian wines.
- There are approximately 5,800 hectares (15,000 acres) of vines cultivated in the province.
- Ontario is the only wine region in the world where grape prices are negotiated before the harvest.

FIRSTS AND BESTS AMONG THE WINERIES

- BRIGHTS: The oldest Canadian winery still in existence was established in 1874 as the Niagara Falls Wine Company, located in Toronto. After the acquisition of Jordan Wines, it became Canada's largest winery. Its list of firsts include: first to make a non-labrusca table wine; the first vinifera varietal wine; the first 7 percent sparkling wine; the first bottle-fermented sparkling wine; the first Canadian "champagne" made strictly from Chardonnay and Pinot grapes.
- CHATEAU-GAI/CARTIER WINES & BEVERAGES: This company introduced Canada to its first wine cooler and wine sold in tetrapaks (bag-in-box); made the first wine-based cream liqueur and Canada's first light wine, "Capistro." Their winemaker, Mira Ananicz, is the only female chief winemaker in Ontario.
- CHATEAU DES CHARMES: Co-owner Paul Bosc was the first commercial wine-grower in the province to plant *Vitis vinifera* grapes extensively, setting the trend for other growers across Canada to follow. He makes the best champagne-method sparkling wine in Canada and the best Gamay Beaujolais Nouveau in Ontario, and was the first in Ontario to perfect carbonic maceration, an untraditional vinification process, as well as the first to import oak barrels from France.
- COLIO WINES: The only winery to use grapes from all three designated wine-growing areas.

- HILLEBRAND ESTATES: Known for the best equipment, facilities, and tours.
- INNISKILLIN WINES: On July 31, 1975 they received the first wine license issued in Ontario since 1929. As mentioned, their 1989 Vidal Icewine won a gold medal at Vinexpo, in 1991; it is the most decorated Canadian wine. The company's president, Donald Ziraldo, was the force behind Niagara's Wine Route signage. Donald Ziraldo and Karl Keiser, co-founders of Inniskillin Wines, were invested in the Order of Ontario, by Lieutenant Governor Henry R. Jackman, in the Spring of 1993. Ontario's most prestigious award was given to the men for being instrumental in shaping the growth and direction of the Ontario wine industry.
- KONZELMANN ESTATE WINERY: The first to introduce Vertico training of the vines to Canada, a method of growing that allows the sun and wind through the vines drying the dew and rain.
- LONDON WINERY: The first Canadian winery to introduce the process for making flor sherry and the first to sell it in a decanter with a glass stopper. Also the first to use the millepore filter.
- MARYNISSEN ESTATES: Ontario's first farm gate winery.
- PELEE ISLAND WINERY: The first in Ontario to produce ice wine (1983) and red ice wine (1989), it has the most extensive vinifera plantings of all the estate wineries.
- QUAI DU VIN: The only winery located in a "dry" zone designated in prohibition days. It is the only company to offer a 25-cent return deposit on its bottles.
- STONECHURCH VINEYARDS: Makes Canada's most expensive, barrel-fermented Chardonnay.
- STONEY RIDGE CELLARS: Has more wines listed with VQA than any other Ontario winery. They are the only winery making raspberry wine.
- VIN VILLA: Canada's first commercial winery on Pelee Island.
- VINELAND ESTATES: First winery to incorporate a wine bistro in their operation.
- Two books highly recommended for understanding and touring Ontario's Wine Country are *Discovering Ontario's Wine Country* by Linda Bramble & Shari Darling, (Boston Mills Press), and *Vintage Canada* by Tony Aspler, (McGraw-Hill Ryerson).

WINE REGIONS OF ONTARIO

Wine Trails Publishing,
P.O. Box 17,
Plattsville, Ont., N0J IS0
TEL/FAX 604-494-7733

An annual publication with insight into what's happening generally in the world of Ontario wines, with profiles of vineyards, wineries, awards, tasting events, etc.

THE WINE COUNCIL OF ONTARIO

35 Maywood Ave.,
St. Catharines, Ont. L2R IC5
TEL 905-684-8070
FAX 905-684-2993

This is an organization whose members are the vineyards. They are a great source of up-to-date information about wine-making in Ontario, Ontario's standings in competitions, etc.

ONTARIO WINE SOCIETY

Ontario Wine Society,
P.O. Box 519, Station K,
Toronto, Ont. M4P 2G9

The Ontario Wine Society (OWS) is a young organization, formed in 1991, and based in Toronto. Several hundred members strong, it's the only "regionally-oriented wine society" in Ontario. Its objective is to "enhance (the) knowledge and appreciation of fine Ontario wines through an emphasis on education, value, and access...to the wineries."

Membership includes organized tours to Ontario vineyards, special club events, bulletins, and a quarterly newsletter, "The Society Pages." It lists wine news in the form of upcoming events, results of competitions, newly available wines, and other tidbits, both wine- and food-related. The OWS expects to expand membership with chapters outside metro.

Best Bottles Wineletter

If you love wine you might think Bill Munnelly has the best job in the province. Self-proclaimed the LCBO's (Liquor Control Board of Ontario's) best customer, he earns his living tasting nearly every wine the LCBO carries, and writing about it. He's the Stratford-based author of *Best Bottles WineLetter*, Canada's first independent consumer wine report. (Munnelly pays for every drop of wine he tastes and accepts no advertisements).

His subscribers, who now number in the thousands, refer to it as "the insider's guide to the LCBO." This is a publication for the novice quaffer, the seasoned sipper, and everyone else in between, even those who don't like wine (the possibilities of converting are immense). This publication is a "must read" if only to savor the Munnelly (rhymes with funnily) sense of humor.

The 16-page, bimonthly newsletter is full of reviews of domestic and imported wines. Munnelly has single-handedly managed to take the snobbery out of the business of choosing and enjoying wine. He leaves the jargon of the oenophile behind and delivers the straight goods with such candor and wit, one can only laugh all the way to the liquor store, Munnelly's "run and grab list" in hand, assured of an appropriate selection.

To read *Best Bottles* is to meet Munnelly on every page. This is a man with a passion for the pen as well as the grape. Of one Riesling he says "This wine is usually pleasant but confusing. I never know what to do with it because I can never figure out if it's reserved, straight forward, or just boring. You know those people you meet half a dozen times of the year but you never get to know them? — something interesting or critical distracts you and you're left wondering, 'should I have tried harder, or is it worth the effort?' I may be mean but I think this wine is plonk." (p. 11, Aug. '93).

Munnelly dispels the myth that good wine has to be French or expensive, or both, to be good. Most of the wines he reviews are affordable, under $10 a bottle. They are assessed not only in terms of price, but season and food accompaniments. He believes people who say they don't care for wine just haven't had a good one, or perhaps they have tried a wine out of season. He's liberal with his food suggestions and will expand the horizons of those caught in the white with seafood, red with meat, trap. "I enjoy sipping a wine like this (1990 Groth Sauvignon Blanc, Napa, Calif.) while I'm chopping onion and garlic. And I'm sure that if Wolfgang Puck ever went to Morocco he'd come up with a dish exotic enough to serve with this wine. Chicken BBQ with ginger, cumin and tons of sweet peppers would be a fine match." (p. 12, Feb '92). With a 1986 Tignanello, Antinori he suggests "A roast bird of some kind and friends in nice sweaters..." (p. 12, Oct. '92).

Munnelly's wit is no disguise for his authoritative viewpoints, just his way of tempering them. He's a graduate of the Dublin College of Catering and Hotel Management with a major in wines of the world. He has worked in hotel management in Britain and Canada and been a wine consultant with Gilbeys. He was also a partner in Rundles Restaurant when it opened in Stratford in 1977, and Toronto's Rosedale Diner in 1980. He has been a wine consultant to the hotel and restaurant trade since 1982 and continues to advise restaurants about their wine lists.

There is no question that Munnelly and *Best Bottles* have influenced the LCBO considerably since the first issue in 1983. As Munnelly educates the consumer, the LCBO responds with better wines and a greater number of varieties. While the relationship between Munnelly and the LCBO has not always been smooth sailing, the rapport between the two seems to have mellowed like a good bottle of wine. Munnelly informs readers when sales are coming up at the Vintages stores and on the occasion of the tenth anniversary of *Best Bottles*, he asked the LCBO "to supply more goody buys than usual, especially Rosé, to put on a sale, and to locate a slew of great local wines."

While most of Munnelly's readers reside in Ontario, out-of-province (including US) subscribers find many of the wines are available in their area. They also benefit from his forays into larger issues like When to Riesling, a Chablis Primer, or tips on setting up a cellar system.

"A Drinker's Diary" features Munnelly's travels, both locally and abroad. For example, his notes on a 50-kilometer (30-mile) Irish pub tour between Gallway and Shannon Airport are just as enlightening for hikers and historians as Guinness guzzlers.

Best Bottles adds to the ease of buying wine by including pictures of many of the labels. Each bottle reviewed is identified according to the name, year, price, country of origin, and government control number. Munnelly reassures those who can't find his suggestions in their local wine section that the LCBO has a toll-free infoline that can locate any item (800-ONT- LCBO).

Munnelly is also the author and publisher of *How to Buy a Bottle*, a 70-page Canadian best-seller, published in 1988 and updated in 1990, 1991 and 1992. A simple guide to wine shopping, Munnelly takes the mystique out of wine and addresses the concerns of most people — "what tastes good? What is good value? And what should be avoided?" He approaches the subject matter from the perspective of two characters — the traditional wine snob and the average Joe. Readers can identify with either stereotype and have a little fun as they shop. Unlike most books and articles on wine, which usually discuss expensive wines, *How to Buy a Bottle* recommends moderately priced wines that best suit the "meals, parties and events" Munnelly himself enjoys most often. The book sells for less than a good bottle of wine!

The book is available through some bookstores or directly from the author. The wine letter is published six times a year, by subscription only. Munnelly is happy to send gift subscriptions and also a free single copy to interested parties.

BEST BOTTLES WINELETTER

Box 503,
Stratford, Ont. N5A 6T7
TEL 519-273-5517

Ferndale Vineyards Inc.

When Fern Cousineau, a former construction company owner, purchased a vineyard in Jordan, heart of the Niagara wine district in 1979, he had no way of anticipating the declining grape market that would beset the wine industry in 1982.

Cousineau purchased the 40-hectare (100-acre) vineyard to escape the rigors of city living and to fulfil a life-long fantasy of owning a farm. It was a dream he had had since his teenage days when he picked fruit in the Niagara fruit belt.

The vineyard had been producing grapes for 80 years and Cousineau hoped to continue the tradition, selling the farm's annual 350-ton harvest to local wineries and juice makers. The grape market continued to slide until growers' costs in Niagara exceeded the price they could get for the grapes. Many growers let their produce rot on the vine.

The future looked grim. In anticipation of Free Trade, the Ontario government predicted grape growers' incomes would be cut in half. Cousineau was determined to come up with an alternative use for his grapes. The result of his dilemma is "Champanade," the "unwine," a sparkling beverage that has captured the taste buds of those looking for an alternative drink to alcohol. It's made of 90 percent juice, blended with natural water trucked in from Caledon and then carbonated. It's the only product of its kind made from start to finish by one producer.

Cousineau had to convert his operation and his thinking from grower to producer. For a time his genteel country lifestyle became more hectic than the city rat race he had left behind. Son-in-law Ken McCarthy uprooted his family to join Cousineau's operation. They built the processing plant themselves with the help of one other person, secured loans, and purchased new and used equipment from across Canada.

The formula for the sparkling beverage was developed with the help of Dr. Tibor Fuleki and his assistants at the Agricultural Research Station in Vineland. The process of making Champanade is similar to wine-making, and uses the same grapes. De Chaunac is made from red grapes and is rose-colored; Concord Champanade is made from Concord grapes; White Champanade is a blending of Niagara and Elvira grapes. There are also blends of white grapes and apple juice and Concord grapes and apple juice. There are six flavors in all.

The grapes are picked and crushed but the grape juice is pasteurized to prevent fermentation. This differs from "non-alcoholic" wine which is allowed to ferment and then has "brutal things done to it" to remove the alcohol. The grape juice for Champanade is stored at a constant temperature of 0 C (32 F) for four months. Bottling is done as demand for the product dictates.

A marketing strategy was planned in consultation with Canadore College Innovation Centre to get Champanade maximum exposure in Ontario. From April to December of 1988, 90,000 taste samples were given out in grocery stores.

With Champanade firmly established, Ferndale launched a second non-alcoholic beverage, Niagara Kooler, a blend of 40 percent juice and carbonated water that comes in five distinct flavors: Perfectly Peach, Apple Cranberry, Very Berry, Orange Mango, and Lemon Lime.

Fern Cousineau's risk-taking paid off. He created a new use for his grapes and those of his neighbours. He developed two products which help in the fight against drinking and driving. Ready to enjoy retirement, he sold controlling interest of Ferndale in April, 1993, to Natural Niagara Inc. which trades on the Toronto Stock Exchange. He will act as a consultant until 1995 and live on the property for twenty years, toasting the fruits of his labor no doubt with Champanade.

Champanade is sold at A & P stores, IGAs, independent grocers, farm markets, and specialty food stores. It's also sold from the vineyard for special occasions like weddings and conferences. A new reception facility is being built at the vineyard and tours may also be booked.

FERNDALE VINEYARDS INC.
3026 8th Ave.,
R.R. #1,
Jordan, Ont. L0R 1S0
TEL 905-562-5779
FAX 905-562-4469

ONTARIO TRIVIA

NEWMARKET is the location of Canada's oldest Quaker Meeting House.

NIAGARA FALLS MUSEUM is North America's oldest museum with more than 700,000 exhibits.

NIPIGON, located at the mouth of the Nipigon River on Lake Superior, was the site of the first permanent white settlement on the north shore of the Lake. On the Nipigon River the world record brook trout was caught. It weighed 6.5 kilograms (14 1/2 pounds).

Pelee Treasures

With four young children, most people would add on a family room to the back of their house. But Cathie and Garry Penner's 4-by-8.5-meter (14-by-28-foot) addition to their white, wood frame home in Kingsville is a caviar plant!

The room has a high ceiling, several sinks, and spotless, stainless steel walls that can be easily hosed down. It's built to Fisheries and Oceans standards and is a registered fish processing plant, so the Penners are licensed to ship their product around the world.

They got into the caviar business by happenstance. A commercial fisherman, Penner and his wife often volunteered their time for the Ontario Fish Producer's Association, meeting the public at food shows in order to promote the local fish industry. Because it was expensive and cumbersome to prepare and cook fish as giveaway samples, it was easier to take prepared fish pâté and caviar. Penner began saving the roe from his whitefish catch. Normally the roe was stripped and fed to the seagulls.

People became interested in the caviar which the Penners were processing in their kitchen. They began to make local sales and met an interested distributor.

For most people, the word caviar conjures up two distinctly different images. Beluga caviar, the lustrous, black pearls heaped in a crystal dish on a bed of crushed ice, is the stuff of James Bond movies and decadent lifestyles. It's the rarest of three types of caviar-producing sturgeon, fish that swim the waters of the Caspian Sea, because a beluga sturgeon can take 20 years to reach egg-producing maturity. A single sturgeon can weigh up to a ton and produce 91 kilograms (200 pounds) of roe, once in a lifetime. Beluga sturgeon produce grains that are larger, softer in texture, and a pearlier hue than the Oesetra and Sevruga sturgeon. Strictly speaking, only roe from these fish can be called caviar and can command prices of $1,500 a kilogram (2 pounds).

But the name caviar is loosely applied to the inexpensive roe of salmon, trout, lumpfish, and whitefish. Dyed black or red, these heavily salted products are responsible for caviar's other persona, the one that makes people shun the thought of this delicacy.

The Penners' roe comes from Lake Erie whitefish that swim to the shoals of Pelee Island in limited numbers to spawn. This is the most southerly range of this species. Their flesh is whiter and brighter, and their roe is truly golden as opposed to the more bronze coloration of some whitefish.

Penner's caviar is superior to other roe because it is processed in close proximity to where it is caught during October and November. It is not pasteurized but frozen so the color is not washed out. Early and late harvest eggs are separated into two distinct varieties. "Pelee Gold," the color of honey, is collected at the beginning of the season. These eggs pop when pressed against the palate. "Pelee Diamonds" is the product of eggs captured towards the end of the spawning cycle. They are crisp, a bright gold in color, and sparkle like diamonds because of their texture.

Whitefish roe is prepared in much the same fashion as sturgeon roe. The eggs are removed from the whitefish in sacs called skeins. There can be up to 10,000 eggs, smaller than a BB pellet, in each fish. The skeins are washed in cold water to remove blood, fat, and membranes, then passed through fine screens to separate the eggs from the sacs. The eggs are washed again and drained overnight. They are weighed and then salted about 4 percent by weight. This is very low compared to 12 percent in other types of fish roe. It's at this point that the eggs become caviar. The salt draws liquid, helping to firm and preserve the roe and the color becomes uniform. It is then frozen to preserve its mild, fresh taste.

Pelee Gold and Pelee Diamonds are sold at select delicatessens and restaurants and retailed at the Penner's plant. They are wholesale distributors in Detroit, Owen Sound, Toronto, and Switzerland and the Penners do their own distribution in Ontario and Ohio. Their caviar has been sold and sampled across Canada and nearly 20 countries world-wide. It is packaged frozen and arrives still frozen, anywhere in Canada and the US within 48 hours.

Prices vary depending upon the distributor and retailer. The 40-gram (1.4-ounce) size ranges between $11 and $20. The 125-gram (4.3-ounce) jar sells for between $30 and $45.

The Penners sell and ship retail gift baskets and cater local parties and banquets. They also make a smoked whitefish pâté, called Pâté de Coregone, a unique blend of smoked and baked whitefish, cream cheese, and spices. The Penner's signature dish is their caviar torte (recipe follows).

PELEE TREASURES
94 Queen St.,
Kingsville, Ont. N9Y 2A2
TEL 519-733-8025
FAX 519-733-9817

Caviar Serving Suggestions

- The mild, delicate flavor of the Pelee caviars can be enjoyed on their own. The Penners teach tasters perfect caviar etiquette, to take it from "nature's spoon," the web of skin that stretches between the forefinger and the thumb.
- Buttered toast points and buttered crackers (low in salt) are perfect accompaniments to caviar. A dollop of sour cream and chopped green onion may be added. Apples and cucumber slices can also be topped with the "Gold." A Detroit restaurant makes what they call the $100 potato with Pelee Diamonds. It's a baked potato with sour cream and 28 grams (1 ounce) of Diamonds on top.

Penner's Caviar Torte

sour cream
cream cheese
Pelee Diamonds
chopped egg
chopped onion
Pelee Gold

- Blend enough sour cream and cream cheese to make a smooth spread and spoon it onto a circular serving dish. Top with Pelee Diamonds in the center to make a bull's eye. Surround the caviar with rings of chopped egg, chopped onion, and Pelee Gold. Serve with crackers or toast points.

ONTARIO TRIVIA

OTTAWA government geographers and cartographers put together the world's first complete national atlas, the Canadian National Atlas, in 1905.

OTTAWA is the place where Dr. Edward Asselbergs of the Canada Department of Agriculture developed the process for making instant mashed potatoes in 1961.

OWEN SOUND is the birthplace of Billy Bishop, Canada's most deocrated serviceman during World War I. The Billy Bishop Heritage Museum is housed in the Victorian home where he was born and raised.

Woolwich Dairy

People either love chèvre (pronounced SHEHV-RUH or SHEHV), or acquire a taste for it. French for "goat," chèvre is goat's milk cheese. It has a delightful, tart flavor, distinct from other cheeses. Goat milk is also made into a variety of other cheeses, including Cheddar; bellisimo, an Italian cheese that's similar to Swiss; gaisli, not unlike Mozarella; and feta, used mostly in Greek salads.

Goat milk cheese has long been a favorite with Europeans, especially the French. Thanks to Woolwich Dairy in Ariss, near Guelph, Canadians and Americans are able to savor some of the finest goat milk cheese made in the world today, and ironically, at prices lower than the imports.

At one time, imported goat milk cheeses cost about 50 percent more than cow milk varieties. They were usually only available at specialty and health food shops. Woolwich Dairy, in operation since 1983, has found a niche in the market and is now Canada's largest goat cheese producer. In a short period of time they have brought the cost of these cheeses down, made them more accessible through supermarket chains, and still manage to produce award-winning products.

Woolwich has won more than 50 awards. Their chèvrai, a smooth, creamy, spreadable cheese, has won top honors in all the Canadian cheese contests including the Royal Agricultural Winter Fair and the Canadian National Exhibition. Gaisli, a mild, meltable cheese competed with cheeses from countries around the world in the open class category and took second place in 1990 at the World Cheese Competition, held every two years in Wisconsin. Their feta and gaisli cheese also won second and third place at the same competition in 1992 in the goat cheese category.

The company is owned by an energetic young couple, cheese-maker Tony Dutra and his wife Olga for whom cheese-making is a family tradition. All but two employees are relatives, so it's not surprising the business operates with a great deal of pride and care. Before buying Woolwich in 1990,

the family ran Nova Cheese, a company that produced *quijo de cabra*, a mild Portuguese cottage cheese, made from goat milk. Prior to that, Dutra's parents ran a small, independent goat cheese operation in Portugal.

One of the secrets of their success is freshness. Many imported varieties are made from frozen curds so that the milk supply is matched to peak consumption times. At Woolwich, the goat milk is picked up fresh from local farmers. The driver of the dairy truck tastes each batch before it is pumped into the holding tank. At the dairy it is pasteurized, then mixed with cultures and coagulants. Curds will form in about 16 hours. Once the solids are separated from the whey, it is hung in cloth bags for 72 hours and is then ready for packaging in a variety of traditional French molds, including rounds and logs which are aged for a couple of months for a slightly stronger taste.

The aged logs and the rounds come plain or coated with a choice of garlic, fine herbs, black pepper, chives, green pepper corns, and lemon dill. The chèvrai comes plain or mixed throughout with the same choice of flavorings.

Woolwich cheeses contain no additives or preservatives, and are rennet free. They are also low in fat. There are 82 calories, 6.8 grams of fat and 4.5 grams of protein in one ounce. Compare this with cow milk cream cheese which contains 99 calories, 9.9 grams of fat, and 2.1 grams of protein an ounce. For the roughly 5 million Canadians with lactose intolerance and lactose-related allergies, goat milk products are a welcome dairy alternative.

Woolwich cheeses are available in Canada, coast to coast, and are now penetrating the American market in New York, California, and New Hampshire. In addition to specialty shops, Woolwich cheese is sold in such major grocery chains as Sobeys, Mr. Grocer, Miracle Mart, and Loblaws.

Cheese is available from the factory and can be shipped by courier. Recipe suggestions are supplied upon request.

WOOLWICH DAIRY

Olga and Tony Dutra,
R.R. #1,
Ariss, Ont. N0B 1B0
TEL 519-836-GOAT
FAX 519-836-4640

DRIVE Highway 401 to Highway 6 north (Guelph). Drive to Highway 7, go left to the first set of lights (Elmira Road) and turn right. Drive for 10 minutes into Ariss, past a hanging yellow flashing caution light, to the first road. Turn right. Drive to next road and turn right. Drive down the dirt road to brown buildings on the left with the Woolwich sign.

STORING TIPS

- Chèvrai keeps for 3 months in the refrigerator and can be frozen.
- Gaisli and Cheddar keep 5 to 6 months in the refrigerator.

Warm Goat Cheese Salad

1 kg (4 cups) torn mixed greens
80 ml (5 Tbsp) olive oil
45 ml (3 Tbsp) lemon juice
10 ml (2 tsp) green onion, finely chopped
5 ml (1 tsp) Dijon mustard
1 egg slightly beaten
75 ml (1/3 cup) seasoned bread crumbs
15 ml (1 Tbsp) grated Parmesan cheese
15 ml (1 Tbsp) sesame seeds, toasted
250 g (8 oz) Chèvrai, sliced into 8 slices
130-45 ml (2-3 Tbsp) butter
8 ripe olives, pitted

- Wash and dry greens. Arrange on platter, cover with plastic wrap and chill. Combine oil, lemon juice, onion and mustard in jar. Cover, shake well and chill. Place egg in a shallow bowl. In another bowl combine bread crumbs, Parmesan cheese and sesame seeds. Dip cheese slices in egg, then coat both sides with crumb mixture. Cover and chill. Just before serving, heat butter in skillet. Add cheese. Cook over medium-high heat 4 to 5 minutes until golden; turn and cook other side until golden. Shake dressing, and drizzle some over greens.

Arrange cheese on top. Add olives and drizzle with more dressing. Serve at once.

Spaghetti with Prosciutto, Italian Parsley and Goat Cheese

30 ml (2 Tbsp) olive oil
15 ml (1 Tbsp) butter
2 cloves garlic, finely chopped
2 eggs
50 ml (1/4 cup) grated Parmesan cheese
30 ml (2 Tbsp) fresh parsley, chopped or 15 ml (1 Tbsp) dried
500 g (1 lb) fresh or dried spaghetti
125 ml (1/2 cup) Chèvrai
6 slices prosciutto, cut into julienne strips
ground black pepper, salt to taste

- Heat oil and butter in a small frying pan on low heat. Add garlic and cook 2-3 minutes. Beat together the eggs, Parmesan, and parsley in a large bowl. Cook the spaghetti in plenty of boiling salted water until el dente. Drain and place in a warmed serving bowl. Add goat cheese, prosciutto, garlic, and egg mixture. Add salt and pepper; toss well. Serve immediately on warm plates or in bowls. 4 servings.

Sugarplums

For anyone who has read Clement C. Moore's poem "The Night Before Christmas," the line "visions of sugarplums danced in their heads," will be a familiar one. But what exactly is a sugarplum? Beatrice Diana Bowyer set herself the task of finding out.

She began with the poet himself, Clement Clarke Moore, an American scholar who wrote the poem in 1822 as a Christmas gift for his children. The poem was originally called "A Visit From Saint Nicholas" but is best known by its first line.

Moore's life spanned tumultuous times, including the American Revolution, the Yellow Fever Epidemic in New York, and the great influx of immigrants to the Americas. It was a time ripe for a poem of hope, surprise, and vision. It was also a time when sugar was a luxury item. So Bowyer knew that this key ingredient in a sugarplum would be used sparingly.

She also discovered that Moore was of British ancestry and in all probability lived in a household of British methods and customs. She concluded the sugarplums of Moore's people would have been the popular sweetmeat of seventeenth-century England, made of fruits and nuts rolled in a sprinkling of sugar.

The English were influenced by the foods brought to them by the Arabians — almonds, walnuts and pistachios, raisins, figs and apricots, and spices, especially ginger.

Keeping all of this in mind, Bowyer began experimenting with recipes to create a sugarplum as close as possible to the one Clement C. Moore had in mind in 1822.

The results are her delicately, handcrafted sugarplums, a combination of dried fruits, nuts, spices and flavorings. The only sugar is that which clings to the outside of the sugarplum when it is rolled.

Bowyer believes there is something very magical about sugarplums. "When you offer someone a sugarplum, it always brings a smile!" They are the perfect accompaniment to share with someone spe-cial, over coffee, tea, or a glass of sherry, a tradition of Christmases past. They also make a wonderful addition to a table setting and can be hung on the tree with ribbon or lace.

Sugarplums come in a rich, burgundy gift box, sized to contain three, eight, sixteen, or thirty-two of the delicacy. They are available in specialty shops throughout Ontario and at events like the Royal Agricultural Winter Fair. They may also be purchased directly from Beatrice Diana Bowyer. She has shipped them throughout Canada with requests as far away as the North West Territories and Newfoundland.

BEATRICE DIANA

Beatrice Diana Bowyer,
R.R. #4,
Simcoe, Ont. N3Y 4K3
TEL 519-426-7262

Chocolate

The best chocolate depends upon two things: the quality of the raw materials and the care taken at each step of manufacturing — the roasting and crushing of the cocoa beans and mixing the "mass," the cocoa paste, with sugar and sometimes milk.

Great chocolate is shiny brown, breaks cleanly, and is free of white specks, lumps, or tiny, burst bubbles. It should melt on the tongue like butter, be neither too sticky nor greasy, and have a distinct aroma of chocolate, not cocoa powder. The more bitter the chocolate, the more flavor it has. The more cocoa butter it contains, the creamier the chocolate will be. The less cocoa butter, the more brittle.

Chocolate connoisseurs seem to agree the Swiss sacrifice rich flavor for smoother texture. The British enjoy their chocolate and its fillings entirely too sweet and the French charge too dearly. This leaves Belgian chocolate as the clear choice for the world's finest boxed chocolates.

Charlinda Fine Belgian Chocolates

When Charlotte Randazzo left her native Holland, with a degree in Fine Arts, and came to Canada in 1954, she never dreamed she would some day make hand-made Belgian chocolates. For thirty years she worked at a variety of arts and crafts, owned a wool shop, designed and sold sweater kits, and taught weaving, knitting, painting, and découpage.

When she moved to Musselman's Lake, about a half-hour drive north of Toronto, she converted a former four-lane bowling alley into a kitchen and European-style chocolate shop with a stained glass window and shop door of dripping "chocolate."

Charlotte consulted a retired, Belgian chocolatier in Toronto and then travelled to Europe where her Belgian mother arranged for her apprenticeship with a professional. The art of making Belgian chocolates cannot be gleaned from a "how to" book or an instructional video. In fact, in Europe, it's a closed, family trade, shrouded in secretiveness.

After serving her apprenticeship, Charlotte returned with original recipes, sources for Belgian chocolate, and Dutch chocolate molds. For the next year, she honed her skills and perfected the unique fillings that ooze from Charlinda's melt-in-the-mouth morsels. Each chocolate is filled with a chocolate cream of dark milk or light chocolate, and among the subtle flavorings are Amaretto, Tiramisu, Mocha, Cappuccino, Hazelnut, Lemon, Raspberry, Ginger, and Praline and Cream.

Anyone who has become frustrated with minor culinary disasters — candy that never reaches the hardball stage, crystallized fudge, perhaps a deflated souffle — make a mental note: The degree of difficulty and the amount of patience it takes to work with raw chocolate is beyond the temperament and skill of most mortals.

Belgian chocolates, like those made by Charlinda, are made from Couverture chocolate. It contains a minimum of 32 percent cocoa butter, which allows it to form its signature thin, glossy shell. Couverture chocolate must be tempered by bringing it to 45 C (113 F) in order to break down all crystals; cooling it to below 32 C (91 F) and then heating it again to 44 C (111 F) for dark chocolate, 42 C (108 F) for milk chocolate, and 40 C (104 F) for white chocolate. The catch is, the chocolate has to stay tempered at the given temperature while it is being worked. If not, the chocolatier must start the process over again. This is a true labor of love. Chocolates are never made in a hurry!

The "Linda" of Charlinda is Charlotte's daughter. She too learned, first hand, the art of Belgian chocolate-making in Europe. She also creates much of the packaging. The sole employees of Charlinda, this mother and daughter team also make 15 flavors of Gourmet Butter Cream Fudge, including a pumpkin fudge for Halloween and Thanksgiving, chocolate-covered ginger and orange skins, and a variety of chocolate wafers and bars, mousse cups, liquor cups, and chocolate dipped fruit. Among the house specialties are Florentines, those cookie-like wafers of almonds, honey, butter and candied fruit that must be cooked in a saucepan before baking and coating on one side with — what else? Chocolate!

Charlinda will arrange trays of goodies for corporate and home entertaining; for weddings the bride and groom may personally select their favorite flavors or request original fillings.

Chocolates are sold loose or by the box and in containers and jars. They are made in a variety of sizes and price ranges; generally they cost $5.98 per 100 g (3.5 oz). Charlinda will also fill a customer's own container.

Products are available at the shop, all year round and by mail order in Canada and the USA, except in July and August. Look for Charlinda at major events like Toronto's One of a Kind Show and the CNE.

CHARLINDA FINE BELGIAN CHOCOLATES

14811 9th Line,
R.R. #2,
Stouffville, Ont. L4A 7X3

TEL 905-640-8089
FAX 905-640-8043

OPEN Tuesday to Friday, 2 p.m. to 7 p.m.
Saturday, Sunday, 10 a.m. to 5 p.m.

CHARLOTTE'S TIPS FOR EATING BELGIAN CHOCOLATE

- Belgian chocolate should never be chewed, eaten in a hurry, or taken during deep conversation!
- Place chocolate on the tongue. It will melt at body temperature, the chocolate giving way to taste and finally aroma.
- Notice the lingering aroma, flavor, and taste after the chocolate has been consumed.

STORING CHOCOLATE

- Chocolate keeps best at a temperature between 15 and 18 C (60 and 65 F), but should always be eaten at room temperature to enhance the aroma and flavor.
- Chocolate may be refrigerated but must be well-wrapped or will pick up odors from other foods.

ONTARIO TRIVIA

OIL SPRINGS, formerly known as Victoria, in Lambton County, is the location of the world's first oil well. It was drilled by James Miller Williams of Hamilton in June of 1858. Williams was the first man in the world to transform crude oil into lamp oil.

OTTAWA'S Sparks Street Mall is the oldest pedestrian mall in the country.

OTTAWA'S Cineplus theatre at the Canadian Museum of Civilization is home to the world's only combination IMAX/OMNIMAX theatre.

Carole's Cheesecake Company Ltd.

If ever there was a Food Hall of Fame, heading up the dessert wing would be Carole's Cheesecakes. Not just because cheesecake is the most popular dessert in North America after apple pie, but because Carole's cheesecakes really are better than anything you can make yourself, all one-hundred-plus flavors, and worth every one of the 300 calories per slice.

As the largest cheesecake bakery in Canada, the main operation on Toronto's Castlefield Avenue uses about 150 tons of cream cheese a year! Carole has made the transition from cottage industry to corporate cheesecake giant without compromising so much as a demitasse of quality. Only fresh, natural ingredients are used in these crustless cheesecakes that take 13 hours to create from preparation to unmolding. Even the fruit on the flans is fresh and placed by hand.

Much of the business's success is due to the high energy level of owner Carole Ogus. After almost 20 years in business, she still works 7 days a week, checking the orders as they go out, selling at the storefront café on Saturdays, and pouring over the books on Sundays.

Carole was an elementary school teacher who loved baking. Her cousin suggested that she sell her cheesecakes and insisted on being her first customer. Carole baked a cheesecake and a fruit flan for her cousin's next dinner party. Women at the dinner placed orders and business grew by word of mouth.

Still teaching, Carole shopped for ingredients, baked cakes, and delivered them in her husband's stationwagon. He redesigned the basement to accommodate a second kitchen with fridge, freezer, oven, and mixer. Carole's three children (now involved in the business) and cleaning lady (who later went to work for Carole's Cheesecakes) helped prepare the ingredients. Cakes were everywhere in the house, cooling.

When production reached 100 cakes a day, Michael Ogus encouraged Carole to move the operation out of the home. She opened her first shop on Eglinton Avenue in 1979, with a $25,000 loan. It was a location that defied all the rules of marketing since her first criterion was a place close to her house. There was no parking and a low traffic flow. Carole hoped that people would go out of their way to get something they really liked.

And they did. Carole now supplies hundreds of hotels and restaurants as well as the Loblaws and Miracle Food Mart chains in Ontario. There is a corporately-owned outlet and eight Canadian franchises at places like First Canadian Place in Toronto and the Rideau Centre in Ottawa, as well as some locations in the United States. Since 1989 the head office/bakery and the Cafe Bakery Bar, are in a renovated sewing machine factory on Castlefield Avenue, still close to Carole's home.

Carole's cheesecakes are sold by the piece or whole, in flavors like Wayne Gretsky's New York Deli (the most expensive variety), New York Naked (the most popular variety), Key Lime, Hazelnut, and Positively Praline. There are also liqueur cheesecakes and regular cakes like Designer Carrot Cake and Black and White Mousse Cake. Prices range from $8.75 to $50.

Carole's cake recipes are top secret but you can try her recipe for honey buns!

CAROLE'S CHEESECAKE COMPANY LTD.
1272 Castlefield Ave.,
Toronto, Ont. M6B lG3
TEL 416-256-0000

Carole's Honey Buns

3 packages active dry yeast
125 ml (1/2 cup) warm water
340 g (3/4 lb) butter, at room temperature
125 ml (1/2 cup) sugar
3 egg yolks
2 ml (1/2 tsp) salt
7 ml (1 1/2 tsp) white vinegar
250 ml (1 cup) sour cream
1375 ml (5 1/2 cups) all purpose flour
FILLING:
125 g (1/4 lb) + 75 ml (5 Tbsp) butter at room temperature
375 g (3/4 lb) light brown sugar
5 ml (1 tsp) cinnamon
30 ml (2 Tbsp) corn syrup
whole pecans
cinnamon and white raisins

- Dissolve yeast in warm water and set aside. In a large bowl, cream butter and sugar, add egg yolks and salt, blend in vinegar and sour cream. Add dissolved yeast, then flour and mix very well. Knead the dough for 8 minutes, until it becomes smooth and elastic. Refrigerate dough for a minimum of 6 hours or a maximum of 3 days.

FILLING:
- Cream butter with 250 g (1/2 lb) sugar. Add 5 ml (1 tsp) cinnamon and corn syrup and mix well. Place 5 ml (1 tsp) of mixture in bottom of each muffin tin. Set a pecan, flat side down, plus 2 raisins, for each honey bun in muffin tin. Take the dough out of the refrigerator. Cut off 1/4 of the dough at a time and roll onto oblong shape, 3 mm (1/8 inch) thick. (Lift dough after rolling so it doesn't stick to the board). Sprinkle dough with brown sugar and cinnamon, roll as for a jelly roll. Cut into 12 mm (1/2 inch) slices for small muffin tins. Place each slice on top of brown sugar and nut mixture in muffin tin. Allow dough to rise in warm place for 45 minutes (the dough should almost reach the top of the muffin tin). Bake 20 minutes at 190 C (375 F).

ONTARIO TRIVIA

PARIS is where the world's first long-distance call was received by Alexander Graham Bell, in Robert White's Boot and Shoe Store, 91 Grand River Street. The call was made from Bell's Brantford home in 1876.

PELEE ISLAND is the largest island in Lake Erie, being 4,000 hectares (10,000 acres).

PEMBROKE was the first town in Canada to light its streets with electricity.

PENETANGUISHENE'S Historic Naval and Military Establishments was the only combined British naval and military base in Canada.

PERTH is the site of the last fatal duel that took place in Ontario. The year was 1833.

PETERBOROUGH is home to Canada's highest jet spray of water. The Centennial Fountain, located in Little Lake shoots water 76 meters (250 feet) in the air. It operates from May to September and during the evening features a cascade of lights.

Dufflet Pastries Inc.

Chances are you've never met Dufflet (Arlene Rosenberg) but you've tasted one of her desserts. She's been a legend in the best dining circles in Toronto for close to 20 years. She's been called a "baking wizard," the "madame of Toronto's number one house of dessert sin," even "Toronto's best baker." Her exquisite creations grace the menus of more than 200 of the city's finest restaurants, gourmet shops cafés and upscale groceries.

Dufflet has a flair for the original and a commitment to quality. She also has an obsession for layering: Cappuccino Dacquoise, for example, combines layers of hazelnut meringue with a rich, coffee butter-cream, mocha whipped cream, and bittersweet chocolate glaze. Even the Banana Cream Cake is four layers of moist banana cake, slices of fresh banana, and a creamy banana icing garnished with coconut.

The petite woman was nicknamed "Dufflet" by her family: a smaller version of her brother Duff. She started the road to sweet success quite by accident. At 20, she quit university and found a job at the Cow Câfé, taking along a sample of her own apple torte and chocolate cake, as if they were her résumé. Needless to say, she got the job.

Word of her tasty fare quickly spread to other restaurants. She was soon in demand, baking for others from the oven in her mother's kitchen. A self-taught natural, she began taking baking courses at George Brown College's night school. She also took a short course at the renowned Le Notre School in Paris. When zoning laws restricted her home kitchen business, she moved her wholesale operation to Queen Street in 1980. Two years later she added her own retail câfé out front and in 1985 moved the production facility to a 1,525 square meter (5,000 square foot) factory on Dovercourt. She now oversees 50 employees, with a repertoire of 100 items, and a client list that reads like the who's who of fine dining.

Dufflet made her reputation on two signature desserts: the Toasted Almond Meringue Torte, an extravaganza of interlayered almond meringue, whipped cream, blueberries, and toasted almonds; and her Chocolate Fudge Cake, a rich, dark moist chocolate that's surprisingly "unsweet." She now stakes her reputation on using only the purest ingredients — butter, whole eggs, fresh fruit, Belgian chocolate, and not too much sugar. Although Dufflet has given up working 80-hour weeks, she still sees that every item that goes out the door conforms to her level of perfection.

Most of the recipes are Dufflet's own creations. Although she no longer does the baking, she continuously experiments to take desserts to the limits of taste sensation and presentation. She also features a number of wedding cakes which can be customized in size and decoration to compliment the color scheme and theme of the wedding.

In 1989 Dufflet Pastries began the "Great Cooks" program, a series of cooking classes that feature more than 30 of Toronto's finest chefs, caterers, and food professionals in a series of day and evening classes for individuals who want to learn tricks of the trade from the experts. Each class is thematic, concentrating on a specific cuisine like Italian, Thai, or Mediterranean or on such subjects as catering, entertaining and of course desserts!

DUFFLET PASTRIES INC.

WHOLESALE:
41 Dovercourt Rd.,
Toronto, Ont. M6J 3C2
TEL 416-536-1330

RETAIL:
787 Queen St. West,
Toronto, Ont. M6J IGI
TEL 416-368-1812

Dufflet's Strawberry Walnut Cream Cake

WALNUT CAKE
375 ml (1 1/2 cups) sifted cake flour
250 ml (1 cup) sugar
2 ml (1/2 tsp) salt
250 ml (1 cup) finely chopped walnuts
4 large eggs
4 egg yolks
5 ml (1 tsp) vanilla extract
zest of 1/2 orange

- Grease and flour two 22 centimeter (9 inch) round cake pans. Line bottoms with silicone paper. Combine the sifted flour, 30 ml (2 Tbsp) sugar, and salt. Stir in walnuts. Whip the eggs and egg yolks at medium speed until blended. Continue beating and add remaining sugar. Continue beating the egg mixture until it has tripled in volume and forms a thick ribbon. Add the vanilla and orange zest. Sprinkle one-third of the flour mixture over the batter. Fold the flour into the batter; add the remaining flour in two more additions. Scrape the batter into the prepared pans and spread evenly. Bake the cakes for 20 to 25 minutes, at 180 C (350 F), until the edge of the cake has pulled away slightly from the sides and the cake springs back when gently pressed. Cool for 10 minutes, then remove from pans and continue cooling.

PASTRY CREAM FILLING:
90 ml (6 Tbsp) sugar
45 ml (3 Tbsp) flour
45 ml (3 Tbsp) cornstarch
6 egg yolks
500 ml (2 cups) milk
30 ml (2 Tbsp) unsalted butter
5 ml (1 tsp) vanilla extract

- Sift together sugar, flour and cornstarch. Add egg yolks and whisk until pale and light. Scald the milk in a heavy-bottomed saucepan. Pour milk over egg yolks, stirring constantly. Return to saucepan and cook over medium heat, stirring constantly until mixture thickens and starts to simmer. Continue cooking for about a minute. Re-

move from heat, strain. Add butter and vanilla extract. Cover with plastic wrap and cool.

SIMPLE ORANGE SYRUP:
75 ml (1/3 cup) water
75 ml (1/3 cup) sugar
30-45 ml (2-3 Tbsp) orange liqueur

- Bring the water and sugar to the boil. Cool and add the liqueur.

ICING AND FRUIT TOPPING
500 ml (2 cups) whipping cream
50 ml (1/4 cup) icing sugar
1 L (2 pints) fresh strawberries
apricot jam

ASSEMBLY:

- Whip the cream with icing sugar until peaks form, but not too stiff. Set aside. Divide each cake layer in half. Place the first cake layer on serving platter. Brush with syrup. Spread one third of the pastry cream over the layer and cover with a handful of sliced strawberries. Continue with the next 2 layers, top with final cake layer. Frost cake with the whipped cream, keeping enough aside for the decorative piping. Cover the top of the cake with the fresh strawberries. Glaze strawberries with melted apricot jam.

Dufflet's Chocolate Mousse Cake

500 g (1 lb) bittersweet chocolate, chopped
500 g (1 lb) unsalted butter, cut into cubes
16 egg yolks
250 ml (1 cup) sugar
10 egg whites
250-500 g (1/2 to l lb) semisweet chocolate, melted into block

- Grease and flour 25 centimeter (10 inch) pan. Line with silicone paper. Melt the chocolate and butter over a double boiler. Stir until melted and remove from heat. Combine the egg yolks and sugar in the bowl of electric mixer. Whip until the mixture is light and lemon colored. Add the chocolate mixture to the egg mixture, stirring to blend thoroughly. Whip the egg whites until stiff but not dry. Add some of the whites to the chocolate mixture and blend thoroughly. Fold in the remaining whites. Pour 3/4 of the mixture into the prepared pan. Set the remaining mixture aside to set. Bake the cake for 1 hour at 180 C (350 F), until cake is set and puffed up. Remove from oven and let cool 10 minutes. Remove from pan to completely cool. Place cake on serving platter. Mask the cake with the reserved chocolate mousse. Scoop the remaining mousse on top of the cake and smooth it over. Make chocolate curls with vegetable peeler, then cover the cake with the curls and dust with icing sugar.

BLUEBERRY SAUCE

500 g (1 lb) frozen blueberries
7 ml (1 Tbsp) fresh lemon juice or to taste
125 ml (1/2 cup) sugar or more to taste

- Combine the ingredients in saucepan. Cover and cook over medium heat until berry juices are released, about 1 to 2 minutes. Stir to moisten all of the berries, cover again, and cook 3 more minutes. Uncover and bring to the boil for one minute. Cool. Adjust flavors.

Glen Farms Herbs & Preserves Inc.

The label on the Glen Farms products says "everything Glen Farms makes is made without pectin, preservatives or compromises." It tells as much about Judie and Dave Glen, the people who stir the stainless steel pots in their farmhouse kitchen, as it does about the superb jams, flavored vinegars and oils, antipasto, and liqueured fruit preserves they create.

The Glen story would make a wonderful made-for-television movie. What began as a means of earning extra money for Christmas is now a cottage industry success story with an innovative approach to the world of fund-raising.

In 1986 Judie Glen was a college student at the University of Guelph, low on cash for books and Christmas presents. A friend suggested she sell her homemade "food gifts" at the local farmers' market. Her husband assisted, making tags on a photocopy machine. The first sales turned a profit of $25, "doubling their entertainment budget." The seeds for Glen Farms Herbs and Preserves Inc. were sewn.

The easy part, according to the Glens, is making the product. All the recipes are from turn-of-the-century cookbooks inherited from grandparents and aunts, written before the days of pectin and additives. They converted the language of bushels and pecks to modern measurements. Everything is made by hand in small batches right in their own kitchen, a 4-by-6 meter (12-by-20 foot) room where everything from cooking to crating is done. The preserves have twice the fruit and therefore half the sugar content of those made with pectin. The product isn't stock-piled, but produced fresh, to order.

Surprisingly there are no barns or out-buildings and no fields of crops at Glen Farms, located on County Road 19 in Grey Township, halfway between the rural hamlets of Molesworth and Ethel.

There is however an herb garden which supplies the flavorings for the vinegars and oils. The Glens realized they could not both grow food and produce a quality product. They sought out first-rate suppliers for year-round fruits, concentrating on expanding their jams and marmalades to 13 flavors which now include cherry, strawberry rhubarb, peach, and four-fruit jam and Scottish, orange, and ginger marmalade.

The Glens marketed their products with a combination of luck and ingenuity. A limited budget necessitated inexpensive craft paper labels and hand lettering which distinguished their product with a down-home appeal that was soon copied by others.

The Glens also learned that the sales representative system didn't work for them. Reps have to carry many lines to make a living. This doesn't always guarantee competent exposure. The Glens let their sales reps go and watched sales soar as they personally called on retailers.

Dave Glen printed a recipe book on his computer and packaged it with the flavored vinegars. This marketing technique had great appeal for gift stores. The Glens generate all their own brochures and a regular newsletter, the *Glen Farms Grapevine*, on their Macintosh computer. It keeps retailers abreast of new products, recipes, sales tips, and promotions.

After seven years in business, the Glens have turned their entrepreneurial spirit to philanthropy. In April 1993, they launched "Special Reserve," a line of 10 new products that includes an antipasto, liqueured fruit, and red pepper and orange jelly. For the next two years The Glens will donate 5 cents for every jar that is shipped to their retailers to the Maitland Conservation Foundation, a non-profit organization working to save the Maitland and Nine Mile River watersheds.

The Glens are also part of a joint venture called JJAMS, a company that originated in the United States to help cultural arts organizations fund-raise. Charities and businesses are supplied with jars of Glen preserves to sell to raise money; a custom label personalizes the product for the organization. JJAMS also provides the "JJAMS Guide to Effective Fund-Raising." Dave Glen's philosophy is that a quality product like theirs can be sold even by school children with the benefit of JJAMS experience. The CIBC National Music Festival fund-raiser was launched with JJAMS and the Listowel School of Dance has teamed up with Glen Farms.

Glen Farms preserves are available in over 150 specialty food, gift, and department stores. They also do mail order and sell product and gift baskets from their home business.

GLEN FARMS HERBS & PRESERVES INC.
R.R. #2
Listowel, Ont. N4W 3G7
TEL 519-887-9704
FAX 519-291-1914
800-565-GLEN (ORDERS)

Catherine's Foods Ltd.

In many households, the word Catherine's has replaced the word antipasto, as in "get the Catherine's from the fridge" or "pick up some more Catherine's." This is antipasto at its finest: thick enough that you can pile it high on a cracker with chopped vegetables like green beans, onions, green and black olives, you can actually distinguish, and a blend of subtle spices that's consistent with every jar.

It's comforting to know, that as the label states, "Yes, there really is a Catherine alive and cooking." She's Catherine Mix, an energetic mother of three, and now grandmother, who began her specialty food line in her own Toronto kitchen in 1982, with the help of her husband who put the labels on the jars at night while watching TV.

In July of that year, Mix opened a kitchen store on the corner of Avenue Road and Brooke Avenue. It was more of a bakery than a specialty food shop where she sold tarts and pies and her first two preserves, the Antipasto and her Traditional Chili Sauce. Both were her grandmother's recipes.

The bakery closed in 1986 to allow Catherine to expand her preserve business. Today there's a staff of 12 people in two licensed kitchens. Catherine's products are distributed nationally to 600 retail outlets, as well as in California and Bermuda.

Despite the phenomenal growth of the business in the past 12 years, Catherine's is very much a family-owned and operated business. The youngest family member, Jennifer, has been sales manager since 1984. Daughter Nancy, who lives in California, designs the labels and all the art work. Son Steven has joined the business in the last year to administer the company. This frees up Catherine to apply her energy and creativity in the promotion and demonstration of her line in the marketplace, and to create new products.

The company produces only seven items. Hors d'oeuvre and Pasta Sauce took a year to create and the Red Pepper Jelly and Cranberry Sauce are only made seasonally. The Peppercorn Garden is a chick-pea-based appetizer, a blend of 15 ingredients. The Port Jelly is the purest of its kind, made without water or grape juice.

Catherine's personal formula for success is "family, quality, and teamwork." Each product is made by hand, in small batches with great care. Only fresh ingredients are used, without preservatives added. They are made the old-fashioned way, with vinegar and sugar and are vacuum-sealed. Look for Catherine's in specialty food shops.

CATHERINE'S FOODS LTD.
3952 Chesswood Dr.,
Downsview, Ont. M3J 2W6
TEL 416-635-0202

Rosedale Preserves Inc.

Former Windsor restaurateur, caterer, and home canning hobbyist, Rob McMillen is now one of Toronto's finest and busiest purveyors of fine foods. What began in the kitchen of a small Rosedale apartment (thus the name) is now a business operated from a 600 square meter (2,000 square foot) warehouse with a professional cooking staff and a product line of almost 30 items.

While working three other jobs to maintain a cash flow, McMillen experimented with a vegetable and seafood antipasto and jams he made from berries picked with his mother in Essex County. He spent two months perfecting a salsa, prevailed on his friends to sample his concoctions and make suggestions and even asked one individual to design a logo. He then went door to door peddling his products to stores. The first taker was a health food store on Parliament Street.

Like all fledgling entrepreneurs, in the early days McMillen did everything himself. He made condiments in small batches, filled the jars, hand labelling them with paper and a glue stick, and added circle tops cut from upholstery material.

The move out of the apartment and into the warehouse in 1992 required more of McMillen's ingenuity in kitchen design and warehouse remodelling. He spent six months searching for ideas to redesign the packaging, including walking the food emporiums of Manhattan.

McMillen settled on earthy colors of soft green, purple, bronze, and black for his packaging. Using an IBM PC and a SATO thermal transfer printer gives him the freedom to create his own labels. He also uses pressure-sensitive labels which can be removed in hot water from the Mason jars and attractive octagonal bottles. Consumers end up with completely re-usable glassware.

Among the Rosedale Preserves are chunky salsas, some made of peach, black bean and pear; pasta sauces of the tomato, cheese, mushroom, and pesto varieties, a Cajun chowchow; and strawberry vinaigrette.

Rosedale Preserves are available in 150 stores throughout Ontario and Quebec including David Wood's and All The Best Foods, in Toronto; Denninger's in Hamilton; Duncan's Fine foods in Collingwood; and Balderson Cheese in Balderson. Mail order is available through Canada's Cupboard. Prices range from $3.99 to $6.99.

ROSEDALE PRESERVES INC.
50 Carroll St.,
Suite 216,
Toronto, Ont. M4M 3G3
TEL 416-778-7208
FAX 416-778-9907

Perennial Splendours

Jeff Ferst of Stratford is the creator, producer, shipper, and only salesperson for his newly created line of products known as Perennial Splendours. The elegant packaging alone is enough to entice you to sample his wares: infused sunflower-based cooking oils with basil, and rosemary, and Eastern spices; cranberry and fine herb vinegars; savory cooking sauces known as "Fruit Splendours" of cranberry and kiwi, peach and mango, and pineapple and banana; and two herbal teas. Recipe suggestions accompany many of these products.

An unusual combination with these taste treats is a line of bath products: scented bath pouches with herbs, oats, and essential oils; and "Scented Splendours," two after-bath fragrances. The common denominator of these diverse product lines is Ferst's commitment to "natural." In the truest sense of the word there is nothing synthetic in his ingredients. Everything is based on herbs, some of which Ferst grows himself. There are no chemicals, synthetic perfumes or flavorings.

Ferst has developed the recipes and formulas for his products, designed the packaging, and drummed up wholesale clientele of more than 30 retail stores between Stratford and Toronto.

The business comes from Ferst's dissatisfaction with chemically laden products in the marketplace and 20 years of working for other people in sales and marketing jobs. He's hoping to add to the product line and hire staff in the near future. His goods are also available through Canada's Cupboard.

PERENNIAL SPLENDOURS
P.O. Box 2305,
Stratford, Ont. N5A 7V8
TEL 519-271-3372

Vicki's More Than Just A Barbecue Sauce

Friends of Vicki Forbes convinced her to turn her family's recipe for a barbecue-style sauce into a business, and so she did. An interior design student raised in Trinidad by Canadian parents, Forbes developed an early appreciation for exotic foods. Now back in Ontario, her sauces satisfy the growing taste for tangier food.

As the label indicates, Vicki's sauce is "more than just a barbecue sauce." It's a blend of Caribbean flavors of sweet, sour, and spices, slowly simmered in small batches to produce a rich, tasty accompaniment to meats, poultry, seafood, and vegetables, or anything edible from meatloaf to tacos.

Vicki's can be used as a marinade, for basting, and as a dipping sauce. It's available in the original recipe (green label) as well as "hot" (red label).

Purists will appreciate the fact that the ingredients are 100 percent pure, as noted on the label. No water, salt, or M.S.G. is added; no artificial preservatives or flavor enhancers are used; and honey, not sugar, is used for sweetening.

Forbes has also combined her talents with Rob Smolka of Butcher's Broil to create two new product lines. "The Right Stuff," as the name suggests, is stuffing for poultry. It comes in six inventive flavors — Plain Jane and Herb, Macadamia Nut Black Currant, Apricot Walnut, Bacon Herb Provençal, Cranberry Cashew, and Apple Cinnamon Raisin. The 200 gram (7 oz) bag is enough to stuff a four and a half kilogram (10 pound) turkey cavity about 1 L (4 cups). This product that will surprise people who are particular (stuffy) about their stuffing. Again, the secret is the finest ingredients and no MSG.

The second line of products is a spiced rub for roasts — one for poultry and one for beef, pork, and lamb.

Forbes and Smolka are in the process of forming a co-op with four fellow "foodies." Look for "All's Fare...Adventures in Foods" outside the North St. Lawrence Market in Toronto.

Vicki's products are currently sold in independent grocery and butcher stores in Toronto, Oakville, and Mississauga, and by mail order through Canada's Cupboard.

HOMEMADE BY VICKI
402-30 Glen Elm Ave.,
Toronto, Ont. M4T 1T7

Canada's Cupboard

Canada's Cupboard wants to share the best Canadian specialty foods with people across the country and south of the border. It's a company that sells only Canadian-made products by mail-order — fruit preserves, honey, spreads, condiments, mustards, dips, wild rice, maple syrup, chocolates and much, much more! It's the brainchild of Shirley Richard and her husband Mike of Barrie, who think consumers deserve the best that can be ordered, all from one toll-free number with one shipping charge.

Shirley, a food and beverage management grad from George Brown College, lost her job when the firm she worked for was bought out and downsized. Mike, a self-employed graphic designer was feeling the pinch from the recession. They decided to combine their skills in a family-run business.

Shirley used her expertise in cooking and food preparation to canvas small independent food producers across Canada. She found that while many have excellent products, their sales are often limited to local markets. She began the difficult task of selecting quality products that would complement each other and represent a complete line of foods for potential buyers.

Mike turned his computer and publishing skills towards developing a catalog, financed by private investors. The result is a 16-page color glossy which features products of 30 Canadian entrepreneurs.

Copies of Canada's Cupboard are available for $2, refundable with a first order.

CANADA'S CUPBOARD

506 Essa Rd.,
Unit 39,
Barrie, Ont. L4N 7L5
FAX 705-733-5717
800-268-5011 (Canada and the US)

Meath Hill Garlic

How do you tell the difference between a "hardneck" variety of garlic and a "softneck" variety? Customers of Sue Parsons' Meath Hill Garlic taste the difference and won't accept substitutes. This Pembroke garlic grower specializes in rocambole, sometimes referred to as red or Italian garlic, a "hardneck" variety. The stem is not pliable to braid like the "softneck" types imported from California. Instead, the plants must be strung together in a 3-D effect. The large, easy to peel cloves taste uniquely different from imports, and produce more oil when squeezed.

Sue Parsons has been an organic gardener for 19 years, growing fruits, vegetables, and flowers for her own consumption. She decided to plant her own garlic for Caesar salad. Friends who tasted the first crop's salad dressing and garlic bread raved about them. The idea for a garlic farm was launched.

Parsons prepared a five-year business plan and purchased 16 hectares (40 acres) of land next to her country home. She sold her first crop in 1990 with the aid of signs placed on the highway, and became an advocate to start a local farmer's market at Cobden. The following year she was selling her product at the Pembroke and Carp farmers' markets as well as Cobden and the Ottawa Byward Market on Saturdays.

Garlic has been cultivated for over 5,000 years and there are more than 300 varieties. It originated in Siberia and was carried to the Middle East by nomadic tribes. The Egyptians, Romans and Greeks enjoyed garlic and it was during the Crusades that garlic came to England.

Garlic is rich in folklore and its medicinal uses have been known since ancient times. Hippocrates mentions garlic as a laxative and a diuretic. Aristotle recommended it as a cure for rabies. The Egyptians worshipped garlic and even traded slaves for it. The Romans believed it had the power to annihilate everything from werewolves to mosquitoes and colds, so soldiers consumed it in great quantities.

The widespread influence of Italian, Greek, and Indian cooking have made garlic popular in North American households since the 1980s. The First World Conference on the Health Significance of Garlic and Garlic Constituents was held in September 1990. The conference revealed there are over 200 medicinal properties in garlic to be studied; that the intake of garlic reduced some tumours by 70 to 90 percent; that it reduced significantly the occurrence of heart attacks and death rate from fatal heart attacks; and that it lowered blood pressure and serum cholesterol. The conference suggested that between one and three raw cloves a day gave the best results, though consumption of more than 25 grams (1 bulb) could actually damage red blood cells.

Currently Meath Hill Garlic has seven acres under garlic cultivation, and expects to harvest more than 65,000 plants. Garlic growing is labor-intensive since it must be planted and pulled by hand. It's more expensive than store garlic because Parsons hires locals and pays Ontario wages, but customers know the price difference is worth every penny.

Food processors are lined up to buy everything Parsons grows. However, she continues to sell local garlic in mesh bags or by the strand at the Ottawa Byward Market from the third week of August until October 31 or until she sells out. She has also shipped her garlic across Canada. Strands come singly or in medium braids (10 giant bulbs with 3 on each side and up the middle); large braids offer 16 bulbs (5 on each side and 6 up the middle). Parsons also grows dried flowers and decorates the strands for a unique gift she sells at a local Christmas craft show.

MEATH HILL GARLIC
Westmeath Road 31,
R.R. #2,
Pembroke, Ont. K8A 6W3
TEL 613-638-0279

Meath Hill Garlic Cooking Tips

- Allicin in garlic is what gives it smell and taste. It's released from garlic only when it contacts the air. The more air contact with cutting or pressing, the more flavor. For a very gentle hint of garlic, use whole cloves; for more flavor, gently crush cloves with a wide knife; for the most flavor, press peeled garlic cloves through a garlic press.
- Boil unpeeled cloves for a hint of garlic in soups.
- Roast unpeeled cloves slowly for a sweet, nutty flavor (this will produce a spreadable clove, excellent on warmed French bread).
- Sautéed garlic requires patience. The smaller the bits of garlic, the more critical the timing. Sauté slowly until mild and tender, without color.
- Burned garlic will taste bitter.

Meath Hill Caesar Salad

1 medium head of Romaine lettuce
125 g (1/4 lb) bacon
3 cloves garlic
30 ml (2 Tbsp) fresh lemon juice
15 ml (1 Tbsp) vinegar
15 ml (1 Tbsp) Worcestershire sauce
.5 ml (1/8 tsp) dry mustard
1 ml (1/4 tsp) each salt and black pepper
1 egg
50 ml (1/4 cup) grated Parmesan cheese
125 ml (1/2 cup) olive oil
125 ml (1/2 cup) croutons

- Wash and dry lettuce. Break into bite-size pieces. Chill. Cook bacon until crisp; drain and place on paper towel. Crumble or cut bacon into small pieces. Rub one clove garlic over the inside of the salad bowl. Crush the other cloves. Combine with lemon, vinegar, Worcestershire sauce, mustard, salt and pepper, egg, and cheese. Whisk in oil. Add the bacon to salad bowl then lettuce. Toss with dressing. Sprinkle on croutons. 5 servings.

Meath Hill Stuffed Garlic Potatoes for Two

2 large baking potatoes
50 ml (1/4 cup) milk
50 ml (1/4 cup) sour cream
2 large garlic cloves, minced
30 ml (2 Tbsp) butter, softened
2 ml (1/2 tsp) salt
50 ml (1/4 cup) grated cheese

- Prick each potato with a fork. Bake potatoes in 190 C (375 F) oven for l hour or until tender. Or microwave 5- 7 minutes, remove potatoes and let stand wrapped in towel for 5 minutes. Cut off 12 mm (1/2-inch) thick slice lengthwise from each potato for lid. Scoop out each potato leaving 6 mm (1/4-inch) shell. Remove the potato from slice leaving shell. Beat the potato pulp until mashed. Beat in milk and sour cream. Mix in garlic and butter, and season with salt. Place mashed potato in potato shell. Sprinkle on cheese. Top with lid. Place in 190 C (375 F) oven for 10 minutes or until heated through and cheese has melted.

Fish Lake Garlic Man

Ted Maczka, the Fish Lake Garlic Man, drives an old blue station wagon with a replica of the largest bulb of garlic the modern world is ever likely to see perched on the roof. The pleasant-natured, grey-haired, bearded man is never without a ball cap or hat, decorated with real garlic bulbs. He's a permanent fixture at the Royal Agricultural Winter Fair and his small farm near Demorestville, south of Belleville, which he refers to as a garlic research and experimental station, has peaked the interest of *Harrowsmith* magazine, CBC's Country Report, and CTV's Regional Contact.

Ted Maczka, Canada's leading authority on garlic, has been spreading the garlic gospel for more than twenty years. He wants Canadians to eat and grow more garlic. He believes Ontario can grow as good a crop as can be found anywhere in the world, rather than importing millions of dollars of garlic (sprayed with chemicals) each year from US growers. He believes that tobacco growers in the province should convert their fields to garlic.

When Maczka first began growing garlic, no-one could tell him how to do it. So he began his own research, collecting data from as far away as India and California. Garlic is grown like a tulip bulb, planted in the fall for harvest the following year. Spring planting can only be successful if started as soon as the frost is out of the ground.

Maczka experiments with different types of garlic on half a hectare (1 acre) of property and grows it in any conceivable type of container in his home.

He is always looking to develop a superior strain. The best garlic he says, is strong, firm, big, and easy to peel.

The Johnny Appleseed of garlic is quick to extol the beneficial properties of the plant. Besides putting "the heart and soul" in food, it thins the blood, detoxifies the body, fights cholesterol, prevents colds, and kills bacteria. As for garlic breath, he recommends drinking milk or cranberry juice, chewing celery or red beets, or getting those around you to eat more of the same!

He ships plant stock all over Canada, the US and Europe, and even the Philippines. His goal is to establish the Garlic Foundation of Canada, an information and development center on world-wide garlic growing methods and its uses.

For $3 and a SASE, Maczka will send a price list of the garlic varieties he sells and his method of successful garlic growing.

THE FISH LAKE GARLIC MAN
Ted Maczka,
R.R. #2,
Demorestville, Ont. K0K IW0
TEL 613-476-8030

Family Tradition Foods Inc.

The average consumer believes that fresh food is always better than frozen. John Omstead, founder of Family Tradition Foods in Wheatley, says that this is a misconception. He's out to educate the public and challenges the consumer to a taste test, comparing his specialty frozen vegetables to those that are fresh or fresh-prepared.

What most people don't realize, according to Omstead, is that much of the produce we consume has been bred for a lengthy "shelf life." The time and distance between growers and consumers is often considerable, typically up to 3,000 kilometers (2,000 miles). Taste, color, and texture has been sacrificed for durability which translates into poor texture, taste, and nutrition.

Omstead points out that the difference between his products and others begins with the seeds themselves. His growers plant seeds that have been specially developed by Asgrow Seed Company, a division of the Upjohn Company. They include small, gourmet vegetables: tiny young peas, petite whole green beans, and a variety of corn known as Even Sweeter. These varieties have been bred not only for size and tenderness, but for taste, texture, and color. They are picked at proper maturity, unlike small sieve varieties which are merely picked small, before reaching maturity. Moreover, certain areas of Ontario are especially appropriate for growing these special crops.

Fresh produce loses most of its vitamin content within three to four days of picking. Family Tradition's vegetables are individually quick frozen (IQF) in a tunnel freezer within hours of harvest, thus locking in vitamins and minerals. For example, frozen green beans contain twice as much vitamin C as raw beans. Quick freezing brings the vegetables through a "temperature window" where ice crystals form: the faster they freeze through the window, the smaller the crystal formation, and the less cell degeneration occurs.

Family Tradition's vegetables are convenient to prepare. Instructions caution not to over-cook them. They have already been fresh-water blanched before being flash-frozen and need only be "wakened up." Kept frozen until ready to use, a serving portion is placed in a colander held under running warm water. They need only be brought to serving temperature by boiling, steaming, or micro-waving, and do not require cooking.

The vegetables are 100 percent natural: no salt, sugar, additives, preservatives, or food coloring has been added. They are also free of pesticides and herbicides, and have been tested by an independent laboratory for residues.

John Omstead is no stranger to the food processing business. He's a fourth-generation member of Omstead's, a company founded by John's great grandfather, Everett H. Omstead, who began a frozen fish operation in 1911. Everett's son Leonard took over the company in 1942, and diversified into onion rings and battered products as well as vegetables. John's father Gerald (Jake) worked on the company fishing tugs until he became personnel manager in 1958. The Omstead corporation was sold to Labatt Foods in 1984 and subsequently the H.J. Heinz Company in 1991.

John Omstead worked his way up to head of the vegetable division before he began his own company in 1989. He longed to get "back to the basics" of the original family-style operation. Realizing he can't compete with the multinationals in the frozen vegetable business, he has carved out his own niche with specialties larger companies have difficulty adding to their processing lines.

Omstead markets his gourmet vegetables in innovative ways, such as vegetable combinations — bags of peas, corn, beans, and carrots; an oriental mix; and a vegetable pasta blend that community groups such as the Sun Parlor Shrine Club and Essex County high school students can sell as a fundraiser.

Family Tradition Foods are carried by independent retailers in Canada and Michigan. You may see these products in neighbourhood bulk stores, such as One Thirty Court in Peterborough. Better restaurants in Canada, and the Great Lake states, and New York serve these gourmet style vegetables.

FAMILY TRADITION FOODS INC.
P.O. Box 869,
Wheatley, Ont. N0P 2P0
TEL 519-825-4673
FAX 519-825-3134

Tomato Capital of the World

Leamington is the Tomato Capital of the World and home to Heinz ketchup. The H.J. Heinz company was founded in the US in 1869 when Henry Heinz began to sell jars of horseradish.

Heinz, believing the factory should be in close proximity to the growers, wisely established a plant in Leamington in 1909. When the first bottle of ketchup rolled off the line a year later, there were only seven people in the Leamington factory and the product was sold by salesmen who came up from the US. There wasn't a sales branch in Canada until 1913.

There probably isn't a home without ketchup and for some people it's a fixture on the table at every meal. Although the tomato plant is native to the New World, North Americans were not the first to discover ketchup.

The Chinese had a brine of pickled fish or shellfish called ke-tsiap. English sailors brought it home from Singapore and Malaysia. In England they tried to duplicate the sauce by substituting mushrooms, walnuts, and cucumbers. The tangy condiment caught on, the name anglicized to "ketchup." Mrs. Harrison warned homemakers in her "Housekeeper's Pocketbook" in 1748, never to be without it. Charles Dickens, in "Barnaby Ridge" speaks of "lamb chops breaded with plenty of ketchup." The praises of ketchup were also sung in Isabella Beeton's "Book of Household Management."

Maine sea captains circling the globe brought together the tomato of Mexico with sauces of the Spanish West Indies. Homemakers trying to duplicate the taste boiled ingredients all day in an iron kettle. In a 1901 edition of the Heinz employee newsletter, "Pickles," a writer noted "the odors of burned preserves and ill smelling sealing wax and the like made living within the house an almost unbearable burden and sleep quite an impossibility." When Henry Heinz first processed ketchup, it was immediately successful, a "blessed relief for Mother and the other women in the household!"

The original Heinz recipe is still the basis for today's Heinz Tomato Ketchup. Roughly 1,200 growers raise over 3 million bushels of tomatoes annually for the company's brew. The Heinz complex sits on a 58-hectare (145-acre) site in Leamington and employs more than 1,500 people.

H.J. HEINZ COMPANY OF CANADA LTD.
North American Life Centre
5650 Yonge St., 16th Floor
North York, Ont. M2M 4G3
TEL 416-226-5757
FAX 416-226-7544

Heinz Burger Sauce

125 ml (1/2 cup) dairy sour cream
50 ml (1/4 cup) Heinz Tomato Ketchup
50 ml (1/4 cup) finely chopped Heinz Dill Pickles
15 ml (1 Tbsp) horseradish (optional)
1 ml (1/4 tsp) salt

- Combine ingredients. Cover; chill to blend flavors. Serve as a topping for cooked meat patties. Makes about 250 ml (1 cup).

Heinz Barbecue Chicken, Southern Style

250 ml (1 cup) Heinz Tomato Ketchup
30-45 ml (2-3 Tbsp) honey
15 ml (1 Tbsp lemon) juice
dash hot pepper sauce
1 kg (2 to 2 1/2 lbs) chicken pieces
salt, pepper

- Combine ketchup, honey, lemon juice and hot pepper sauce. Brush on chicken during last 5 to 10 minutes of grilling or broiling. Season with salt and pepper. Makes about 300 ml (1 1/4 cups) sauce. Serves 4-6.

Strub Brothers Limited

Strub's of kosher dill pickle fame is a Canadian family success story. It began in a kitchen in Hamilton in 1921, and is now in its fourth generation of family management.

Michael Strub, a butcher by trade, and his wife Sophie immigrated to Canada from their native Russia shortly after the Revolution. Sophie brought her special recipe for kosher-style dill pickles that she made in a pungent brine. The popularity of the pickles prompted sons Daniel and Irvin to move the pickle operation out of the kitchen to a small facility in the back of a Dundas warehouse. They sold at first to the restaurant trade, but increasing demand led to merchandising in stores where the pickles were kept in giant wooden barrels. Customers took their pick from the murky depths of the barrel at five cents a piece.

By 1956 the company had moved to larger facilities and began bottling the pickles in jars. In July 1991, they built a processing plant in Brantford which has set the industry standard for refrigerated pickles. It is the only facility of its kind in Canada.

Pickle aficionados identify four types of dills: fermented (usually in brine); unfermented (packed in brine with vinegar); sour (prepared in fermented salt stock, then packed in vinegar); and sweet (packed in brine, then drained and packed in a sugar syrup with vinegar). Strub's makes a full-sour dill pickle.

Strub's also launched two new products to commemorate the move to the new building. Their Garden Fresh Pickles have 25 percent less salt than the whole dills and are cut in half lengthwise. Tzatziki is an entirely different product, a yogurt-based cucumber and garlic dip and spread.

All Strub's products are kosher and all natural without preservatives. Their product line includes horseradish, hot mixed pickles, hot banana peppers, dill tomatoes, sweet pimento peppers, herring products and sauerkraut. They are sold in grocery stores across Canada and the USA.

STRUB BROTHERS LIMITED
100 Roy Boulevard,
Brantford, Ont. N3R 7K2
TEL 519-751-1717

ONTARIO TRIVIA

PETROLIA is the site of Canada's first oil gusher. It was brought in by Hugh Nixon Shaw in 1862. The flow was 2,000 barrels per day.

PICKLE LAKE at the end of Highway 599 is the most northerly road-accessible town in Ontario.

POINT PELEE NATIONAL PARK is the most southerly tip of Canada's mainland. It's on the same latitude as northern California.

PORT COLBORNE is Canada's flour-milling centre.

PORT DOVER on Lake Erie is the largest freshwater fishing port in the world.

PORT DOVER'S Harbour Museum is the only marine museum on the north shore of the Great Lakes dedicated to the history of commercial fishing.

PORT DOVER is home to the only cantilevered bridge in Canada, located near the Port Dover Harbour Museum.

Peipps' Wild-Game-Farm

The wild boar is one of the four heraldic beasts of venery — the sport of hunting — especially associated with King Richard III of England. The boar's head was considered a delicacy and was the Christmas dinner of noblemen. Even King Arthur's Christmas table, consisted of "...salmon, venison, and wild boars,/by hundreds, and by dozens and by scores."

In Ontario, there is only a handful of wild boar farmers who can supply you with this most noble food. Among them are Hans and Erica Peipps.

The Peipps came to wild boar farming in an unusual way. Hans Peipps studied the habits of wild boar as a hobby for thirty years in Germany. He came to Ontario in 1984 in search of a farm to raise wild boar in their natural habitat. The ideal location would be acreage covered with weeds and that included a portion of bush and marsh. He found the perfect 80-hectare (200-acre) parcel near Badjeros, just south of Collingwood, in a farm that hadn't been worked for 15 years.

Finding the property was easy. The difficulty was locating stock that could be raised in the wild, boars that had not been cross-bred or barn-raised. Unable to find animals in Ontario, he purchased 23 sows and 10 boars from a hobby farmer in Quebec.

Today the Peipps have 75 sows and 20 breeding boars. The animals roam enclosed areas that consist of pasture, marsh and bushland. One sow and her piglets occupy half a hectare (1 acre). This allows for their sense of territory with enough space to protect their habitat.

The greatest expense in raising wild boar is fencing the enclosures. These four-strand fences run 9,000 volts of electricity through each strand with a generator for back-up. Each morning the Peipps walk the fence lines that ensure the boars stay in and the wolves keep out. However, there are no expensive buildings to maintain and no pens to clean out. The wild boar is a hardy animal that adapts well to any climatic conditions and does not require medi-cating. In nine years, Peipps has yet to pay a veterinary bill!

In summer the boars eat roots, leaves, and grass. Peipps seeds areas of pasture with corn and mixed grain which he opens to the boars once the plants break ground. In winter a ration of grain, along with carrots corn, hay, and apple pulp, provided free by a local cider mill, are scattered for the animals to search and root for.

Wild boars can live as long as 16 years. The sows produce one or two litters a year, for about 12 years. The meat is best when the animal is between two and four years of age.

At two, wild boar meat is the same quality and texture throughout the carcass. A boar that weighs between 70 and 72 kilograms (150 and 160 pounds) will dress at between 36 and 45 kilograms (80 and 100 pounds) of meat.

The flavor of wild boar meat is somewhere between beef and pork, with a somewhat nutty taste. Unlike domestic pork which is pink in color, wild boar is dark red. It is high in protein and low in cholesterol. Roasted whole it makes for a spectacular barbecue.

Peipps' wild boar meat is government inspected. It is available in cuts similar to pork: ribs, loin and shoulder chops and roasts, and stewing meat. The Peipps sell it by the pound at their farm gate and are hard pressed to keep up with the demand.

PEIPPS' WILD-GAME-FARM
R.R. #1,
Badjeros, Ont. N0C IA0
TEL 519-923-3145

DRIVE Highway 24, south from Collingwood to Osprey Concession 1 NDR. Go west on this concession and look for the sign on the north side of the road.

Uplands Pheasantry

Pheasants originated in the Orient and were confined to that part of the world until the Romans brought them to Europe in 1250 BC, and later to England. Benjamin Franklin's son-in-law, an Englishman, brought pheasants to North America in 1790, but he was unsuccessful at breeding them. In 1881, the US Consul in Shanghai sent 28 Chinese pheasants to Oregon. This species thrived and, with the introduction of more breeding stock, the birds multiplied quickly. By 1892 they found their way to Ontario where they became so plentiful a two-week open hunting season was declared. The greatest number of pheasants recorded in the world was at turn-of-the-century Pelee Island, a place where they are still abundant.

There are 16 genera of pheasants consisting of 170 different species and subspecies. The most popular pheasant in Canada is the English ringneck, the result of crossing several species in England.

Pheasants have been released throughout Ontario and have populated the countryside south of a line from Owen Sound to Brockville. They are also found on the Niagara Peninsula, in Essex County, in the Erie and South Huron districts, around Lake Simcoe, and along the northern shores of Lake Ontario as far as Prince Edward County.

With very few exceptions, pheasants live and breed well in captivity. The English ringneck, the Chinese ringneck and the melanistic mutant are the most common ones reared. The ringnecks are excellent for hunting and are used extensively on hunting preserves. With the loss of public hunting lands, hunting farms have become popular in Ontario. There are also farms committed to meat production for the restaurant trade and specialty food business, and farms that supply hunting farms and hobbyists. The sport in Ontario generates about 20 million dollars annually.

The largest pheasant farm in Canada is Uplands Pheasantry, located south of Aylmer. It was established in 1956 by Mike and Brenda Streib and was the first commercial pheasant hatchery and farm in the country.

The Streibs began modestly with 200 birds the first year and now annually hatch approximately 125,000 chicks. They primarily supply birds for the hunting market and service a small trade in the restaurant and food industry. Their pheasants are sold in every province across Canada and in some American states, in Europe, and the Caribbean.

Individuals may also purchase oven-ready pheasant from Uplands, year-round. They are vacuum packaged and ship well. A single cock bird will serve three to four people. A brace — that's an English term meaning a pair (a cockbird and a hen) — will serve six to seven people. The birds range in size from a kilogram to a kilogram and a half (1 pound 12 ounces to 3 pounds). At Christmas, they are packaged with rice for gift-giving in woodgrain boxes.

Uplands pheasants are raised naturally in large, outdoor pens, without the use of growth stimulants. Pheasant meat is primarily white meat, without a "gamey" taste. It contains no cholesterol and has very little fat. Visitors to the farm are welcome.

UPLANDS PHEASANTRY
R.R. #2,
Aylmer, Ont. N5H 2R2
TEL 519-773-8151
FAX 519-765-3673

DRIVE south from Aylmer on Highway 73, past County Road 45 and Concession 2. The Uplands Farm is on the west side of Highway 73, about 11 kilometers (6.8 miles) south of Aylmer.

Streib's Pheasant Supreme

2 pheasants
60 ml (4 Tbsp) oil
1 onion, quartered
2 apples, quartered
3 stalks celery, in 5 cm (2") pieces
butter, salt, pepper to taste

- Cut birds in serving portions. Place in a roasting pan and add salad oil, onion, apples, and celery. Dot with butter, salt, and pepper. Cover and bake at 160 C (325 F) until tender, approximately 2 hours. Drain fat and discard vegetables and apples. Place pheasant in open pan and prepare glaze.

GLAZE

175 ml (3/4 cup) brown sugar
250 ml (1 cup) crushed pineapple
125 ml (1/2 cup) sherry (optional)

- In a mixing bowl, combine all ingredients. Pour over pheasant pieces and glaze in a 200 C (400 F) oven until golden brown. Turn to prevent burning. Reduce heat to very low temperature and cover until ready to serve.

Streib's Roast Pheasant with Wild Rice

250 ml (1 cup) brown or wild rice, cooked 5 minutes less than directions on package
50 ml (1/4 cup) butter
1 onion, diced
125 ml (1/2 cup) celery
1 small can mushrooms, drained and sliced, reserve liquid
5 ml (1 tsp) salt
.5 ml (1/8 tsp) pepper
2 ml (1/2 tsp) marjoram
3 pheasants
butter
50 ml (1/4 cup) sherry (optional)

- Sauté vegetables in butter and add to rice with seasonings. Stuff cavities of birds. Wrap each pheasant with foil. Bake at 160 C (325 F) until tender, approximately 2 hours. Unwrap birds and brush with butter. Brown in a 200 C (400 F) oven 15 minutes. Prepare gravy from pan drippings and mushroom liquid. Correct seasonings. Add sherry to gravy if desired, just before serving.

New Frontier Meats

St. Catharines is not a place where you'd expect to find extraordinary, old-fashioned, European-style sausage, but that's where you'll find Nestor Zacarelli who holds the title of "Ontario Sausage King" (1992, 1993, 1994). He moved there from Toronto, but learned the art of sausage-making in his native Argentina from Italian grandparents. They slaughtered their own pigs and taught Zacarelli their secrets, beginning with the use of superior meat.

Zacarelli doesn't raise his own animals but being a butcher by trade, he personally selects Grade A-1 carcasses. He uses only natural casings, and fresh garlic, and grinds his own spices.

On site at his butcher shop, he smokes the sausages in an old-fashioned smokehouse with natural smoke from cherry wood or apple wood. This is a slow process that produces hot or cold smoke and takes a great deal of patience.

The word sausage, derived from the Latin "salsus" means salted or preserved. It's a food born of necessity, a method once used to preserve all of the animal trimmings decades before the days of refrigeration. The Greek poet, Homer, mentioned roasting a sausage about 2,800 years ago. Some 1,500 years ago the Babylonians consumed large numbers of sausages and by the 5th century BC, there are references to salami, a sausage thought to have originated in the city of the same name on the east coast of Cyprus. Around AD 228 someone wrote a cookbook with sausage recipes. Today you'd be hard pressed to find many cook books with a single recipe for sausage-making, although there are recipes that use sausages.

Local customs, ingredients, even the climate influenced the size, taste, and look of the link. The names of today's sausages reflect their place of origin: Milano sausage from Milan, Bologna from Bologna, Genoa salami from Genoa, Thuringia sausage from Thuringia, and Berliner from Berlin.

Traditionally, sausages were made with pork or pork combined with other meat. Today they can be made entirely from pork, beef, veal, lamb, chicken, or game animals, or a combination thereof. They can be fresh or cured with salt or smoke, or both; this is what extends their shelf life. Sausages are also dried. Drying can vary from a few days to as much as six months. The longer a sausage dries, the firmer it becomes.

Zacarelli makes 32 varieties of smoked sausage. Grape Grower's sausage made with local wine, Beer sausage made with beer, and Polka sausage, a blend of beef and pork, are among the fare. He also makes fresh sausage like Octoberfest and Italian — flavored hot, mild, honey garlic, onion, and parsley. While many of the traditional types are from family recipes, Zacarelli also likes to experiment, developing his own recipes with ingredients like hot pepper and spices. He prepares special orders for customers from their own favorite formulas or will develop something special with a client. He often works with hunters combining game with pork and beef to create a less gamey sausage.

The Segovia Restaurant in Toronto asked Zacarelli to duplicate a Spanish chorizo they couldn't find elsewhere. One diner who frequents the restaurant and enjoys this specialty is Julio Iglesias.

In addition to making sausages, Frontier Meats carries a full line of deli meats as well as sides and hinds of beef and pork, cut and wrapped in full view of the customer.

Look for Zacarelli when he defends his Ontario Sausage title at the next Ontario Sausage Festival, the first weekend in July. Out-of-towners can place phone orders (shipping extra). Zacarelli's famous sausage and prime meat cuts are currently shipped from Sioux Lookout to New York State.

NEW FRONTIER MEATS
16 Oakdale Ave.,
St. Catharines, Ont. L2P 2B9
TEL 905-988-5762

- Simmer fresh sausage in a small amount of water (125 ml (1/2 cup)) to enhance the spices, before barbecuing. Place smoked sausages directly onto the barbecue. Turn sausages constantly over a low flame, about 20 minutes.
- Smoked and dry sausages are best served with beer, Italian sausage with dry, red wine.

ONTARIO SAUSAGE FESTIVAL

- The first weekend of July, St. Catharines hosts the Ontario Sausage Festival. Bus-loads of sausage savorers come from all over Ontario as well as parts of the USA to appreciate the culinary efforts of the lords of the links. The two-day, annual event has been a success since 1982. This is a weekend of music, entertainment, and plenty of succulent sausage sampling for the entire family. Along with the judging there are a variety of sausages available for sale.

ONTARIO SAUSAGE FESTIVAL

P.O. Box 723,
St. Catharines, Ont. L2R 6Y3
TEL 905-684-2961; 905-684-3215; 905-685-8300

Russell Jones Popcorn

There is a right way and a wrong way to pop corn. That's why Russell Jones prints instructions on every bag he produces from his farm near Leamington, in the Canadian popcorn belt.

A full-time worker at Chrysler in Windsor, Jones has been growing popcorn since 1971. He takes his annual holidays in October to harvest the crop, but the year-round operation employs the whole family. Wife Marg makes deliveries to supermarkets and children Roy and Beth work bagging and packing the kernels.

There isn't much Russell Jones doesn't know about popcorn, from its folksy history to the scientific aspect of what makes corn pop. The first five years of business, he bought his seed from Orville Redenbacher of Indiana fame (then switched to an Iowa supplier when Redenbacher was bought out). Jones learned Redenbacher's techniques and has since added a few of his own.

He plants his corn the last two weeks of April unless delayed by cool weather. At peak production he has 142 hectares (350 acres) planted with seven farmers under contract. Currently about 80 hectares (200 acres) are under cultivation, producing between 40 and 50 bushels of popcorn an acre. Jones has the capacity to store and dry about 20,000 bushels in four bins.

Most supermarket shelves contain imported popcorn, grown in the American mid-west. It's a low-grade mix of hybrid corn. A good deal of it is machine-harvested which scratches the kernel shells resulting in unpopped duds. The superior taste and popability of Jones' corn is in part due to the fact that it is ear-picked and air-dried.

Jones planted his first acre of popcorn in 1979. To celebrate 20 years in business in 1990, he began marketing popcorn by the ear, selling four ears for a dollar along with microwave bags. He also promotes his product through farm tours which he likes to conduct himself.

Jones was the first to employ ziplock-style, reusable bags, an industry innovation that helps keep moisture in the bag. His popcorn is dried to a 13.75 percent moisture content. The moisture turns into steam when heated. Twenty layers of photo cells hold the pressure of the soft starch core until it can no longer be maintained. The center skin cracks and expands up to 40 times its original size.

Jones sells microwave popcorn that is added to the bag with butter, just before popping. Pre-packaged microwave popcorn found in the marketplace contains a mixture of salt, oil, and corn that makes for soggy popcorn.

Popcorn is a uniquely North American product. It was first grown as maize in Mexico thousands of years ago. An 80,000-year-old grain of pollen, carbon-dated in Mexico City, is believed to be that of corn.

Popcorn became popular in the nineteenth century as a home-grown treat that caught on at country fairs, carnivals, and circuses. Popcorn machines were installed in movie theatres during the 1920s; it's difficult now to watch any cliffhanger movie without the sound of crunching accompanying the soundtrack.

Today popcorn is touted by everyone from nutritionists to the Dental Association as being among the most nutritional snacks, high in fibre and low in calories — only 110 in 1 liter (4 cups) without butter!

Jones popcorn comes in 500 gram (1 pound), 1 kilogram (2 pound) and 2 kilogram (4.4 pound) and 20 kilogram (44 pound) bags, emblazoned with color-coded maple leaves: red for yellow butterfly, blue for white popcorn and green for mushroom popcorn (hot air). He also sells his own brand of coconut oil and salt. The products are available at A & P, Knechtels, and N & D stores in southwestern Ontario.

Tours of the operation can be arranged by calling ahead.

RUSSELL JONES POPCORN

R.R. #5,
Leamington, Ont. N8H IX3
TEL 519-326-7128

RUSSELL JONES POPPING TIPS

- As a connoisseur of popcorn, Jones prefers the traditional, stove-top cooking, oil method. Dry air poppers dry out popcorn.
- Select a high quality oil, preferably coconut oil, for a richer taste.
- Choose tender, butterfly popcorn for eating; prefer the larger-popping mushroom popcorn for popcorn balls and confectionary treats.
- Refrigerate corn in airtight containers.
- Heat oil in a pan to 230 C (450 F). Drop 2 kernels in and cover until they pop. Now add a single layer of corn and re-cover. Shake the pan during popping. Corn should be popped in 2-3 minutes.
- Add salt to taste only after popcorn has finished popping.

Popcorn Medley

90 ml (6 Tbsp) butter or margarine
15 ml (1 Tbsp) Worcestershire sauce
5 ml (1 tsp) seasoned salt
2 ml (1/2 tsp) garlic powder
1 L (1 qt) unsalted popped popcorn
375 ml (1 1/2 cups) (13 oz. can) chow mein noodles
375 ml (1 1/2 cups) bite-sized shredded wheat biscuits
250 ml (1 cup) pecan halves
5 ml (1 tsp) basil

- Melt butter or margarine in large skillet. Add Worcestershire sauce, salt and garlic powder. Add popcorn, noodles, bite-sized wheat biscuits, and pecans; toss gently until well-coated. Sprinkle with basil. Place on cookie sheet and heat at 120 C (250 F) for 45 minutes, stirring occasionally. Cool. Yields 2 L (2 qts)

Peanut Farming

Peanuts have been raised commercially in the tobacco-producing areas of southwestern Ontario since 1980. As tobacco consumption decreases, peanuts have replaced it as an alternative cash crop. Peanuts don't grow as well in Ontario as they do in the American peanut-producing states of Georgia, North Carolina, Texas, Virginia, and Oklahoma, but the cooler temperature here means less herbicides, fungicides, and pesticides are used. Aflatoxin, a carcinogenic mold, doesn't develop on peanuts grown in this climatic zone. Peanuts are environmentally friendly in other ways. There is no waste and immature peanuts are sold as bird feed and the hulls used as livestock bedding by local farmers.

Before the peanut became so popular in North America, it took a long, circuitous route from the New World to the Old World and back again. By the time sixteenth century explorers and missionaries came to the New World, peanuts grew as far north as Mexico. Portuguese navigators introduced 2-seeded peanuts from Brazil to both African coasts and the Malabu coast of southwest India. Spanish explorers took 3-seeded peanuts from Peru to the Philippines, China, Japan, and eastern India.

Portuguese slave traders used peanuts as rations on board ships carrying Africans to America. Once in America, slaves planted peanuts throughout the southern states. The first commercial crops were raised in South Carolina around 1800.

At one time peanuts were only cultivated in tropical and subtropical parts of the world. Superior strains and farming methods now enable them to grow in areas where the growing season is at least four months long.

Peanuts are the seeds of an annual plant that resembles the common garden pea. Botanically speaking it's a vegetable, a member of the legume family related to peas and beans. True nuts grow on trees.

Peanuts are the only plant said to plant its own seeds. Once the bright, yellow, self-pollinating flowers bloom on their leafy bush, they swell and wither, pulling the vines to the ground. The withered blossoms or embryos push down several inches into the soil where the peanut pods develop with their delicious nuts inside. From this comes the name ground nuts, ground peas, earth nuts, goobers, and goober peas. The Valencia peanut grown in Ontario is the most flavorful of all the peanut varieties.

The peanuts are planted in mid-May and harvested in late September before the frost. Harvesting usually takes six weeks. Once brought in from the fields, the peanuts are washed and hand-graded, then transferred to bulk kilns for drying, before being stored in temperature-controlled cooler units. Thousands of pounds of fresh raw peanuts are sold to Asian buyers in Toronto. The yield in Ontario is about 1,300 kilograms per hectare (1,500 pounds per acre).

Picard Peanuts

Just 4 miles north of Simcoe is the "home of the Canadian peanut." Picard Peanuts were the first commercial peanut shelling plant in the country and have been leaders in the industry to promote this relatively new Ontario crop. They store their peanuts in the shell for freshness, then shell and roast them weekly.

Picard's offer a complete line of peanuts and peanut products. They are also the creators of a unique Canadian snack food, the Chipnut. This is a peanut covered in a crisp potato shell. They sell all varieties of imported nuts and manufacture their own candy. They carry an extensive line of baking products, dried fruit, and party supplies.

Group tours of the plant can be arranged. There's a retail store at the plant location and in St. Jacobs.

PICARD'S PEANUTS LTD.
R.R. #1,
Windham Centre, Ont. N0E 2A0
TEL 519-426-6700
FAX 519-443-7779

OPEN Monday to Saturday 9 a.m. to 5 p.m.; Sunday 12:30 p.m. to 4:30 p.m.

DRIVE Highway 401 to Woodstock. Take Highway 403 east to Highway 24. Drive south on Highway 24. Picard's is located on the west side of the highway, north of Simcoe.

Kernal Peanuts

The Racz family grew tobacco from 1947 to 1986. They began growing test plots of peanuts in 1977 in conjunction with the University of Guelph to help develop a suitable variety of the crop for southwestern Ontario. Ernie Racz also became involved with Agriculture Canada to lend his expertise to the creation of a peanut harvester suitable for use in the province. Called the "once-over," it digs, separates, and collects the peanuts, unlike harvesters designed for warmer climates which leave the peanuts in the fields to dry.

The Racz family began growing peanuts commercially in 1982 and opened a wholesale and retail operation on their farm the same year. They now have 60 hectares (150 acres) in peanut production.

While Ernie Racz looks after the crops, his wife Nancy handles business sales. They sell roasted peanuts that are salted, unsalted, and garlic flavor, bagged in a variety of sizes from 100 grams to 10 kilograms (4 ounces to 22 pounds). They make their own peanut butter (crunchy and smooth) sold by the jar and pail, and four types of peanut candies — buttercrisp, peanut clusters, peanut brittle, and pralines. They also make up an assortment of gift baskets which can be custom ordered in any size. Pre-arranged tours of the plant are welcomed. The best time to visit is in mid to late summer when the plants are growing, or during fall harvest.

KERNAL PEANUTS LTD.
R.R. #1,
Vittoria, Ont. N0E IW0
TEL 519-426-9222
FAX 519-426-9229

Hilton Whole Grain Millers

Anyone who starts their day with a steaming bowl of oatmeal, eats granola, or bakes with oats, will want to taste a revolutionary, whole grain oatmeal called Hilton Toasted Oats. Barry and Karen Mahon of Perth County have developed a process of milling oats that's very different from the traditional "steam cooked" method used by most millers. The Mahons actually toast their oats whole. For the consumer that means a healthier, fresher, tastier product. The price is lower than supermarkets prices too!

What's even more exciting for parents is that children like the nutty-toasted flavor. And what's good news for everybody is that you can buy your oatmeal by mail order no matter where you live. Hilton Toasted Oats go by mail to every province and as far away as Labrador and the Territories. They have become a popular specialty item with bed and breakfasts, are making breakfast eaters out of kids, and gaining a loyal following among committed porridge advocates.

The Mahons didn't set out to revolutionize the oatmeal market. They left their dairy farm on the Niagara Escarpment when their land was expropriated, and took the herd with them to the town of Staffa. But the dairy business became unprofitable when interest rates soared. They converted their operation to a custom seed-cleaning plant to provide a service for area farmers. They also formed a company to supply nutritional lunches for school children. However, the seed-cleaning business was only seasonal and didn't have long-term potential as farmers were beginning to plant seed without cleaning it to save money. The lunch business proved too labor-intensive.

The Mahons decided to take their seed-cleaning one step further and process the grain into edible food. They chose oat flakes as their specialty, mainly because Karen bought large quantities for her own baking. She also adds the nutrient-filled grain to meat loaf, patties, fruit breads, muffins, cakes, and dessert toppings.

The Mahons came up with their own method of heat stabilization, a gentle, less intense way of processing the oats so they don't become rancid. The result was a nutty-flavored oat that Karen found greatly enhanced her baking.

The Mahons were also committed to a whole grain product. With the recent discovery that oat bran lowers cholesterol, most milling companies are separating all or a part of the bran from the oat and selling it separately. Coupled with the fact that the steaming method of processing leaches out minerals and nutrients, oatmeal in the market place is less nutritious than Hilton Toasted Oats. To give your oatmeal the bran test, look at its color. The whiter it is, and the faster it cooks, the less oat bran is left on.

Hilton Toasted Oats contain 100 percent of the natural oat bran and are rich in carbohydrates, protein, vitamin E, seven B vitamins, and nine minerals. The oats store the same as other oatmeal, up to a year in a sealed container in the cupboard, or indefinitely if frozen. They cook the same way on the stove or in the microwave, but are darker in color.

Unlike commercial oatmeal which may sit for long periods of time in warehouses, Hilton Toasted Oats are available fresh daily, made as demand requires. The oats come in three flake sizes (regular, large and small), in 5 kilogram (11 pound) and 10 kilogram (22 pound) packages. Recipes are included with each order. They are available by mail order or sold in local stores in and around Stratford and at the Farmer's Market in Waterloo.

HILTON WHOLE GRAIN MILLERS
R.R. #2,
Staffa, Ont. N0K 1Y0
TEL/FAX 519-345-2582

Oat Honey Corn Crunch with Hilton Toasted Oats

125 ml (1/2 cup) white sugar
125 ml (1/2 cup) brown sugar
75 ml (1/3 cup) honey
75 ml (1/3 cup) water
5 ml (1 tsp) vinegar
90 ml (6 Tbsp) butter
1 ml (1/4 tsp) salt
500 ml (2 cups) Hilton Toasted Oat Flakes
1500 ml (6 cups) popped popcorn
125 ml (1/2 cup) broken walnuts

- Boil the sugars, honey, water, vinegar, butter, and salt slowly in a large saucepan. Heat slowly and stir constantly until a little of the syrup will form a hard ball when dropped from teaspoon into cold water. Quickly pour syrup over the cereal, popcorn, and walnuts in a large bowl and toss with two large spoons until evenly mixed. Spread mixture onto buttered cookie sheet. Let stand until cool and break into chunks. If sticky, dry a little longer in oven. Store in tightly covered containers. Makes half a kilogram (1 1/4 lbs).

No-Flour Oat Monster Cookies

250 ml (1 cup) butter
625 ml (2 1/2 cups) packed brown sugar
500 ml (2 cups) granulated sugar
500 ml (2 cups) peanut butter
6 eggs
20 ml (4 tsp) baking soda
4 Tbsp vanilla
7 ml (1 1/2 tsp) corn syrup, honey, or molasses
2.25 L (9 cups) Hilton Toasted Oats
500 ml (2 cups) chocolate chips or raisins, or peanuts, or whatever

- Cream butter, sugars, and peanut butter until smooth. Beat in eggs. Stir in baking soda, vanilla, and corn syrup. Mix well. Add Hilton Toasted Oats and whatever. Roll in walnut-size balls and space well on lightly oiled cookie sheet. Bake 15 to 18 minutes at 160 C (325 F). If your oven is too hot lower to 160 C (325 F) and cook longer. Makes lots and freezes well.

Royal Agricultural Winter Fair

Each year the Royal Agricultural Winter Fair gets bigger and better. In 1993 it was a $6.5 million production, not counting the inestimable value of thousands of volunteer hours. When the "country comes to the city" for twelve days in mid-November, some 350,000 individuals delight in the sights, sounds, and smells of Canada's rural roots. For those who love the fragrance of fresh cut hay and horse sweat, this is the place to be. It's here by the tractor-trailer load — about 1,800 bales of hay, 3,000 bales of straw, and 3,000 bales of dry wood shavings — brought in to facilitate roughly 3,000 cattle, 2,000 horses, 800 sheep, 450 goats, 300 pigs and 300 rabbits, all vying for the prestige of a Royal ribbon.

Although there are four aspects to the fair — agriculture, the Royal Horse Show, the Winter Garden and commercial vendors — it's the emphasis on agriculture and learning that makes the Royal special.

Fairs are the oldest agricultural organizations in Canada. Farmers have always wanted to know which are the best breeds and which are the best of those breeds. They say the first question has never truly been answered. However, in response to the second question, standards for each breed were established for the show ring around 1850. As the show window of Canadian agriculture, the Royal has been responsible for contributing to the improvement of Canadian livestock and agri-products and the development of Canadian export trade.

The first Royal Agricultural Winter Fair was held in 1922, a year late due to construction delays in building the Coliseum. The Fair was largely the brain-child of W.A. Dryden who owned a short-horn breeding farm in Brooklin. Dryden and a group of three other men, George Pepper of Toronto, D.C. Flatt of Millgrove, and Professor E. Day of Guelph, formulated most of the plans. Their idea was to attract the best animal breeds and agricultural products from every province by featuring competition in all classes. This way, national standards would eventually filter down to the provincial

fair level. Toronto was selected as the location, winning out over Hamilton by a deciding vote cast by Dryden and the horse show was added as a means of attracting more people.

The *Toronto Star* dubbed the Royal as "The Best and Biggest of its kind on the Continent of America if not in the World"; The Globe headline read "Royal Winter Fair Greatest On Earth" (November 1922). More than 200 box cars of livestock arrived from across Canada via the CPR and Grand Trunk Railway. Twenty-five car loads of cattle came up from the US. Three passenger trains arrived daily at the grounds from Hamilton, Brantford, London, Woodstock and beyond. There was even a special train from Prince Edward Island with 200 people on board.

On opening day 22,000 people passed through the gates. The cost was five cents for children and another twenty-five cents to see the horse show. It was a time when draught horses and shorthorns were in their hey-day, and prize money of $70,000 enticed competitors.

Today, the emphasis on agriculture and its educational role is still paramount at the Royal. In 1993, a full-time director of education developed a dozen special, hands-on learning centers for students, in co-operation with teachers and educational facilities. Among the close-up views of rural life were field crops, swine, egg grading, maple syrup, and sausage-making.

Food is always front and center at the Royal in raw and cooked form with judging in every category including field crops, vegetables, honey, cheese, fruits, jams, jellies, pickles, and chili sauce, one of the most competitive categories. All the preserves are auctioned at the end of the Fair, and a cookbook titled "The Royal Country Recipe Collection" was published in 1993, featuring the recipes of many former winners.

The Royal Horse Show is still the highlight of the social calendar. The Fair officially opens at the horse show, usually with royalty presiding. Part of the tradition and the charm of the Royal lies in the contrasts of jewels and top hats amidst dungarees and horse flesh. The Fair is the finale event for the top Canadian and American riders who have competed all summer in show jumping trials across North America. There are also competitions in dressage and horse showing for every age and level of rider.

For anyone planning a garden or wanting a retreat from Ontario's winter, the Winter Garden brings the outdoors inside. Fountains and waterfalls, gazebos and greenhouses, trees, flowers and bird houses abound, with plenty of shopping ideas for the gardener in your life.

The commercial displays and vendors have quality items for sale — everything imaginable to eat, wear, and play with. It is a perfect place to start Christmas shopping.

THE ROYAL AGRICULTURAL WINTER FAIR

The Coliseum,
Exhibition Place,
Toronto, Ont. M6K 3C3
TEL 416-393-6400
FAX 416-393-6488

ONTARIO TRIVIA

ST. CATHARINES had the first electric street car system in North America.

SAINT THOMAS has a life-size statue of the famous circus elephant, Jumbo, killed here by a train in 1885.

ST. WILLIAMS Forest Station is Canada's first Provincial forestry station, established in 1908. Its purpose was to provide nursery stock to farmers for planting on sandy and idle land for windbreaks around farm buildings, orchards, and fields. Currently, about six million trees are shipped annually to landowners.

SAULT STE. MARIE is home to Forestry Canada's Great Lakes Forestry Centre, the largest forest research complex in Canada.

International Plowing Match and Farm Machinery Show

The International Plowing Match and Farm Machinery Show is an annual event that takes place every September in a different county or region of Ontario. It brings the agricultural community together, challenging the abilities and techniques of its members in competition, as well as an exposition that celebrates the history of farming and the latest developments in technology and the land. The show attracts some 100,000 people from across Canada, the US and Europe, appealing to both urban and rural people alike. It's the largest event of its kind in Canada and the second largest in North America.

The match is sponsored by the Ontario Plowmen's Association (OPA) in co-operation with an annual host. It first took place November 11, 1913 at Sunnybrook Farms, Eglinton, the current site of Sunnybrook Hospital in Toronto. However plowing matches were very popular in the province as early as 1824, and were often held in conjunction with local fairs.

In Europe, plowing matches can be traced back to the sixteenth century when plowing was a great source of rivalry among agricultural people. Plow Monday, the first Monday after Twelfth Night or Epiphany, marked the first day of the farmer's year, when the ground was thawed sufficiently to be ploughed. This celebration was observed in England up until the seventeenth century, then revived 300 years later in 1945.

The Ontario Plowmen's Association formed because farmers recognized the short-comings of their own poor ploughing techniques. Poor tillage resulted in low yields and encouraged weeds. There was a common desire among the farming community to learn better farming techniques, generally, and share that knowledge.

What's significant about the OPA and their matches is that their 80-plus-year history is very much the history of agriculture in Ontario. The OPA was front and center in every aspect of farming from educational activities to government legislation. For example, it was the OPA who lobbied the Department of Agriculture during World War I to leave one capable farmhand on every 40-hectare (100-acre) farm so that farm production might be increased during wartime. It pressed for standardization of farm machinery, especially for parts that could wear out or break. And the OPA backed such legislation as the Weed Act in the late 1920s which promoted government support of seed cleaning plants.

The Plowing Matches became the OPA's vehicle for showcasing everything that would contribute to the rural way of life in a positive way. "The midway, the fakir and the wheels of fortune men" were barred. On the rounds of the Ontario Agricultural College in Guelph, in 1915, between 4,000 and 5,000 people were attracted to see the featured demonstration — the tractor. In 1922, the Hydro-Electric Commission demonstrated the value of electricity for farms and homes at the County Farm in Lindsay, and in 1943 at the Oxford Match, a home-made electric lawn mower was among the many labor-saving devices.

Moving the Match around the province has triggered change and innovation. In 1945 in Peterborough, the success of the wind-up dinner began a tradition of such events. 1960 was the first year a woman's program was initiated, at the match in Elgin. It was sponsored by Ontario Hydro and featured the use of electrical appliances in the home. It was also the first crowning of the Queen of the Furrow. Seventeen young women were judged on their ability to identify the parts of a plow and tractor and answer questions about plowing.

The annual Plowing Match has only been cancelled during World War II and in 1918 due to the influenza epidemic. In 1954, it survived Hurricane Hazel which struck the site on the Friday evening of the match. There was a great deal of damage to exhibitors, but despite heavy rain and mud, all but 5 of the 46 classes of events were completed.

So what exactly takes place at the modern-day, International Plowing Match? The competition is open to plowing contestants from around the world, but those from Ontario must qualify at branch level matches. Competitors are classified according to points they have accumulated, age, the size of their plow, and whether it is drawn by tractor or animals.

Contestants plow in their category over the course of several days so there is a good deal of tension and anticipation among plowers. The judges look for the split, straightness, and uniformity of the crown; the firmness, packing, closeness, and depth of the seed bed; the straightness, neatness, depth, and width of the finish; and over-all, the ins and outs, the burying of grass and stubble, and the straightness and uniformity of the furrows. If all that farm talk seems confusing, head for the tented city where hundreds of exhibitors display goods that relate to the farm and the home, from giant tractors to home-made crafts. There are dozens of food caterers, and a range of exhibits and demonstrations like dog trials and antique shows that appeal to young and old.

ONTARIO PLOWMEN'S ASSOCIATION

367 Woodlawn Road,
Unit 8,
Guelph, Ont. NIH 7K9
TEL 519-767-2928
FAX 519-767-2101

Fergus Truck Show

Billed as the 40-million-dollar weekend, the Fergus Truck Show is now in its 9th year and continues to be considered the best truck show in Ontario, attracting contestants from across Canada and the United States.

What exactly is a truck show? In Fergus, an estimated 40 million dollars worth of trucks, exhibits and displays are featured, with over 200 trucks entered in 30 different classes of Show and Shine competition. These working trucks—the kind you see every day on the highway—provide a spectacle of chrome, accessories, custom paint jobs and murals. Each truck in the competition is closely examined by a team of judges. However, it's the public who chooses the much coveted award of "Best Truck of the Show."

There are truck pulling competitions for stock, street legal, modified 4 X 4s and heavies with pullers, competing for money.

There's also plenty of music, great food, and entertainment during this 2-day volunteer event. All proceeds from the show go to the community of Fergus and the volunteer groups themselves, who help organize the event.

FERGUS TRUCK SHOW

P.O. Box 412,
Fergus, Ont. NIM 3E2
TEL 519-846-0983 (Days)
FAX 519-843-3412 (Evening, days)

WHERE: Fergus & District Community Centre,
550 Belsyde St.,
Fergus, Ont.
WHEN: 4th weekend in July

Minden Techni-cal Challenge

In Minden, a community of 1,200 people in the Haliburton Highlands, a world class event takes place every January. The Minden Techni-cal Challenge is the largest limited-class sled-dog race in the world. It's also the largest sled-dog race of any kind in Ontario. It attracts the world's top competitors, both canine and human. The 60 dog teams comprising about 1,000 dogs come from as far away as British Columbia, Alaska, and Idaho, to vie for more than $25,000 in prize money.

The race is sanctioned by the International Sled Dog Racing Association (ISDRA) who have deemed the Minden course as the most physically challenging on the ISDRA circuit.

A two-day event, racing begins each morning at 10 a.m. The start and finish is on Minden's main street so there's plenty of free, ring-side viewing. The action begins with the 4-dog teams. Each team bolts out of a giant starting chute at 2-minute intervals. After lunch, the 8-dog teams run. The sled-dogs get so excited it takes four or five volunteers to hold a team back until the musher gives the starting signal.

If you have never seen a sled-dog race, you will be surprised at the small stature of the dogs and their lean constitution. Unlike the 40-kilogram (90-pound) pet malamutes, often mistaken for huskies, sled-dogs weigh between 18 and 23 kilograms (40 and 50 pounds). They are bred for their high energy and agility and, like all great athletes, spend hundreds of hours training for the racing season.

Even before the snow flies, the teams begin indoor training on homemade 3-wheel training rigs. The dogs begin slowly after a summer of inactivity when it's too hot to train. They run about 4.8 kilometers (3 miles) over a 15 to 20 minute period. By the time they move outdoors they'll average 29 to 32 kilometers (18 to 20 miles) an hour.

Each position on the team, from lead dog at the front to wheel dogs at the back, requires a particular skill. Early training gives the musher a chance to se- lect the appropriate dog for each position. Back-up dogs are trained along with the chosen team.

The event is very much a family attraction. After the 8-dog teams have raced there is a "kid-and-mutt" race for children. Spectators can visit the race headquarters and are welcome to stroll the dog yards where they can talk to the mushers and look over the dogs and puppies. Yearling huskies are brought along to experience the atmosphere and excitement of the race as part of their training.

MINDEN TECHNI-CAL CHALLENGE

Haliburton Highlands Chamber of Commerce
P.O. Box 147,
Minden, Ont. K0M 2K0
TEL 705-286-1760
FAX 705-286-6016

DRIVE Highway 35 to Minden, about 200 kilometers (124 miles) north of Toronto.

Rockhound Gemboree

Bancroft, in the highlands of Hastings, is the mineral capital of Canada. This village of 2,200 people is at the edge of the Precambrian Shield, where approximately 300 different minerals can be found, roughly 80 percent of all of Canada's minerals.

Specimens from Bancroft are present in fine mineral collections and museums throughout the world, including the Smithsonian Institute. Bancroft supplied graphite, in demand during World War I, and corundum, mined at the turn of the century for sandpaper. Marble in the Royal Ontario Museum and the Whitney Block at Queen's Park also came from Bancroft.

Underlying the Bancroft area is the Grenville Province of the Canadian Shield. Millions of years ago, a mountain-building process laid down layers of volcanic, sedimentary, and intrusive rocks. Many unusual minerals formed as a result.

Mining began with iron ore in the mid-1800s; a railway was built to carry it to Trenton. In 1866 Ontario experienced its first gold rush when the mineral was discovered at Richardson mine, Eldorado. There was also a corundum rush at the turn of the century and most recently uranium was discovered near Bancroft. All these mines are now closed.

Collectors are still drawn to the "Bancroft assemblage of minerals," an area that stretches north of the town. The old pits, quarries, and underground workings produce a great variety of simple, complex, and rare species, including a respectable list of many of the "world's best" individual minerals, such as uraninite, uranophone, ellesworthite (discovered here) and betafite. Also there are excellent specimens of apatite, betafite, candrinite and diopside, as well as more common gems like garnet and zircon.

Bancroft hosts the Rockhound Gemboree annually during the last weekend of July. It's the largest commercial mineral and gem fair in Canada. Mineral collectors come from around the world to display and swap polished rock slabs, slices, and precious and semi-precious stones. Items range from nickel grab bags to gems worth thousands of dollars. Throughout the day there are demonstrations like gem cutting, polishing, and gold-wire work.

Geologists lead field trips to some of the choice sites in the Bancroft vicinity where access to the minerals is easy. Collectors don work boots or comfortable shoes and safety glasses and pack a lunch and a geologist's hammer for the trip. Rockhounds can explore a range of venues from the stockpile dumped at the station in the 1940s, to Eagle's Nest and Quirk Lake, known for mica and hematite; Faraday Hill for calcite, pyrite, and marble; and McCormack Mine where everything from a to z, allanite to zircon, can be chipped away. Also of interest is the Bancroft Museum which once housed a logging firm in the 1800s. Local minerals and those from around the world are on display. It's open daily.

ROCKHOUND GEMBOREE

Bancroft & District Chamber of Commerce
P.O. Box 539,
Bancroft, Ont. K0L 1C0
TEL 613-332-1513

DRIVE Highway 401 to Belleville and go north on Highway 62.

Biggest Battle

Every year in the third week of July, Prescott's Fort Wellington on the St. Lawrence River hosts Canada's grandest military pageant. Re-enactors, people with a passion for military history, come together from all over North America. They bring with them their flint-lock muskets and military paraphernalia and wear authentic military uniforms, correct down to the plumes on their shakos. They re-enact large-scale, mock battles of the border wars, the War of 1812 or the Revolutionary War, and demonstrate military tactics and aspects of camp life. Entire families come together; even the children wear authentic dress. During the re-enactment weekend, there are usually three mock battles by the river. The grassy field next to the fort is abloom with the canvas tents of a military encampment, and crafts and trades of the era are demonstrated and displayed. The event attracts close to 15,000 spectators.

Fort Wellington, designated a National Historic Site in the mid-1920s, is where British and Canadian militia have stood guard for more than 170 years. There's a spectacular view of the St. Lawrence River from the ramparts that surround the fort. Two 24-pounder cannons, mounted on traversing platforms and once intended to destroy enemy ships or the buildings of Ogdensburg on the American side, still face the river. The stone caponnière is still in place to stop opposing cannon ball fire.

During its military lifetime, there were two Fort Wellingtons. The first, built during the War of 1812 when the US declared war on England was meant to protect British shipping between Upper and Lower Canada. The fort was constructed on the St. Lawrence River, upstream from an 80-kilometer stretch of rapids where bateaux and Durham boats transferred their goods to lake vessels. The fort was abandoned and eventually deteriorated as relations improved between Britain and the US. However, a second fort, parts of which remain today, was built on the same site to deal with the re-bellions of 1837. Although the fort was never attacked, the British garrison was part of the Battle of Windmill in 1838, one kilometer east of the site. It remained a British stronghold until the 1850s. From 1866 to 1870, it was again garrisoned because of the threat of attack by the Fenians, Irish-Americans hostile to Great Britain.

As an historical site, under the jurisdiction of Parks Canada, the original 1813 fortifications have been preserved along with the 1838-39 blockhouse, officers' quarters, and latrine. The buildings have been refurbished to the era of 1846, when the Royal Canadian Rifle Regiment was stationed here.

Other special events at Fort Wellington include a Victorian "Garrison Christmas" in December, and the "Shadows of the Fort," a first-person animation of the fort's history, which is held in the month of August. There is a Young Volunteer Program which involves children between the age of 7 and 14 as participants in the fort's historical programs, and an Extension Program that takes relics and discussion of the fort's early days to organizations such as schools, that cannot visit the area. During the summer, guides in period costume bring to life the daily activities of the fort.

FORT WELLINGTON NATIONAL HISTORIC SITE
370 VanKoughnet St.,
P.O. Box 479,
Prescott, Ont. K0E 1T0
TEL 613-925-2896
FAX 613-925-1536

OPEN May 21st to September 30th, 10:00 a.m. to 5:00 p.m. (subject to change)

Canadian Tulip Festival

The world's largest tulip festival isn't in Holland, but Ottawa. However, Ottawa's tulips do have a Dutch connection. During World War II, Princess Juliana (later Queen Juliana) of the Netherlands took refuge in Ottawa with her family. Her daughter, Princess Margriet, was born there. The hospital room had to be made an official part of the Netherlands by an Act of Parliament so Margriet would be eligible as heir to the Dutch throne. After the war, the Royal Dutch family presented Ottawa with a gift of tulip bulbs. Since that time, more than 10,000 additional bulbs have arrived every year.

The third weekend of May, Canada's capital city blooms with millions upon millions of tulips, laid out in a giant carpet of every color of the rainbow. Tulips adorn city parks, streetscapes, and every conceivable container in the city.

The Canadian Tulip Festival embraces the entire town in a multi-cultural celebration. Among the activities are cruises on the Rideau Canal; train excursions through the Gatineau Valley; live entertainment; international food, dance, and song; and even a run, walk, and wheelchair race weekend.

The festival is recognized as one of the top 100 events in North America and was awarded the Top Event for Ontario in 1993 by the American Bus Association. It attracts roughly 600,000 people during the week.

CANADIAN TULIP FESTIVAL
P.O. Box 394, Station A,
Ottawa, Ont. KIN 8V4
TEL 613-562-1480
FAX 613-562-1479
800-66-TULIP

Leacock Heritage Festival

Every summer since 1988, on the shores of Lake Couchiching, a celebration of culture, humor, and history honors Canada's foremost humorist, Stephen Leacock. Tea in the rose garden, a concert in the park, a cruise along the lake are just some of the activities reminiscent of Leacock's turn-of-the-century Orillia.

The highlights of the event are two literary competitions which draw "humorous interest" from around the world — the Leacock Limerick Awards, a competition for unpublished limericks, and the Leacock Humorous Short Story Competition. If Leacock were alive today, he would be pleased to be remembered in this way, in the place where he spent most of his summers. For what pleased him most was making people laugh.

Leacock wrote nearly forty books of humor, all in his spare time. He was a university professor and writing was a hobby to entertain himself and his friends. Yet there are more of his books in print today than any other Canadian writer, living or dead.

His writing ranges from nonsense to humor to satire. His special gift was to see the fun in the everyday elements of mundane life. His satire was never mean or cruel, but funny. Perhaps his best known book is *Sunshine Sketches of a Little Town*.

Leacock was always in demand as a speaker, captivating audiences wherever he travelled. Born in England, he emigrated to Canada with his parents when he was seven. Educated at Upper Canada College and the University of Toronto, he taught school for a time at the college until he received his PhD in economics and political science. He lectured at McGill University in Montreal until his retirement in 1936, dividing his time between his home in Montreal and his summer place at Old Brewery Bay, near Orillia. The town now maintains his summer house as the Leacock Memorial Home.

The Leacock Heritage Festival runs for about ten days towards the end of July. There is a long schedule of events with activities for every member of the family.

LEACOCK HERITAGE FESTIVAL
P.O. Box 2305,
Orillia, Ont. L3V 6S3
TEL 705-325-3261
FAX 705-325-7666

Port Elgin Pumpkin Festival

The World Pumpkin Confederation (WPC) Weigh-off, is a competition designed to locate the largest pumpkin, squash, and watermelon in the world. There are twenty "weigh-off" stations world-wide. The only official WPC weigh-off station in Ontario is at Port Elgin, now christened the Pumpkin Capital of Ontario. This is the town's largest event, and has received national and international acclaim.

Giant pumpkin growing has its roots firmly established in the province. At the turn of the century, Goderich farmer William Warnock attained international acclaim with his 182 kilogram (400 pound) pumpkin at the Paris World's Fair. The French government awarded him a special medal and diploma. Warnock topped his own world record with a 183 kilogram (403 pound) specimen in 1903 at the St. Louis World's Fair.

The Rennie Seed Company paid Warnock $5 for one of his giant pumpkins and sold seeds at the unheard-of price of five cents a piece. At the time, the average wage was thirty cents an hour. It was from these early seeds that Maritime farmer Howard Dill began the specialized breeding of his pumpkins known as the "Atlantic Giant."

Today, the name Howard Dill and the Atlantic Giant are synonymous with these behemoths of the garden. Dill's seeds have been the source of all record pumpkins grown since 1979. Weights have surpassed the 363 kilogram (800 pound) mark and it's predicted that by the turn of the twenty-first century, the record for this giant member of the gourd family will exceed 454 kilograms (1,000 pounds).

Port Elgin's Pumpkinfest is usually held during the first weekend of October. There are prizes for the heaviest pumpkin, squash and watermelon, as well as the longest gourd, the tallest sunflower, and the heaviest cabbage. Should the heaviest pumpkin at Port Elgin also be a world record, as was the case of a 380 kilogram (836 pound) beauty grown by Stouffville's Norm Craven in 1993, there's an additional prize of a new truck.

Official entry forms and pumpkin growing tips are available by calling the Pumpkinfest hotline.

PORT ELGIN PUMPKIN FESTIVAL
515 Goderich St.,
Port Elgin, Ont. N0H 2C5
TEL 519-389-3714
800-387-3456

Sioux Lookout Blueberry Festival

Blueberries have been called perfection in a bowl. They are one of nature's ideal convenience foods requiring no peeling, hulling, or pitting. They are also one of Ontario's great natural resources. The round smooth-skinned, blue-black berries are plentiful in the province's Canadian Shield.

There are two types of bushes — those that can grow up to 5 meters (15 feet) high, and the low, hardy, 1/3-meter (1-foot) variety. It's the latter that grow wild in Ontario.

Nowhere are they more plentiful than in Sioux Lookout, where the annual Blueberry Festival has been celebrated since 1983. What was begun by three local entrepreneurs to promote tourism and to utilize one of the area's favorite renewable resources, is now a popular ten-day event.

The festival takes place around the beginning of August when blueberries are at their best and most plentiful. This is a family celebration with activities for every age and interest, including a Blueberry Social, the Blueberry Triathlon, and a prize for the heaviest blueberry. Food, especially blueberries, is bountiful at events like the Pancake Breakfast, the Fish Fry, the Barbecue, an Old Fashioned Picnic, the Pie Wagon, and of course the Bake-off.

Those who can't go to the festival can get a feeling for it with recipes from the event, especially Ann Donnelly's winning blueberry pie recipe from 1993.

BLUEBERRY FESTIVAL COMMITTEE
P.O. Box 577,
Sioux Lookout, Ont. P0V 2T0
TEL 807-737-1937
FAX 807-737-1778

BLUEBERRY TIPS

- Select plump, firm berries, fully ripe when picked, as they will not ripen at room temperature.
- Store in the refrigerator, unwashed, for up to two weeks.
- Freeze loose, then seal tightly in plastic bags. Do not wash before freezing.

Ann Donnelly's Winning Blueberry Pie

1 22-cm (9") baked pie shell
1 L (4 cups) blueberries
250 ml (1 cup) sugar
250 ml (1 cup) water
45 ml (3 Tbsp) cornstarch
2 ml (1/2 tsp) salt
15 ml (1 Tbsp) butter
whipping cream
45 ml (3 Tbsp) icing sugar
1 ml (1/4 tsp) almond flavoring

- Place 250 ml (1 cup) of berries in saucepan. Chill remaining berries. Add sugar, water, cornstarch, and salt to saucepan. Cook over low heat until clear. Remove from heat and add butter. When butter has melted add chilled berries. Mix well. Cool combined mixture for 1/2 hour. Pour into pie shell. Let stand until set. Whip cream, icing sugar, and flavoring. Top pie before serving.

Wild Blueberry Breakfast Cake

500 ml (2 cups) flour
250 ml (1 cup) sugar
15 ml (3 tsp) baking powder
1 ml (1/4 tsp) salt
125 ml (1/2 cup) solid shortening
2 beaten eggs
250 ml (1 cup) milk
375 ml (1 1/2 cups) fresh or dry-pack frozen wild blueberries

- Sift dry ingredients together. Cut in shortening with knives or pastry cutter. Combine beaten eggs with milk and add to pastry. Flour blueberries and fold gently into batter. Pour batter into a greased 2.5 L (9" X 9") loaf pan and bake 60 minutes at 185 C (370 F).

Groundhog Day

Without a shadow of a doubt, Wiarton, a small town of about 2,000 people, located at the gateway to the Bruce Peninsula, is indisputably the best place to celebrate Groundhog Day. The tradition began there in 1953; and today Wiarton hosts the largest Groundhog Festival in North America.

Unless you've actually visited the home of Wiarton Willy, you may not realize this pug-nosed prognosticator of the weather is an albino groundhog, and he's real! He lives with two cousins, also albinos, under the care of Jenny and Sam Brouwer at Wiarton Willy's Motel.

Willy has been predicting spring's arrival for more than 30 years. His supporters say he's about 90 percent accurate. It's believed that his white fur doesn't interfere with the white snow when he's checking for his shadow each February 2nd. His rare skill is thought to have something to do with his birthplace, in a field just north of Wiarton, on the 45th parallel, midway between the equator and the North Pole.

On February 2, Wiarton residents don white tuxedos and gowns and visit Willy's lair about dawn. He usually emerges between 7:30 and 8:00 a.m. If he sees his shadow, winter will last another six weeks. Willy usually whispers the verdict in the ear of Wiarton's Mayor, who then makes the announcement to the media. It seems only the Majors of Wiarton are able to understand Groundhogese.

February 2 falls halfway between the winter solstice and the spring equinox. It has been celebrated in folklore for centuries as a time to turn one's back on winter and look forward to spring. Groundhog Day in medieval Europe was known as Candlemas Day, a day to light candles. The following rhyme explains how to predict the weather on this day:

If Candlemas Day be fair and bright;
Winter will have another flight,
But if Candlemas Day brings cloud and rain,
Winter is gone and won't come again.

Europeans noticed that many hibernating rodents began to stir in early February and thus they became associated with predicting the weather. The settlers who came to North America brought the legend with them. The most common rodent in southern Canada, from the Peace River to the Maritimes just happens to be the groundhog.

Groundhog celebrations were the brain-child of Oliphant native Mac McKenzie, aide to Ontario Health Minister, Dr. MacKinnon Philips, in the 1950s. Mac discovered the Native legend of Klionda the Mohawk, and Nawgeentuck the Groundhog, who saved his life. The Ojibwa Natives of the Bruce Peninsula believed the groundhog was an offering from the Great Spirit and that the animal possessed spiritual powers that would sustain human life.

Mac thought it would be a great idea to celebrate Groundhog Day not only in honor of the Native legend, but as a way of breaking up the long Canadian winter with a celebration. He also saw the potential for local businessmen. He sent out invitations to people in Canada and the United States. Reporter Frank Teskey of the *Toronto Star* concocted a story on the event. The rest, as they say, is history. One of Canada's first winter festivals was launched.

Wiarton's Groundhog Day Festival is sponsored by the local Lions Club and takes place over an entire weekend. Indoor and outdoor activities are planned for the entire family.

Naturally the highlight of the weekend is when Willy makes his prediction on the grounds of Wiarton Willy's Motel. That day the motel is transformed into a media mecca, complete with four hog lines for incoming calls. The event attracts attention internationally with roughly 400 incoming calls, including the predictions from Willy's rivals, Punxsutawney Phil in Pennsylvania and Staten Island Chuck in New York.

WIARTON WILLY'S MOTEL
Jenny and Sam Brouwer,
R.R. #1,
Wiarton, Ont. N0H 2T0
TEL 519-534-3907

WIARTON & DISTRICT LIONS CLUB
P.O. Box 427,
Wiarton, Ont. N0H 2T0

Oktoberfest

The Kitchener-Waterloo Oktoberfest is the largest Bavarian Festival in North America, the second largest in the world. Only the original Oktoberfest held in Munich is bigger! In 1984, the American Bus Association named it the "number one tourism event in Canada."

The first Oktoberfest, held in 1810, was a celebration of the wedding of Ludwig, the 24-year-old Crown Prince of Bavaria. Horse races, feasting, and the drinking of toasts were the order of the day. The horse races became an annual event in honor of Ludwig's bride. With each year's celebration, new activities were added. In 1818, one of the events we associate most with an Oktoberfest celebration was added — mammoth beer tents.

Kitchener-Waterloo's Oktoberfest is now the third largest festival in Canada. Its unique spirit of *Gemutlichkeit*, a German word that means everything from good times to warm hospitality, attracts more than 600,000 people from around the world. An annual event since 1969, much of its popularity is due to the area's rich, German heritage which lends it an authentic Munich flavor.

Celebrations get under way with the ceremonial tapping of the keg and continue with Canada's largest Thanksgiving Day Parade which is televised. Over 50 cultural and sporting events include the Miss Oktoberfest Ball; fun runs; antique, arts, and crafts displays; and demonstrations of Mennonite traditions. There are also around 25 Festhallen — clubs and halls set up with their own unique flavor of food, music, and entertainment.

Oktoberfest begins on the Friday of Thanksgiving weekend and generally runs nine days.

KITCHENER-WATERLOO OKTOBERFEST
17 Benton St.,
P.O. Box 1053,
Kitchener, Ont. N2G 4G1
TEL 519-576-0571
FAX 519-742-3072

Robbie Burns Day

Robbie Burns was born January 25, 1759, in Ayrshire County, Scotland. The son of a poor farmer, he wrote poems that were clever and witty, that sympathized with the poor and the down-trodden; poems that some even believed "were dangerous to read and so to be severely left alone." Much of his writing was obscene and bawdy verse. Nonetheless, Scotland's bard is loved by millions throughout the world. His poetry has been translated into most languages, including Russian and Chinese, and more than several hundred years later, his birth is still celebrated worldwide.

A "Nicht Wi' Burns" in Fergus begun in 1977 is the most authentic and popular Robbie Burns Night in the province. Visitors arrive from all over southern Ontario including a busload that arrives each year from Toronto. What makes the celebration particularly special is the Scottish heritage of the town, founded in 1783 by Adam Fergusson for Scottish immigrants in Upper Canada.

This picturesque site on the Grand River is also home to the Fergus Highland Games. The town is dominated by Scottish limestone architecture in over 200 nineteenth-century buildings, including the local farmer's market and the Breadalbane Inn.

The Burns celebration takes place at the Legion and is organized by a very active Friends of Burns Committee. The first year of the celebration, the town was blessed with a Scottish baker who knew how to make the haggis, and an individual who knew the Toast to the Haggis.

Haggis is a national Scottish dish, served on high holidays such as Hogmanay, and especially present at Robbie Burns celebrations, as he wrote an "Ode to Haggis." The name is thought to come from the verb "haggen," meaning to hack. Haggis is a sheep's stomach stuffed with a spicy mixture of its heart, liver, lungs, onions, oatmeal, and mutton fat. It's usually boiled for several hours in stock and then served with a purée of turnips or the vegetables that were boiled with it. Typical accompaniments are beer or pure malt whiskey.

The Fergus chef usually makes about 59 kilograms (130 pounds) of the celebrated dish, for the sell-out crowd. The haggis is piped in (carried by haggis bearers and accompanied by a sword carrier), followed by the traditional Address to the Haggis, grace, and a toast to the Queen. The meal also includes other Scottish delights like tramped tatties and bashed neeps.

Toasts include one to the lassies and a reply for the lassies as well as plenty of song, including all-time Scottish favorites like "I Belong to Glasgow," and "Roamin' in the Gloamin'" and of course Burns' immortal classic, "Auld Lang Syne."

FRIENDS OF BURNS
610 St. David St. S.,
Fergus, Ont. N1M 2L9

Fall Leaves

Move Ontarians out of the province and what they miss most is the changing of the seasons. For many, autumn is their favorite when shorter days and cooler nights trigger the changing of the leaves. The pageant of colors lasts only two or three weeks, often peaking over the Canadian Thanksgiving holiday weekend when there's plenty of time to motor the wine district, board the train for a ride through the Agawa Canyon, cruise through cottage country, or attend a fall fair.

Queen's Park publishes the "Ontario Fall Auto Tours" guide, available for free from tourist offices. The booklet breaks down the province by geographical area, complete with maps, clear driving directions, "best color" dates for each area, and highlights of things to see and do in each locale. There is also a toll free number to call which continuously updates the Fall Colors Report.

Different colors predominate in different parts of the province. In southern Ontario for example, the yellows of the sugar maples dominate the landscape as do the species of the Carolinian forest of Point Pelee National Park, the sycamores, hickories, black walnuts, and butternuts. In northern Ontario colder temperatures encourage redder tones, the crimsons of Thunder Bay and the reds and bright oranges of Sault Ste. Marie.

The first leaves to change color are the deep reds and magentas of the sumacs, followed closely by the yellow-green tones of willows and ashes. Sugar and red maples display red, yellow, and orange leaves. The male species of the red maple shows its deep brilliant tones; the female, turns yellow. Last to change are the oaks, ranging in tones from red to various shades of brown. Elms and alders generally fall to the ground green.

Timing of the color change varies from one location to another depending not only upon the type of flora, but changes in temperature and precipitation. A wet, warm spring precedes an earlier show, whereas a late spring or summer drought can delay the process.

Mother Nature is still pretty much in charge of what happens and on a biochemical level it remains a mystery. What is known is that chlorophyll, the green pigment in leaves that traps sunlight to help manufacture food, breaks down, exposing the colorful yellow and orange pigments known as carotenoids. The color red comes from a third type of pigment known as authocyanim. As the leaves change color, minerals and nutrients return to the main part of the plant to be utilized next spring. The leaves eventually fall off due to a lack of moisture and the shorter photosynthesis period.

FALL COLORS REPORT and to order the ONTARIO FALL AUTO TOURS, call:

From Canada, continental USA, and Hawaii
English 800-ONTARIO (668-2746)
From Canada
French 800-268-3736

seeing ontario

Most Northerly Highway

Highway 599 begins at the town of Ignace and goes to Pickle Lake: the end of the road. This 300-kilometer (186 mile) stretch of pavement, known as the 599 Corridor, is the province's most northerly highway and the gateway to Ontario's last frontier.

This is not a drive for people seeking coffee shops or souvenir stands. The four-hour meander through rugged terrain has only two coffee shop/gas station stops along the way. The land is boreal forest, untouched by the logger's axe, and is interspersed with miles of rivers and lakes. The only sound you will hear, outside of the hum of your own tires, is the cry of the loon or the drumming of a partridge. During the summer, when traffic is heaviest, you might expect to see another vehicle every 30 or 45 minutes.

There are a number of reasons people venture onto this highway, some 482 kilometers (300 miles) from the coast of Hudson Bay, in addition to being attracted to the physical landscape and its tranquillity, and its geographical and historical interest. It is one of the few remote regions, excellent for fishing, hunting, and naturalist activities accessible by car. Others make the trek to reach a number of fly-in outfitters for primitive wilderness fishing, some 80 to 241 kilometers (50 to 150 miles) outside of Pickle Lake.

The Corridor was formed during the last ice age. The ridges or moraines are the result of glaciers receding and halting. Geological records indicate the area was occupied during the Laurel Period (500 BC to AD 1000) by Natives who made a unique type of blackduck pottery. The earliest European maps of the region, dated 1788, show Lake Sturgeon, a neighborhood scouted by the Hudson Bay Company in 1794 for potential post sites.

The Corridor is also known for its gold mines. During the early 1900s, it produced more gold than all the mines in Ontario combined. Gold bricks from St. Anthony's Gold Mine were shipped by sleigh to Fort William (Thunder Bay) until the route was opened up by the Grand Trunk Pacific Railroad in 1908. The mines between Sturgeon Lake and Pickle Lake became known as the "Gold Belt" of Ontario.

There are still several active mines at Pickle Lake, but today the village is known as the last bastion of civilization for those wanting to advance further into the frontier towards James and Hudson Bays.

A fishing paradise, this is the place to catch walleye, northern pike, lake trout, speckled trout, sauger, perch, bass, sturgeon, whitefish, burbot, and suckers. It's also replete with big game, including moose, black bear, wolves, lynx and woodland caribou, and a destination for birdwatchers with bald and golden eagles, hawks, owls, partridge, ducks, geese, and songbirds.

Naturalists will be amazed that the landscape isn't scarred with logging roads or clear cut areas. For canoe and kayaking enthusiasts, the vast arctic watershed surrounding Pickle Lake is among the most challenging, yet one of the best kept secrets of the paddling world. For the gourmet, the boreal forests provide a variety of tasty wild mushrooms; wild rice is a local Native industry.

A gravel road, known as Highway 808, stretches further north and west of Pickle Lake to Windigo Lake, providing access to boat launching sites and picnic areas. The community has an Annual Ice Worm Festival in February and March, and a Black Fly Festival on July 1 weekend!

Those driving the Corridor are advised to do so in a road-worthy vehicle, equipped with water and supplies in case of mechanical problems.

HIGHWAY 599 CORRIDOR
Township of Ignace,
200 Beaver St.,
P.O. Box 248,
Ignace, Ont. P0T 1T0
TEL 807-934-2202
FAX 807-934-2864

Algoma Central Railway

One of the most spectacular train excursions in North America is on the Algoma Central Railway, between Sault Ste. Marie and the town of Hearst. The experience is unforgettable, whether you travel in the luxury of one of the restored, private cars, take the day excursion into the Agawa Canyon during the fall color season, board the Snow Train for a panoramic view of snow and crystal ice in an area that averages 480 centimeters (189 inches) of snow annually, or drop off at one of the mileposts for a wilderness adventure. This is Laurentian shield country: rugged walls of granite, part of the oldest rock formations in the world, dominated by eastern white pine, yellow and white birch, sugar and red maple, and white and black spruce.

Between 1918 and 1923 members of the Group of Seven painted the Algoma landscape. Lawren Harris, A.Y. Jackson, Frank Johnston, J.E.H. Mac-Donald, and Arthur Lismer rented a boxcar that was outfitted like a cabin. It was shunted to choice areas for painting. The Group then travelled on foot and by canoe throughout the area, painting this virgin wilderness for the rest of the world.

The Algoma Central Railway Company was incorporated August 11, 1899. The name was changed to the Algoma Central and Hudson Bay Company in 1901, and to its present name in 1965. Construction of the line began in 1899 and was not completed until 1914. There are 476 kilometers (296 miles) of track between Sault Ste. Marie and Hearst and a 42 kilometer (26-mile) line from Hawk Junction to Michipicoten Harbour on Lake Superior. Trainloads of iron ore en route from Wawa to Algoma Steel in the Sault, and forest products destined for mills in Canada and the US, still flash by the passenger windows.

The train track is marked by white mile boards on telephone poles adjacent to the tracks. Passengers can request to be dropped off and picked up at any of these points on the regular train schedule. It is not unusual to travel with a snowmobile in winter or a canoe or backpack in summer, to venture into the hinterland. Here are 26,000 square kilometers (16,000 square miles) of vacation wilderness offering some of the country's finest backpacking, camping, canoeing, fishing, and hunting.

Algoma Central Railway is the largest owner of privately held forest land in Ontario, holding some 344,000 hectares (850,000 acres) in scattered blocks. The company also operates a marine division of vessels on the Great lakes. Its fleet of self-unloading vessels is the second largest in carrying capacity under Canadian registry and continues the tradition of the oldest Canadian bulk freight carrier with continuous service on the Great Lakes today.

While the trip to Hearst and back takes a day each way, the Fall Color Train and the Snow Train offer day excursions. Between mid-September and mid-October the changing leaves are ablaze with color, visible through large panoramic windows.

There are three trestle bridges, the most noteworthy being the curved trestle at mile 92. It's 46 meters (150-feet) long and 40 meters (130-feet) high over the Montreal River. The highlight of the trip, however, starts at mile 102 as the train begins its descent, 152 meters (500 feet) over 19 kilometers (12 miles), to the floor of the Agawa Canyon. Here there is a two-hour stopover at Agawa Canyon Park, an area maintained by the railway. One can picnic along the Agawa River or climb to the main lookout, 76 meters (250 feet) above the picnic grounds. Within walking distance are Otter Creek Falls, Black Beaver Falls, and Bridal Veil Falls. There are three lakes a short walk from the rim of the canyon and an opportunity for a self-guided nature walk.

In winter, the atmosphere is entirely different. Waterfalls and cliffs turn to masses of ice in the crystal clear air. Pines and spruce are burdened with layers of snow. The train moves beyond the canyon to where the gorge narrows and there is only enough room for the track alongside the river. It travels to Eton at mile 120. Here passengers transfer to a

southbound train for the return trip to Sault Ste.
Marie.

Two private vintage rail cars are available for the
day excursions: the refurbished "Michipicoten,"
built in 1910 by the Pullman company of Chicago,
is ideal for parties up to eight. The "Agawa," a
Barney and Smith car from 1913, accommodates up
to twelve people.

The Snow Train operates Saturday and Sunday
from January 1 to March 13. The Agawa Canyon
Train operates daily from June 6 to October 10.
There is also a regular train schedule north and
southbound to and from Hearst.

ALGOMA CENTRAL RAILWAY
129 Bay St.,
Sault Ste. Marie, Ont. P6A IW7
TEL 705-946-7300
FAX 705-946-7382

Sainte-Marie Among the Hurons

Sainte-Marie Among the Hurons, in Midland, is the site of the first European community in Ontario. It was founded in 1639 by French Jesuits in the land of the Wendat, or Huron people. The site was first visited in 1615 by Samuel de Champlain, who suggested to the French Crown that the 25,000 Hurons in the vicinity be converted to Christianity. It was a decision that would set in motion events which would ultimately destroy the Huron tribe.

Father Jerome Lalemant, following in the footsteps of Father Jean de Brébeuf, established the mission on the banks of the Wye River as a retreat for missionaries and a home for Christian Wendat and the French. Each brought aspects of their own culture to the community. The French brought in livestock from Quebec by canoe and planted gardens. The Jesuits had their own wooden residence while the Wendat lived in longhouses and wigwams, a total of 20 buildings in all. By 1648, one-fifth of the European population of New France lived at Sainte-Marie.

For almost 10 years Sainte-Marie prospered, but rivalries among the Wendat and Iroquois, coupled with epidemics of influenza, measles, and smallpox eventually led to its downfall. After the Iroquois attacked the village of St. Joseph and many Wendat and Jesuits lost their lives, the village at Sainte-Marie waited with trepidation for an attack that never happened.

In the spring of 1648, the village was abandoned and set on fire by the Jesuits and Wendat. They travelled by canoe to what is known today as Christian Island and established Sainte-Marie II. This mission was eventually abandoned and those who survived the hardships of winter returned to Quebec in 1650.

With the aid of archaeological evidence, Sainte-Marie Among the Hurons was restored to its seventeenth century likeness in 1967 as a heritage project during Canada's Centennial year. The replica is complete with wooden palisades that encircle longhouses, wigwams, bastions, stables, gardens, and the dwellings of the Jesuits and French, as well as the shops of local tradespeople.

A visit to Sainte-Marie begins with an audio-visual presentation that sets the tone of life in the seventeenth century. The village is an interpretive museum with men and women in period dress carrying on the activities of the day.

There are special programs throughout the year, including an adventure on the Wye River in an historic canoe.

SAINTE-MARIE AMONG THE HURONS

Huronia Historical Parks Resource Centre
P.O. Box 160,
Midland, Ont. L4R 4K8
TEL 705-526-7838
FAX 705-526-9193

Oil Springs

Thirty-five kilometers (22 miles) southeast of Sarnia is the quiet hamlet of Oil Springs. Few people would ever guess that here in the 1800s was launched one of the world's greatest industries: the oil and petroleum business. It was a boom and bust town that rivalled the excitement and spirit of the gold rush.

The Enniskillen Swamp area around Oil Springs was known for its patches of black, sticky crude oil, called "gum beds." For centuries, Native peoples used the surface oil for medicinal and ritualistic purposes. French explorers noted the existence of these oil slicks, but it was Charles and Henry Tripp of Woodstock who used the oil to make caulking for ships, asphalt, varnish, and burning fluid. The Tripp brothers incorporated the first oil company, the International Mining and Manufacturing Company, in 1854. Their products were technically innovative and recognized at the Universal Exhibition in Paris in 1855, which made them the first men to develop petroleum commercially. However, their venture wasn't viable economically because of the lack of road or rail transportation out of the swamp to the marketplace. The Tripps sold out to James Miller Williams, a 39-year-old businessman who made fine carriages and railway cars in Hamilton.

Williams was clever enough to dig below the surface of the gum beds to find the source of the tar-like substance. At 4 meters (14 feet) he struck oil. He immediately set up a small refinery pumping 50 barrels a day by hand. His timing was perfect. The kerosene lamp had just been invented and the Great Western Railway completed a line between London and Sarnia through nearby Wyoming.

In 1858 the world's first commercial well and refinery were the exclusive domain of Williams and his associates. The drilling of a second well that provided 60 barrels a day attracted the attention of the outside world. As fast as horses could run, prospectors arrived from all over Canada and the US. The swamps that once repelled settlers attracted people with picks, shovels, and buckets. By 1861, 400 wells were producing between 50 and 800 barrels of crude per day.

The wells were dug deeper and deeper, some even into bedrock, with a primitive spring pole rig, a long, ash tree trunk placed parallel to the ground over a Y-shaped fulcrum. A heavy drill bit was suspended from one end of the pole. Drillers jerked the bit up and down by jumping on a treadle.

No one noticed Hugh Nixon Shaw come into town. He had $50 in his pocket and title to one acre of land. He began digging in July of 1861; by January he was into bedrock 157 feet down, with enough sweat, it was said, to fill the hole. He was mocked and laughed at. No one had drilled as deep and ever found oil. He decided to drill one more day and quit.

On January 16, 1862, as he dug down one more foot, a large crack sounded from the bottom of his well that could be heard across the entire field. Moments later a thick, heavy spout of oil shot as high as the tree tops, splintering Shaw's rig and blackening everything in site. The world's first gusher spewed 2,000 barrels a day and couldn't be brought under control until early February. In all, about 100,000 barrels of oil were lost before it could be capped.

Other drillers scrambled for sites near Shaw's. More than 30 large wells were brought in that year, some with a greater flow than Shaw's. The giant of them all was the Black and Mathieson well, producing 7,500 barrels a day.

Land prices skyrocketed from $2 to $100 an acre. Oil sold for $10 a barrel at the railway and $1 at the well. The *Oil Springs Chronicle*, Canada's first oil paper, was launched and the main street was planked for a mile and a half with a double width and double thickness of white oak, proclaimed to be the first and finest paved street in Canada. Lamps set on ornamental posts lit up the entire main thoroughfare. It was the only totally kerosene-lit road anywhere, even ahead of the larger cities in Europe and America, at a time when many settlers were still using tallow candles.

Oil Springs reached a population close to 4,000 people. There were nine hotels, twelve general stores and horse-drawn buses that ran the length of the town every five minutes. A telegraph service was installed and two carpenters worked overtime to service the oil barons.

J.H. Fairbanks, who came to the town in 1860, introduced the "jerker-rod system" of pumping crude. One hundred wells or more could be pumped from a single central steam power-house. This proved to be highly economical and completely replaced the spring pole.

The boom didn't last. The price of oil deflated to less than a dollar a barrel with the glut of oil in the marketplace, including oil found in the USA. Many of the wells were short-lived. When steadier producing wells were discovered in Petrolia, eight miles to the northwest, the population fell to 550 almost overnight.

However, it was the technical expertise and innovative equipment developed in Oil Springs that opened up the rest of the world to the petroleum industry. Drillers from the area travelled to Europe, Russia, Iran, Mesopotamia, Egypt, Java, New Guinea, Trinidad, Venezuela, and Peru.

Today, Oil Springs, with a population of about 700 people, is still involved in oil, petro-chemical, and related industries. About 300 oil wells yield about 25,000 barrels of crude each year. Many of the jerker line systems developed in 1862 are still operable. The area has also been drilled for gas wells. It's estimated only one-third of the oil reserves have been extracted.

Visitors to Oil Springs will want to take the 20-minute driving tour of the oil heritage district where ancestors of the oil pioneers still harvest the black gold. Among the stops is the Oil Museum of Canada, located on the site of the first commercial well dug by Williams. There are indoor and outdoor exhibits depicting the first hundred years of the industry. Among the artifacts is the only remaining kerosene lamp that helped shed light on Main Street. Along the way is the last remaining receiving station, a board and batten construction built in 1915; cribbed and modern holding tanks; jerker lines developed by Fairbanks; the site of Shaw's gusher; the plank road; and modern, working wells.

THE OIL MUSEUM OF CANADA

Kelly Road,
R.R. #2,
Oil Springs, Ont. N0N IP0
TEL/FAX 519-834-2840

DRIVE from Sarnia, east on Highway 7 to Reece's Corners. Go south on Highway 21 to Oil Springs.

Huron Historic Gaol

The Huron Historic Gaol (pronounced "jail," the old English term popular in the 1800s and early 1900s) is a unique edifice located in the town of Goderich. The unusual, octagonal palladium-style building was constructed between 1839 and 1842 of stone from the nearby Maitland River Valley. Most prisons then were primitive, usually made of logs, and so insecure that the inmates used to leave at night and return in the morning.

The Huron Gaol led the way in prison reform and is a symbol of the humanitarian considerations of the mid-nineteenth century. Its structural design allowed for prisoners to be segregated according to sex and severity of crime, which greatly advanced the rehabilitative process. In addition to functioning as a jail and a courthouse, it housed the aged, the insane, and the poor at a time when there were no old age homes, no hospitals, and no public buildings in the county.

Although the Gaol opened in 1842, the first prisoner committed for a criminal offence didn't arrive until 1843. Sometimes a white flag was flown to indicate that no prisoners were incarcerated.

To discourage people from escaping, primitive walls, 6 meters (18 feet) high and extending 1.5 meters (5 feet) into the ground, surrounded the jail in the same octagonal shape as the building. The walls were mortared smooth to prevent attempts at scaling. From time to time prisoners did escape but many returned for the comforts of food and lodging rather than face the surrounding rugged terrain.

The only successful escape was made in April 1880 by two prisoners convicted of forgery. From a set of keys that had been left hanging in a door they made soap impressions and then keys of wood and metal. The two men unlocked their way to the courtyard at night and piled furniture, which was being painted in the yard, to scale the walls. They used blankets to climb down the outside of the wall and were never seen or heard of again.

The Huron Gaol imprisoned the infamous James Donnelly of the Black Donnelly clan of Lucan in 1885. He was on trial in Goderich for murder and, when convicted of manslaughter, was sentenced to seven years in the Kingston Penitentiary.

It was also the site of the last public hanging in Canada, which took place in the park on the north side of the building in 1865. The culprit was from Seaforth and had killed his father and step-mother.

The facility was closed by the provincial government March 31, 1972. Remaining prisoners were sent to the jails at Walkerton and Stratford. Between 1972 and 1974 the "Save the Gaol Committee" rescued it from becoming a parking lot. It opened as an historic site in 1974 and was declared a National Historic Site in 1975.

HURON HISTORIC GAOL
181 Victoria St. North,
Goderich, Ont. N7A 2S9

FOR INFORMATION CONTACT: THE HURON COUNTY MUSEUM
110 North St.,
Goderich, Ont. N7A 2T8
TEL 519-524-2686

Bethune Memorial House

The town of Gravenhurst is in the heart of Muskoka cottage country but it's best known in China as the birthplace of Dr. Norman Bethune.

Long before Bethune's childhood home was designated by the federal government as an historic site in 1973, a steady parade of Asian tourists had become an increasing nuisance for the occupants of 235 John Street. It is ironic or perhaps fitting that there was nearly as much controversy surrounding the historical designation of the house as there was surrounding the tumultuous life of Dr. Norman Bethune himself. To appreciate the controversy, a little background may suffice.

Bethune was born in the two-story, yellow clapboard house in Gravenhurst in 1890 and lived there for the first three years of his life. His father was a Presbyterian minister and the family moved to six different parishes by the time Norman was 14. He studied biology at the University of Toronto, but left in 1911 to work at Frontier College in Northern Ontario, setting up classes for immigrant workers in a bush camp. He enlisted in the Royal Canadian Army Medical Corps during World War I and was wounded in Ypres, France. He became a doctor, married, and set up a private practice in Detroit, Michigan. Two years later, in 1926 he contracted tuberculosis. He read about a controversial treatment for TB, in which air was pumped into the diseased lung cavity. He insisted on having the risky operation, recovered within a month and dedicated himself to eradicating TB.

He worked in thoracic surgery for a number of years in Montreal, writing articles, and improving and creating new surgical instruments like the "Bethune Rib Shears," still made today. On a personal level he was a complex, unorthodox man, described by one friend as "some meteor passing." During the Depression, he became concerned about the health of the poor and opened a free clinic for the unemployed in 1935. Travels to the Soviet Union convinced him that socialized medicine was the only way to ensure treatment for all

people. He set up the Montreal Group for the Security of the People's Health and joined the Communist Party.

When the Spanish Civil War broke out in 1936, Bethune designed on the battlefield a mobile blood transfusion service, later called the greatest innovation in military medicine. When Japanese forces invaded China, he left Canada for the last time on January 8, 1938, with a Canadian nurse and $5,000 worth of medical supplies. He was asked by Mao Tse-tung to supervise the army hospital, but felt he would be more effective in the field. He travelled to the border mountain ranges where he taught classes in first aid, sanitation, and basic surgery. In the next year he covered more than 3,000 miles, often on foot and by mule, into remote areas of China. Once he operated on 115 cases in 69 hours without stopping, even when under heavy artillery fire. Known as Pai Ch'iu-en, he became a legend throughout the country.

Bethune died of blood poisoning on November 12, 1939. The country extolled the man who was "without thought of self..." and Mao wrote a famous essay in his honor, "In Memory of Norman Bethune." His image was placed on postage stamps, fêted at memorials, and graven into statues.

While few Canadians liked Bethune's politics, they recognized and admired his humanitarian efforts. Local citizens and the United Church Board in Gravenhurst failed to elicit official recognition of him even in the form of an historical marker. When a Maoist group from Toronto wanted to hold a pro-Bethune rally for Ontario communists at the site, the town became alarmed. Shortly thereafter the Ontario government decided to dedicate an historical marker.

The flourishing wheat trade with China eventually prompted the federal government to have a change of heart and designate the building a National Historic Site. There was even some speculation that the Chinese government was prepared to purchase the manse. It was finally purchased by the federal government in 1973 and restoration began immediately. It was furnished to represent the appearance of an 1890s home with some artifacts that belonged to Bethune.

Bethune House is open year-round with special events at Christmas and a summer Victorian social. Group tours are welcome.

BETHUNE MEMORIAL HOUSE

235 John St.,
P.O. Box 2160,
Gravenhurst, Ont. P0C 1G0
TEL 705-687-4261

OPEN year-round (except statutory holidays in winter) 10 a.m. to 5 p.m.

DRIVE Highway 169 (Bethune Drive) to the Bay Street Exit. Go west on Bay Street and turn right (north) on John Street.

Woodside House

Canada's tenth Prime Minister, William Lyon Mackenzie King, lived at Woodside House in Kitchener, then known as Berlin. He resided there with his parents and three siblings during five years of his adolescence, between 1886 and 1891, before leaving to attend the University of Toronto, and spent subsequent summers there until 1893. This was home to King's fondest childhood memories. "...of all the time of my boyhood, the early years that left the most abiding of all impressions and most in the way of family association were those lived at Woodside."

The Kings moved from Woodside when Mackenzie King's father, also a barrister, left Berlin to lecture at Osgoode Hall. The house was built in 1853 by James Colquhoun and subsequently changed hands a number of times.

In September 1947, Prime Minister William Lyon Mackenzie King revisited his boyhood home. He was greeted by four-year-old Marilyn Kilbasco, who lived there with her family. Dressed in a tartan skirt and a white blouse, she placed a pink carnation in the Prime Minister's lapel and kissed his cheek. It was a warm moment captured in a picture that Mackenzie King treasured all his life. In December young Marilyn wrote to him that her father had died. He responded with a touching letter of comfort and sent her a framed copy of the photo to brighten her Christmas. Marilyn remained in King's thoughts and he wrote her several dozen letters before his death in 1950.

Over the years the home fell into disrepair. In the 1940s it was destined for demolition. It was secured on a trust basis by the North Waterloo Liberal Association in 1944 and in 1950 the Mackenzie King Woodside Trust was incorporated to restore the grounds and buildings to the conditions of King's boyhood.

The crumbling brick structure was demolished and rebuilt with a new foundation and a basement for modern heating in 1952. Architects were able to consult with King himself, guided by his recollections and those of his sister Jennie (Mrs. H.M. Lay) who also provided some of the original late Victorian furniture and bric-a-brac.

Unique among the possession are relics from King's famous ancestor, William Lyon Mackenzie. (The Prime Minster's mother was the youngest daughter of this crusading journalist/politician who led the Rebellion of 1837 in Upper Canada.) The large marble-topped table in the parlor is said to have been carved by the rebel. King retained the Vice-regal Proclamation offering a £1,000 reward for the capture of his grandfather, dead or alive.

Woodside House was declared a National Historic Site in 1954. Today it recreates the lifestyle of an upper-middle-class family in late Victorian times in the ten-room house and on the 4.65-hectare (12-acre) grounds which include a parkland of woods, marsh, rolling lawns, and herb and flower gardens.

Guides in period costume demonstrate nineteenth century cooking, crafts, and music. The 50-seat theatre in the basement features an interpretive display of King's life. There are also special events held annually, on Canada Day, Easter, and Thanksgiving and a Victorian Christmas in December. A series of educational programs developed in co-operation with the Waterloo County Board of Education are given in both official languages. School tours should book six weeks in advance. Picnic tables are available May to late Autumn.

WOODSIDE NATIONAL HISTORIC SITE
528 Wellington St. North,
Kitchener, Ont. N2H 2L5
TEL 519-742-5273

OPEN 10 a.m. to 5 p.m. daily.
CLOSED statutory holidays during the winter.

DRIVE according to the signs posted on the major roads entering Kitchener. Visitors using the Conestoga Parkway (Highway 86) take the Wellington Street West exit.

Laurier House

Most Canadians immediately recognize 24 Sussex Drive in Ottawa as the official residence of the Prime Minister of Canada. Few, however, know the significance of 335 Laurier Avenue. It's the address of Laurier House, the residence occupied by two of Canada's longest-serving prime ministers, Sir Wilfrid Laurier and William Lyon MacKenzie King. Unlike 24 Sussex Drive, Laurier House is open to the public as a National Historic Site, maintained by Canada's Parks Service.

The house was constructed in 1878 by an Ottawa jeweller and is located in what was then the fashionable residential area known as Sandy Hill, situated approximately ten blocks east and five blocks south of Parliament Hill, an easy walking distance.

Following the election of Sir Wilfrid Laurier in 1896 as Canada's seventh prime minister, the Liberal party purchased the property to become his home. Laurier resided there from 1896 until he died in 1919. His widow remained in the house until 1921. She bequeathed the house to William Lyon MacKenzie King who had succeeded Laurier as the leader of the Liberal Party.

King resided in the dwelling from 1921 until his death in 1950; during twenty-one of those years he was Prime Minister, making Laurier House truly the seat of power in Canada. The heart of the house centered on the third floor attic study is where King spent most of his working time, rarely opting to occupy his Parliament Building office. He had a staff of about five who, with secretarial assistants, worked with him at Laurier House, directing the affairs of state. A typical schedule started at 9:00 a.m. and continued until about 11:00 p.m., seven days a week. It was also in this house that King entertained many dignitaries of the era, including Churchill, Roosevelt, DeGaulle, and Nehru.

Following King's death in 1950, the property was bequeathed to the "people of Canada" and fortunately has been maintained as a museum for later generations to enjoy.

The building reflects the Second Empire style fashionable in the years following Confederation and recognizable by its mansard roof, ornate dormer windows and solid brick character. The King attic study has been left largely as it was during his occupancy and the house is crammed with mementos such as Churchill's cigars, the painting of King's mother, his famous crystal ball, and furniture given to him by King George VI.

The second floor of the house is more reflective of the Laurier period and contains a number of the original furnishings removed from the house following Laurier's death and subsequently returned. Also on the second floor in a separate wing is a replica of Lester B. Pearson's study. It contains furniture and memorabilia from his time in office as Canada's fourteenth prime minister.

LAURIER HOUSE NATIONAL HISTORIC SITE
335 Laurier Ave. East,
Ottawa, Ont. K1K 6R4
TEL 613-692-2581 (information)
TEL 613-992-8142 (group reservations)

OPEN April 1 to Sept 30, Tuesday to Saturday; 9:00 a.m. to 5 p.m.
October 1 to March 31, Tuesday to Saturday; 10:00 a.m. to 5:00 p.m.
Year-round, Sunday; 2:00 p.m. to 5:00 p.m.

Queenston Heights

Queenston Heights is the site of one of the major battles of the War of 1812, the only significant, international conflict to have been largely fought on Ontario soil.

The Niagara National Historical Sites branch of the Canadian Parks Service maintains a recreational park where visitors can explore the battlefield and the 56-meter (183-foot) monument of the hero of Upper Canada, Major-General Sir Isaac Brock who, together with thirteen British troops and 300 American soldiers, perished on a cold October morning about 200 years ago.

The Heights are located at the point where the Niagara Escarpment meets the Niagara River, a cliff towering some 110 meters (360 feet) above the village of Queenston, midway between Niagara Falls and Lake Ontario.

In the early 1800s, control of the village was crucial to maintain supply routes and to defend the access point of the overland portage route around the Falls to the western ports on the Great Lakes.

In the summer of 1812, as much of Europe was embroiled in the Napoleonic Wars, the US declared war on Britain with the objective of capturing the rest of British North America.

On the morning of October 13, 1812, a numerically superior force of Americans attacked the village of Queenston from across the river. When the invading army failed to capture the village, a small group of Americans managed to reach the crest of the cliff and in a surprise attack, temporarily defeated the defending British troops, killing General Brock in the process.

Later that same day, British reinforcements arrived from Fort George and the American forces were trapped on the Heights between the British and the cliffs. Rather than jump to their deaths, 925 American invaders surrendered and the British, along with local Canadian militia, won the day.

That victory had the immediate benefit of convincing the somewhat sceptical residents of a then sparsely populated Upper Canada that a separate colony with British protection could be successfully defended.

As the subsequent history of Canada and Ontario unfolded, many look back to that cold October morning as symbolic of a desire of those who inhabit the northern portion of the continent to maintain an independent and distinct Canadian existence.

Even a brief visit to Queenston Heights evokes the battle scene. The tranquillity of the vista overlooking Ontario and the State of New York enhances an appreciation for the fact that for more than 180 years we have peacefully shared an undefended border with our neighbors to the south.

Among the historic sites in the area is Fort George, a short distance downriver from Queenston Heights on the edge of Niagara-on-the-lake. The Fort is an historically accurate reconstruction of the major British fort that existed at the mouth of the Niagara River at Lake Ontario at the time of the War of 1812. During the summer months, staff in period uniforms acquaint visitors with a sense of military life in early nineteenth century Ontario.

A self-guided walking tour takes about 45 minutes.

NIAGARA NATIONAL HISTORIC SITES

Niagara Court House,
P.O. Box 787,
26 Queen St.,
Niagara-on-the-Lake, Ont. L0S 1J0
TEL 905-468-4257
FAX 905-468-4638

DRIVE the QEW, taking Highway 405 to Brock's Monument or Highways 55 and 87 to Fort George.

OPEN from Victoria Day to Labor Day, daily from 10 a.m. to 6 p.m.

Fort Malden

Flying in a southwesterly direction from Toronto, the western third of Lake Ontario, all of the Niagara River and the eastern half of Lake Erie unfold below in one expansive panorama. Looking down on these large bodies of water which modern aircraft traverse in little more time than it takes to drink a cup of coffee, it is hard to imagine that two centuries earlier great warships plied these lakes and their shores were dotted with great military installations.

One of these was Fort Malden (also known as Fort Amherstburg) located in Amherstburg on the east shore of the Detroit River where it empties into Lake Erie.

Jay's Treaty of 1794 provided that the British were to relinquish all territory lying to the south of the Great Lakes. The fort and naval dockyards at Detroit had to be surrendered and the British moved to Fort Malden across the river.

The facility initially served three functions: it was the new military garrison for the British on the Detroit River; a new naval base for the British Navy on Lake Erie, including a dockyard where naval vessels could be serviced and constructed; and a meeting place for the British and their Native allies, including the Shawnee Chief Tecumseh.

During the period from 1799 until 1813, numerous warships were launched from the dockyards at Amherstburg, including the 400-ton *Queen Charlotte* in 1810. It was a large 3-masted, square-rigged frigate, 30 meters (100 feet) in length with a beam of 8.5 meters (28 feet) and capable of carrying a crew of 126 men and armaments that consisted of 17 cannons. Prior to its construction (and the similar ship, *Royal George*, launched a year earlier from Kingston for service on Lake Ontario) the British had never attempted to build large square-rigged vessels for the Great Lakes.

It should be remembered however that naval engagements in that era consisted of broadside cannon fire which could more easily damage the large fore and aft sails of a smaller vessel. Because the square rigged warships carried smaller but more numerous square sails, set at right angles to the mast, these vessels were less susceptible to damage by broadside fire.

With the outbreak of the War of 1812, General Isaac Brock led his British troop from Fort Malden, together with colonial militia and Native allies, to the successful attack and capture of Detroit. However, in the early fall of 1813, following the British loss at the Battle of Lake Erie, the British were forced to abandon Fort Malden and retreat eastward, so the fort was burned before it was abandoned.

American forces occupied the facility briefly until July 1815, when it was returned to the British by the Treaty of Ghent that ended the war. Its strategic significance declined when the British relocated their naval establishment to Lake Huron. It enjoyed a brief resurgence in 1837 with the outbreak of the Upper Canada Rebellion when a new fort was built and re-garrisoned. However, by 1851, the last British regulars were withdrawn.

In 1937, having recognized the historical significance of Fort Malden, the federal government acquired land for a park and today the facility is operated by the Department of Canadian Heritage as the Fort Malden Historic Site.

Visitors may tour the 4.5-hectare (12-acre) park that includes remains of the 1840 period earthworks and four buildings, a visitor Orientation Centre with a small auditorium, and exhibits relating to the fort. There is also a restored barracks, circa 1819.

FORT MALDEN NATIONAL HISTORIC SITE
P.O. Box 38,
100 Laird Ave.,
Amherstburg, Ont. N9V 2Z2
TEL 519-736-5416

OPEN 10 a.m. to 5 p.m. daily
CLOSED statutory holidays, November to April

White Otter Castle

Over the years, people have come by canoe, boat, plane, helicopter, and snowmobile to see an imposing structure known as the White Otter Castle, built in the wilds of northwestern Ontario.

The mystery and romance surrounding the castle and the man who built it, Jimmy McOuat (pronounced Mckewitt) has inspired poetry, music, paintings and etchings. It has given new meaning to the saying "a man's home is his castle."

Jimmy McOuat was born January 17, 1855, the seventh child of Scottish homesteaders living in the Ottawa Valley. The youngest of six sons, there was little chance he would inherit the family farm, so at the age of 31, he ventured west and established his own homestead on Rainy River near Emo.

McOuat was a successful pioneer. He bought two neighboring farms, then, seduced by gold fever, he sold all three homesteads, only to lose his life savings when the mines closed in 1900.

In 1903, he came to White Otter Lake, then known as Big Clearwater. The closest town for supplies was Ignace, some 48 kilometers (30 miles) away, a canoe trip with more than 15 portages, including one with a 92 meter (300-foot) hill.

McOuat built a small shack on the shore. He trapped and caught fish and at one time worked for a commercial fisherman on Clearwater West Lake. It isn't know the exact year he began to build his castle but in 1914, at the age of 59, he had the walls up and the roof on when he was visited by an Indian guide and a journalist named Hodson, who wrote for a magazine called *Rod and Gun*:

"A hundred yards back from the lake it stands, on the edge of a small clearing. In the background dark pine woods. In the foreground a mile expanse of crystal lake. No one speaks but with one accord the paddles pause here. Eyes strain. Heartbeats quicken. In the very air is mystery....

Three stories high, a massive structure of heavy logs, at one corner rises the tower, log upon log. Yes, it must be all of forty feet high, but tell us not that its building was accomplished by the unaided strength of one old man!"

Even by modern standards, the castle is considered a structural masterpiece. Its main diagonal faces exactly due north and overall the proportions of the building, including the 26 windows, are perfectly symmetrical.

The architectural style bears the imprint of McOuat's Scottish heritage and his pioneering roots. The 4-story, 13-meter (41-foot) tower, the feature that gives it the name "Castle," served as a look-out, with a spectacular view of the lake. The 3-story house resembles a frontier home and barn with living quarters on the ground floor and a loft for sleeping. The main building is sizeable by pioneer standards, being 7 by 9 meters (24 by 28 feet) and the kitchen 4 by 6 meters (14 by 20 feet).

The castle was made from green pine logs McOuat cut from the site and "snaked" out with a homemade winch and a 30 meter (100 foot) line. The logs averaged 11 meters (37 feet) in length and weighed between 726 kilograms (1,600 pounds) and one ton each. There are 21 logs to the eaves, 30 logs to the peaks, and 43 logs on each side of the tower. They are cut square on the interior and left rounded on the outside. Each has been chinked with a mixture of lime and beach sand, and at every corner, the logs are not merely notched, but dovetailed. No one can imagine how one small elderly man could hold the logs up to "pinch" them in.

All 26 windows came ready-made in sashes. Old timers say McOuat carried them in himself, over all the portages.

What motivated him to build the Castle? Some say he built it for a lost love, Jane Gibson of Clifford, Ontario, a woman who turned down his mail order bride offer. Others say he was once wrongly accused of throwing an ear of corn at a man who cursed him and told him he would die in a shack. McOuat never forgot the angry man's prediction and was determined to build himself a house.

McOuat only lived in the house four years. He disappeared in October 1918; his badly decomposed body was discovered the following summer, entangled in his fishing nets in front of the Castle. He is thought to be buried in a grave beside the tower.

For more than a decade, friends and curiosity seekers visited the slowly deteriorating castle. In 1986, a group of concerned citizens formed The Friends of White Otter Castle, with the aim of preserving it as an historic site.

After years of red tape, fund-raising, government assistance, volunteer man hours, and creative ingenuity that included designing a special lifting device to enable the logs to be repaired, the White Otter Castle has been restored. McOuat was never able to obtain the rights to the land the property sits on from the federal government. Today, it's part of the Turtle River-White Otter Lakeway Provincial Park, and continues to be accessible only by boat, plane or snowmobile.

THE FRIENDS OF WHITE OTTER CASTLE
P.O. Box 2096,
Atikokan, Ont. P0T 1C0

WHITE OTTER CASTLE
Township of Ignace,
200 Beaver St.,
P.O. Box 248,
Ignace, Ont. P0T 1T0
TEL 807-934-2202
FAX 807-934-2864

The Mildred M. Mahoney Silver Jubilee Dolls' House Museum

If dollhouses conjure up a particularly female, childhood whimsy, think again. The earliest dollhouses, popular since the 1700s, were miniature replicas of homes of the wealthy, exhibited as status symbols by their owners. Their furniture was oversized in proportion to the rooms (unlike modern dollhouses whose furniture is to scale) so they could be carved and adorned with more detail. Children were allowed to view the houses on holidays and Sundays, from whence came the nickname, "Sunday House." It wasn't until the 1830s that dollhouses were introduced for children to play with, a trend which began in England.

Today, next to stamps and coins, the collecting of miniatures is the third most popular hobby in North America, generating over $100 million worth of business annually. It's a hobby that's financially out of the league of most children.

Mildred Mahoney has expanded her hobby so that she now has the reputation of an experienced collector and expert restorer. What began with an orange crate for a dollhouse in 1926 has become the Mildred M. Mahoney Silver Jubilee Dolls' House Museum, the world's largest collection of its kind, with over 200 dollhouses and over a million miniatures, with a value of several million dollars.

The houses range from stately manors to rustic cottages, constructed from 1780 to the present. Mrs. Mahoney collected them over the years at auctions, estate sales, and through agents and buyers as well as friends. The houses are of European, Canadian, American, and Japanese origin.

Finding and purchasing a house is only the beginning. Mrs. Mahoney meticulously restores and furnishes each one with antique miniatures of the appropriate period. This requires a great deal of investigative work of the historical era, as well as the background of the dollhouse itself. The value of the houses increases with an "inherited pedigree" (one in which the collector can trace the generations of family owners and the pieces added by each).

No detail is overlooked in the restorative process. Bed linens are hand embroidered, silk damask graces the walls of some mansions. There is Chippendale furniture, carved newel posts on the stairs with needlepoint carpets and tiny stair rods, crystal chandeliers, thumb-size oil paintings, an ivory chess game, a leather-bound set of Shakespeare. The price of such detail is not cheap. One gold-and-enamel livingroom suite was $20,000. Glass and china in miniature costs almost as much as full-sized dishes.

The pride and joy of the collection is Marygate House, a five story English manor, valued around $40,000. It's complete with servants' quarters, a nursery, and a sewing room, accessorized down to tiny spools of thread. Built in 1810, the manor is furnished with authentic, German Beidermeier pieces, the Rolls Royce of dollhouse furniture.

Also among the treasures is a replica of the Kensington-Kerr House, made in 1809, a duplicate of Queen Victoria's dollhouse. There's a Dutch sea captain's house with a roof-top hoist for loading barges canal-side, a French palace shaped like a bird cage, a Japanese palace finished with a courtyard, and the American-made Mystery House, so named because little is known about it, filled with turn-of-the-century furniture made from cigar boxes by tramps who exchanged them for a meal or a night's lodging.

In addition to the houses, the Museum has a collection of other buildings such as a toy shop with dozens of tiny dolls. (No dolls appear in the houses as Mrs. Mahoney believes they distract from placing oneself inside.) There's also a general store with more than 5,000 products, a toy shop with miniature trains, a toy maker's shop, and a barn with animals.

Appropriately enough the Dolls' House Museum is housed in Bertie Hall, a red brick mansion built in Fort Erie in 1826. The house has nearly as much history as its contents. King Edward VII slept there in 1865, and from 1875 to 1892, it was a hotel, operated by John Crabb.

The four meter (twelve foot) deep basement is said to have secret tunnels that formed one link of the Underground Railroad, which brought black slaves to freedom between 1826 and 1865. The tunnel is also thought to be the route by which Chinese workers were smuggled into the USA after the Canadian National Railroad was built, and was used by bootleggers during Prohibition.

Bertie Hall is owned by the Niagara Parks Commisson. It is leased to Mrs. Mahoney who has bequeathed her collection to the provinical and federal governments.

Allow yourself a good two hours to view the collection. Find out why each house contains a pair of slippers and be sure to look for Mrs. Mahoney's first dollhouse, the 1926 orange crate.

MILDRED M. MAHONEY SILVER JUBILEE DOLLS' HOUSE MUSEUM

Bertie Hall,
657 Niagara Blvd.,
Fort Erie, Ont.
L2A 3H9
TEL 905- 871-5833
OPEN: May 1-Dec. 31, 10 a.m. to 4 p.m.

DRIVE the QEW to Fort Erie. Exit at Central Avenue. Turn right on Phipps Street, left on Niagara Boulevard.
PARKING at rear of building.

Niagara Falls

Niagara Falls is one of the seven natural wonders of the world. It's also the biggest tourist attraction in North America, with nearly 12 million people visiting annually in the summer months alone.

Considering the tens of thousands of visitors who annually crowd the rail to view this spectacle of water over rock, the daredevils in barrels who challenge its height amidst the outcroppings of collapsed shale, its reputation for attracting honeymooners from around the world, and given the intrusion of the urban landscape, it's interesting to contemplate the vision of early explorers who came upon Niagara in all its natural splendor.

The first written account of Niagara Falls was in French, given by Jesuit missionary, Father Louis Hennepin in 1678:

"...we entered the beautiful river Niagara, which no bark ever yet entered....Four leagues from Lake Frontenac (Lake Ontario) there is an incredible Cataract or Waterfall, which has no equal. The Niagara river near this place is only an eighth of a league wide, but it is very deep in places, and so rapid above the great fall, that it hurries down all the animals which try to cross it, without a single one being able to withstand its current. They plunge down a height of more than five hundred feet, and its fall is composed of two sheets of water and a cascade, with an island sloping down. In the middle these waters foam and boil in a fearful manner.

They thunder continually, and when the wind blows in a southerly direction, the noise which they make is heard from more than fifteen leagues. Four leagues from this cataract or fall, the Niagara river rushes with extraordinary rapidity especially for two leagues into Lake Frontenac."

Hennepin's exaggerated estimate of the Falls' height, "more than five hundred feet," perhaps best expresses his awe. The Horseshoe Falls on the Canadian side measures 48.2 meters (158 feet); the Rainbow Falls on the American side is 50.9 meters (167 feet). The four upper Great Lakes contain 20 percent of the world's fresh water: this is the outflow that plunges over these Falls.

One of the most moving accounts of the Falls was written by British writer, Charles Dickens, who visited Niagara in 1842. His words capture what many feel but perhaps cannot express.

"When we were seated in the little ferry-boat, and were crossing the swoln river immediately before both cataracts, I began to feel what it was: but I was in a manner stunned, and unable to comprehend the vastness of the scene. It was not until I came on Table rock, and looked— Great Heavens, on what a fall of bright- green water!— that it came upon me in its full might and majesty.

Then, when I felt how near to my Creator I was standing, the first effect, and the enduring one — instant and lasting — of the tremendous spectacle, was Peace. Peace of Mind: Tranquillity: Calm recollections of the Dead: Great Thoughts of Eternal Rest and Happiness: nothing of Gloom or Terror. Niagara was at once stamped upon my heart, and Image of Beauty; to remain there, changeless and indelible, until its pulses ceased to beat, for ever...

To wander to and fro all day, and see the cataracts from all points of view; to stand upon the edge of the Great Horse Shoe Fall, marking the hurried water gathering strength as it approached the verge, yet seeming, too, to pause before it shot into the gulf below; to gaze from the river's level up at the torrent as it came streaming down; to climb the neighboring heights and watch it through the trees, and see the wreathing water in the rapids hurrying on to take its fearful plunge, to linger in the shadow of the solemn rocks three miles below; watching the river as, stirred by no visible cause, it heaved and eddied and awoke the echoes, being troubled yet, far down beneath the surface, by its giant leap; to have Niagara before me, lighted by the sun and by the moon, red in the day's decline, and grey as evening slowly fell upon it; to look upon it every day, and wake up in the night and hear its ceaseless voice: this was enough. "

Today there is talk of the Falls eroding, but there is no need to worry that they will disappear in our lifetime. Some 12,500 years ago the Falls were at the site of Queenston Heights. At the time of Christ they were slightly down river from the Rainbow Bridge.

Views with a Difference

CN TOWER

Toronto's CN Tower is the world's tallest free-standing structure. This communication tower is 553 meters (1,815 feet) high from the reflecting pool at the base to the top of the transmission mast. There is an indoor and outdoor observation deck as well as the world's largest revolving restaurant located at the 351-meter (1,150-foot) level. At the 447-meter (1,465-foot) level is the world's highest observation deck. On a clear day, visitors can see 160 kilometers (100 miles).

CN TOWER

301 Front St. West,
Toronto, Ont. M5V 2T6
TEL 416-360-8500

DAVID DUNLAP OBSERVATORY

At night, two curved shutters on a giant dome in Richmond Hill slide apart to make an opening skyward that's 4.6 meters (15 feet) wide. Even though it weighs 72 tonnes, the upper structure of the Dome can be rotated in any direction, enabling the 23-tonne telescope inside to point to any place in the sky. On a clear evening, depending upon the time of year, one can see Mars, Jupiter, Saturn, the moon, double stars, star clusters, and all the galaxies in between. This is the largest optical telescope reflector in Canada.

The David Dunlap Observatory belongs to the University of Toronto but is open to the public. It was presented to the school in 1935 by Jessie Donalda Dunlap as a memorial to her husband. The observatory is used for astronomical research, training advanced students at the university, and fostering the public's interest in astronomy.

The telescope has a reflector mirror with a 2-meter (74-inch) diameter. At the time of presentation, it was the second largest telescope in the world. It plays a major role both nationally and internationally in research in astronomy and astrophysics.

The site of the observatory is the highest point of a farm located 25 kilometers (15.5 miles) from the University of Toronto's downtown campus. The administration building on the grounds houses an astronomical research library, laboratories, machine and electronics shops, and an auditorium for teaching purposes and public lectures. There is also an illuminated display of stellar photographs.

The observatory hosts two types of tours for the public, which must be pre-booked about three weeks in advance. Wednesday morning tours begin at 10 a.m. and run about an hour and a half. The telescope is demonstrated but there is no viewing through the dome. On designated Saturday evenings, from April to October, tours include a slide presentation and telescope viewing if the sky is clear. Members of the Toronto Centre of the Royal Astronomical Society of Canada set their own telescopes up outside for public viewing in good weather. This enables people to view objects that are low in the sky and many celestial bodies which can't be viewed comfortably with the larger instrument.

DAVID DUNLAP OBSERVATORY

P.O. Box 360,
Richmond Hill, Ont. L4C 4Y6
TEL 905-884-2112; 905-884-9562

DRIVE Highway 7 to Bayview Avenue. Go north on Bayview Avenue 3 kilometers (1.8 miles) to Hillsview Drive, then west on Hillsview Drive to the entrance gates.

Highlands Cinema

In the heart of cottage country, Hollywood North takes on new meaning for those visiting the Highlands Cinema. With the purchase of a ticket, movie buffs not only see first run movies, but gain entrance to the largest collection of movie memorabilia and equipment in Canada. The theatre/museum is located in the home of Keith Stata in Kinmount, a town of three hundred people in the Haliburton Highlands.

For Stata, there has been no business like show business since the age of six, when his mother purchased an 8-mm movie projector. He began showing movies in the woodshed and charged neighborhood children 2 cents a piece. In high school, he made films with separately recorded sound, but never pursued his dream of becoming a movie producer, going into the construction business instead.

The Stata household always had a projection room, so when he built his current home, it seemed natural to include a 50-seat theatre. What began as a hobby quickly turned into a successful commercial venture. As more and more people wanted to come and see movies, he began expanding the seating capacity. The original theatre now seats 75. A second 100-seat addition was added in 1986 and a third theatre built in 1988 was expanded in 1990 to accommodate 150. In total, that's more seats than there are people in Kinmount!

In the 460-square-meter (1,500-square-foot) lobby are more than 150 projectors used between 1890 and 1960, including hand cranked models, those taken from town to town in a suitcase, and one that belonged to Irving Berlin. About 4,000 posters and lobby cards recall super stars like Rudolph Valentino and Carol Lombard. Memorabilia abounds from ticket stubs to theatre signage to ticket windows.

Each of the three theatres has a different decor. Everything including the seats, curtains, doors, and exit signs have all been rescued from theatres that closed from as far away as Hollywood to Haileybury.

Highlands Cinema is open in the summer months until Thanksgiving weekend, and operates seven days a week. Movie-goers can find out what's showing by calling ahead and listening to a regularly updated recording.

When Stata isn't busy as the owner, manager, projectionist, and usher, or talking to the patrons, he runs around the continent picking up more memorabilia. He'd be pleased to hear from anyone with any collectibles.

HIGHLANDS CINEMA
P.O. Box 85,
Kinmount, Ont. K0M 2A0
TEL 705-488-2107

DRIVE from Bobcaygeon take Highway 649 until it meets Highway 121. Turn right on Highway 121 to Kinmount. In the village, cross the bridge over the Irondale River and continue on Highway 121. The cinema is north of the main street, left off Highway 121, just past Rokeby's Lumber. Parking for 120 cars behind the theatre.

Pembroke Heritage Murals

It isn't always necessary to visit an art gallery to view the work of local and national artists. A stroll through the downtown streets of Pembroke reveals extraordinary works of art in the form of large- scale paintings. These murals with themes that celebrate the area's rich culture and heritage have become a great source of enjoyment and pride for the citizens of Pembroke. They are both a tourist attraction and a means of beautifying the city.

Visitors to the community can conduct their own self-guided tour with the aid of a map and information brochure available from the town's merchants. There are currently fourteen murals on the walls of buildings with more planned for the future. They vary considerably in style, detail, and depth of color, but not in quality.

The themes are varied and mark milestones in the city's development. For example, artist Robert Ganeau depicts Peter White and his family outside their log cabin. They were the first European settlers to come to Pembroke in 1828.

Pierre Hardy's mural celebrates Pembroke as the first community in Canada to have commercial electricity with pictures of the first three generations of street light styles in an engaging 1920s streetscape.

Artist Stefan (Cesare) Bell pays tribute to three of Pembroke's citizens who were among the original inductees into the Hockey Hall of Fame. During the 1920s, Hugh Lehman played for Vancouver, Frank Nighbor for the Ottawa Senators and Harry Cameron for the Saskatoon St. Pat's.

Subjects include local businesses, the Canadian Armed Forces, a style of log boating unique to Pembroke, ice cutting on the Ottawa River, and explorer Samuel de Champlain.

Canada's largest three-dimensional mural, and the only one to incorporate lit stained glass, honors Marguerite d'Youville who founded the Grey Nuns community.

Pembroke's largest mural is 34 meters by 23 meters (112 feet by 40 feet). It's also Canada's largest multi-level, multi-angle mural. Made to look like an old photograph, it illustrates loggers at work using the tools of their trade.

These are not the work of amateurs. Each piece is a commissioned work of art by Stefan Bell, Neil Blackwell, Robin Burgesse, Craig Campbell, Randy Chester, Robert Garneau and Pierre Hardy among others. An ever expanding group of volunteers along with the generosity of residents, merchants, and corporations have funded these additions to the cityscape. Pembroke has set the standard by which other communities might recall their past and beautify their city at the same time.

PEMBROKE HERITAGE MURALS

1 Pembroke St. East,
P.O. Box 277,
Pembroke, Ont. K8A 6X3
TEL 613-735-6821
FAX 613-735-3660

Royal Botanical Gardens

Horticulturalists, gardening enthusiasts, students of science and nature, and everyone who wishes to spend the day in a rich, natural environment will find the Royal Botanical Gardens (RBG) in Hamilton an extraordinary place to explore and learn about the world of plants.

The size of the RBG is overwhelming. It takes in 1,100 hectares (2,700 acres) of land and contains 40,000 recorded plants. There are 50 display collections, showcased in six garden areas and 50 kilometers (30 miles) of marked trails through natural sanctuaries, divided into six unique study areas.

The RBG has something to offer everyone in every season. The Rock Garden blooms with 125,000 spring bulbs in April, followed by azaleas and summer annuals until October.

Iris are the feature of the Laking Garden. 250,000 blooms display color unequalled by any other plant genus which is why the iris is named for the Greek goddess of the rainbow. Here also are the perennial collection, peonies, and the Heritage Garden, a southern Ontario, turn-of-the-century display.

In the Arboretum are conifers from around the world, the Avenue of Trees, and shrubs displayed in alphabetical order. The lilac dell is home to approximately 800 cultivars, making it the largest lilac collection in the world. The RBG is the International Registration Authority for new lilac varieties which means that anyone, anywhere in the world, who creates a new lilac must contact the RBG to name and register the plant.

In Hendrie Park, a one hectare (two-acre) display features 2,000 modern hybrid and 650 shrub roses, ablaze with color from June to October. Here also are clematis, lilies, medicinal plants, and a sneak preview of new cultivars of annuals in development.

From January to April, the Mediterranean Garden is at its best. This interior display will hold your interest for hours and is a great place to go on a rainy day.

The Teaching Garden has a summer collection of herbs, plants that are edible as well as ornamental, and a display known as the Plant Lover's Garden, where one can discover what grows in various soil and light conditions.

Throughout the year, the RBG hosts a number of special events for the entire family. There are festivities like the Cherry Blossom, Rose, and Herb festivals; picnics; brunches; a croquet tournament; and sales of plants by organizations like the Rhododendron, Iris, and Rose societies. The RBG also conducts an extensive education program, with more than 120 courses and 100 different programs.

In the heart of the RBG's center is the Floral Art Shop which sells dried and silk flower arrangements, books, gifts, and gardening tools. There is also a Nature Interpretive Centre, a library, and the RBG quarterly magazine called the *Pappus*.

The RBG is a registered charity. It is funded in part by the province through the Ministry of Culture, Tourism, and Recreation, and by the regional counties of Halton and Hamilton-Wentworth of which it is a part. RBG has an extensive list of members and donors who contribute annually, in addition to the thousands of visitors who frequent the gardens.

ROYAL BOTANICAL GARDENS

680 Plains Road West,
P.O. Box 399,
Hamilton, Ont. L8N 3H8
TEL 905-527-1158 8:30 a.m. to 5:00 p.m. weekdays
FAX 905-577-0375
800-668-1158 in Ontario, Quebec
INFOLINE 905-527-8938

OPEN year-round except December 25

DRIVE from Toronto, take the QEW west, then take Highway 403 west, following the signs for Hamilton/Brantford. Exit at Highway 6 north, turn right at the first traffic light and watch for the signs.

DRIVE from Niagara, along the QEW past Hamilton. Cross the Burlington Skyway Bridge and exit at Plains Road. Turn left at the traffic light and watch for the signs.

ONTARIO TRIVIA

SIMCOE'S Eva Brook Donly Museum holds one of Ontario's finest and largest collections of books and microfilms for genealogy in old Ontario, Canada, and early America. The Loyalist Library is supported by the Grand River Branch of the United Empire Loyalists.

SUDBURY has the largest-known concentration of nickel in the world.

SUDBURY is home to the Big Nickel, a replica of the 1951 Canadian commemorative nickel. The statue is 9 meters (30 feet) high.

SUTTON, a small town at the south shore of Lake Simcoe is the burial place of writers Stephen Leacock and Mazo de la Roche. They are buried in the cemetery of St. George's Church.

STREETSVILLE resident William Chester Shaw built the IMAX, the most technically advanced projector, which displays a picture on a screen 6 stories high and 24 meters (80 feet) wide, with sound in six-track stereo from 80 speakers. It was first used at Expo '70, Ontario Place, and the Smithsonian Institute.

Brickman's Botanical Garden

Perth County Road 12, on the way to Wartburg, is an unremarkable vista of farmers' fields. Suddenly to the right, off a gravel road, there's an incredible burst of color.

This vision of brilliant splendor entices you off the road and into Gerry Brickman's perennial garden. Begun in the fall of 1988 for his personal pleasure, this is now one of the largest, privately owned gardens in Canada and has a reputation as one of the best.

What started out as pasture land is now 2 hectares (five and a half acres) of fragrant elegance, with more than 3,000 varieties of perennials from around the world, some of which are horticultural rarities. Brickman knows each one of them by their Latin and common names. There are flowers of every hue and colour, plants of every shape and stature: 400 kinds of free-flowering daylilies, 80 types of radiant delphiniums, 187 varieties of peonies, 125 types of roses, some of royal lineage, and just about every other type of flower that will grow in this part of the world, as well as some that won't! There are wild flowers, water plants, ornamental grasses, and herbs.

Horticulturalists have deemed the style of Brickman's garden as "natural," a true gardener's garden. There are no walls or arches, paving stones or intricate borders. The flowers don't line up like soldiers in meticulous rows, but cascade over one another as if painted in by an artist's brush.

Brickman lacks formal training in gardening although he comes from a family that has been in the nursery business for several generations. His country oasis is the culmination of a great deal of research and inspiration gleaned from books and other notable gardeners, like Gertrude Jekyll, and Claude Monet.

From Bloomsbury's member, Vita Sackville-West, came the inspiration for Brickman's White Garden. After the delicate white of early spring crocuses and narcissus comes the parade of tulips, daffodils, and the ground cover, snow-in-summer, whose foliage stays silver after its blooms have faded. Stately white irises continue the sequence, followed by peonies, clematis, Queen Anne's lace, shasta daisies, and calla lilies: 100 different perennials in all.

The Queen Mother's Garden was inspired by a book of her favorite flowers and includes nasturtiums, honeysuckle, and gooseberries. It honors her passion for roses, such as the Blanc Double de Coubert and William Shakespeare.

A Biblical Garden displays 116 plants named in the Bible. Palm and fig trees tower above plants from the Holy Land — papyrus, spikenard, hyssop, and Moses' bulrushes.

The garden is at its peak of beauty in July, but even later in the season there's plenty of color, and the place is abuzz with birds, butterflies, and insects. Pens around the garden center hold swans, ducks, and geese.

Visitors are advised to take plenty of film and a sun hat for the heat of the day. Each of the perennials in the garden may be purchased from a nursery on the premises run by Brickman's sister. There is a modest admission fee which helps support the garden. Bus tours are welcome.

BRICKMAN'S BOTANICAL GARDENS

R.R. #1,
Sebringville, Ont. N0K 1X0
TEL 519-393-6223
FAX 519-393-5239

OPEN May to September 9:00 a.m. to 5:30 p.m. daily

DRIVE west on Highway 8 out of Stratford to Sebringville. Turn right onto Regional Road 12 to Wartburg. Follow the signs to Brickman's, before Wartburg.

BRICKMAN'S GARDENING TIPS

- In late fall, Brickman mulches his beds with Canadian sphagnum peat moss to hold the moisture and keep the weeds down.
- Use natural fertilizers, bone meal, bloodmeal, and sheep manure mixed with droppings from farm-raised chickens, ducks, and geese. Brickman builds his beds up by at least an inch with these products.
- Plan the garden before planting, looking at the area in both sun and shade.
- Plant a few plants at a time rather than trying to plant a large number all at once.
- Don't plant perennials too close together the way you would annuals. Be patient.

Northern Kiwi Nursery

There's good news for people who like kiwi fruit, that decorative green ingredient in fruit salads that surfaced in the import section of the grocery store around the time of nouvelle cuisine. Now you can grow your own kiwi right in your own backyard. It's not the brown, furry fruit that comes from New Zealand, known botanically as *Actinidia Deliciosa*, but a cousin, *Actinidia Arguta*. It's hardy up to -40 C, so it will grow almost anywhere in Canada.

Kiwi vines are available from Peter Klassen and his two brothers, peach farmers in Niagara-on-the-Lake. They opened Northern Kiwi Nursery as an experiment in 1988 and have more than half a hectare (1.5 acres) in vines, propagating 20 different varieties of kiwi. In 1992 they produced over 10,000 kiwi vines which they shipped across Canada from BC to Newfoundland; in the USA, including Alaska; and as far away as Jamaica, Lithuania, and Greece.

The entire Klassen family is involved in the business now that they are close to producing enough fruit to be commercially viable in the marketplace.

The fruit of the hardy kiwi possesses the sparkling, green flesh of its New Zealand relative, but the flavor combines the distinctly kiwi taste with a mixture of pineapple, strawberry and grape. It looks different too, smaller than the egg-sized New Zealander, more like a very large grape, averaging between three-quarters and one-and-a-half inches in length and an inch in diameter. It weighs between 5 and 10 grams, and makes for a wonderful bite-sized treat, because it doesn't need peeling. Unlike its fuzzy cousin, the hardy kiwi is smooth-skinned. On the Brix scale of sweetness, the measure of sugar in fruit, the fuzzy averages 12 to 14 while the smooth is much sweeter, between 17 and 22.

Kiwi vines are easy to grow. Like grapes, they require a supporting arbour, trellis, or fence and have been know to climb trees. They aren't fussy about soil requirements. While moist, rich soil is desirable, they will also thrive in heavier clay soil. The roots are shallow and the vine doesn't like wet roots, but may need water in arid summers.

The kiwi is a vigorous plant. At the peak of the growing season it can grow up to two-and-a-half centimeters (an inch) a day. The plant was initially introduced to North America for its decorative dark green color and heart-shaped leaves. Small, white fragrant blossoms are attractive to bees.

Self-pollinating varieties are becoming available but for the most part there are male and female vines. Each male vine which bears no fruit will pollinate up to eight females. Females produce in three to five years and continue to propagate for up to 60 years. Mature vines yield about 45 kilograms (100 pounds) of kiwi a year.

Northern Kiwi Nursery sells two sizes of kiwi vines. One-year-old vines are shipped in 10 centimeter (four-inch) pots. Two-year-old vines growing in 4.5-liter (1 gallon) pots are shipped bareroot. Orders received before March 31 will be shipped in a dormant state some time in April, which is preferable for the health of the vine. Orders received after the end of March are processed as quickly as possible.

Vines are shipped UPS. Those with no street address arrive via Canada Post. Vines may also be picked up by calling ahead for an appointment.

Complete instructions on planting, pruning, watering, fertilizing, and supporting the vines are included with purchase. The Klassens are available to assist with any difficulties.

NORTHERN KIWI NURSERY
R.R. #3,
181 Niven Rd.,
Niagara-on-the-Lake, Ont. L0S 1J0
TEL 905-468-5483
   905-468-7573

Campberry Farm

Pecans, almonds, apricots, persimmon, pawpaw: these are trees we associate with climates of the southern USA. Now there are hardy varieties of these species, available right here in Ontario.

Campberry Farm in Niagara-on-the-Lake has been experimenting with new crop introductions since 1969. The business started as a hobby for owner Doug Campbell whose interest began with unusual ornamental shrubs and berries. Word of mouth increased demand for his rare plants. That, coupled with being laid-off from his city job, prompted Campbell to go into the nursery business on a full-time basis.

Some of Campberry's most unique species are the Southern magnolia, evergreen azaleas and silk trees. The nursery specializes in new hybrids of nut trees, with 810 hectares (2,000 acres) in the early stages of cultivation. Among the varietals are the American chestnut, American hazel, black walnut, English walnut, filbert, hardy almond, northern pecan, shagbark hickory, the sweet kernel apricot, persimmon and the pawpaw. There's also a selection of blackberries, raspberries, and strawberries, noteworthy species not found at local greenhouses, and a dozen or more unusual species like the Kentucky coffee tree, scarlet oak and black ash.

Campberry provides consultation and site inspection services for growers interested in commercial nut tree production and discounts for those buying in hundred or thousand lot quantities. Trees are for sale only during the digging season, usually between March 25 and May 15. They are dug bareroot and packed in moist peat and moisture-proof wrappings. Trees are always freshly dug for each customer so orders should be placed three weeks before pick-up or delivery. Several nursery lists are issued each year. Pickups and visits are by appointment only. It's best to telephone between 8:00 and 10:00 p.m.

CAMPBERRY FARM
R.R. #1,
Niagara-on-the-Lake, Ont. L0S IJ0
TEL 905-262-4927

DRIVE the QEW east from St. Catharines. Take the Highway 405 exit to the Queenston-Lewiston Bridge, but exit onto the Niagara River Parkway. Drive approximately 1.5 kilometers (.9 miles) north on the Parkway. The nursery is on the left side, away from the river.

Richters

Richters call themselves "Canada's herb specialists," but in fact their reputation as one of the top sources for herbs in seed, plant, or dry form is worldwide. They offer hundreds of varieties of herbs from the more traditional — dill, oregano, basil, French tarragon, sweet marjoram, and ginger — to the specialized growing of Chinese, medicinal herbs like ginkgo, ginseng, fo-ti, reishi mushrooms, and Chinese senna.

Richters are also a source for gourmet vegetables, wildflowers, alpine flowers, everlastings, organic plant foods, natural pest controls, beneficial insects (yes they actually sell bugs by the box, including ladybugs, wasps, and green lacewings), herb garden kits, books about growing and using herbs, and gardening supplies (including the popular Potmaker, a tool which recycles newspapers, molding them into plant pots — an invention of the late Otto Richter, founder of the company).

Richters have always been a family business. After emigrating from Austria where they operated a nursery, Otto and Waltraut Richter began growing and selling herbs in Locust Hill in 1969. With the publication of their first seed catalog in 1970, their mail order business flourished.

Today Richters ship anywhere in the world. Their creation of a specialized carton allows the plants to travel and arrive in first rate condition. All plants are grown organically without the use of chemicals. Even the dried herbs are "guaranteed pure," without fumigation.

Visitors are welcome at the greenhouses in Goodwood, where Waltraut Richter rhymes off information about the herbs with the ease of someone reciting poetry. She carries on the business with son Conrad. They hold lecture series in the months of March, April, August and September and produce an annual, 80-page catalog, a source of useful information in itself.

RICHTERS
Goodwood, Ont. L0C IA0
TEL 905-640-6677
FAX 905-640-6641

OPEN seven days a week, 8:30 a.m. to 5:00 p.m.
CLOSED Mondays in November and December and some holidays.

LOCATED half an hour from Toronto, 2 miles east of Goodwood, on Bloomington Road.
Catalogue available.

Stokes Seeds Ltd.

In both Canada and the USA, the name Stokes is synonymous with seeds. Stokes Seeds Ltd. of St. Catharines is one of the oldest mail order operations in North America, and the largest mail order seed house in Canada. Each year Stokes sends out roughly 5 million packages of vegetable and flower seeds — over 600 varieties — to more than a quarter of a million gardeners and 38,000 commercial growers in Canada and south of the border. They specialize in seeds for the more northerly climates of Canada, the northern USA and the Great Lakes area, and developed many of the varieties themselves.

Walter P. Stokes and Herbert Johnson started Johnson & Stokes in Mooretown, New Jersey in 1882. Harry Gayle, a Canadian cauliflower farmer, applied for a sales job with the American company and was told he had to get 5,000 customers in Canada. In 1927 he achieved his quota and hung out a shingle in St. Catharines. During the Depression, he bought out the Canadian arm of the company for $4,000 and changed the name to Stokes Seeds. During World War II, he arranged for Asian and European seed growers — those producing most of the world's flowers and vegetable seeds — to send him their parent stock for safekeeping. In return, he offered them one-quarter of the seeds produced from the stock once the war was over. During peacetime, Stokes had seeds when they were in short supply.

Much of Stokes' success can be attributed to Dr. Ernie Kerr, renowned Canadian seed breeder, who ranks among the top 10 seed breeders in North America, and among the best in the world when it comes to his specialty, sweet corn and tomatoes.

Stokes remains very much a family operation, despite the fact that there are close to 300 employees in peak season, with 60 IBM terminals running six days a week on double shifts to fill the seed orders and a crew in Buffalo to process orders for the American market. At the helm is Gayle's son John and grandson Wayne.

On the same premises where Harry Gayle first began the business there's an old-fashioned retail seed store; the first controlled-atmosphere seed storage facility, still used today; a warehouse where the seeds are tested, packaged and stored; 20 hectares (50 acres) of research and trial grounds and a seed laboratory.

Stokes imports seeds from Japan, Taiwan, Denmark, Sweden, Switzerland, Holland, Hungary, the Philippines, and the USA, and they own a portion of a seed business in Budapest. All new seed is tested for purity, vigor, and germination. Almost all Stokes' seed is rated at a germination of 90 to 95 percent.

Stokes produces what is considered to be the most useful seed catalog in North America. Aimed at market gardeners, it details the relative merits of each flower and vegetable and the color, size, disease resistance, and purpose for which each variety was bred.

STOKES SEEDS LTD.

39 James St.,
P.O. Box 10,
St. Catharines, Ont. L2R 6R6
TEL 905-688-4300
FAX 905-684-8411

Lawn Star Rake

Stella Quesnelle of Penetanguishene suffered from a chronically sore arm that made lawn and garden work a difficult chore. As a result, she got the idea for the Lawn Star Rake, a revolutionary garden tool.

Her husband Al, a welder, made the first prototype in the basement and the Quesnelles applied for a patent. As the name implies, this lawn implement is a rake, but a rake with a difference: it has wheels. It can be pushed away from the raker with ease, without the constant lifting action. The rake's teeth push up, out of the way, as the Lawn Star is pushed forward and come back down in place when the rake is pulled back.

The Lawn Star is built for comfort. It has a 56-centimeter (22-inch) sponge grip to ensure raking without blisters. A loop holds it handy on the arm without gripping. It pushes easily over piles of garden debris and leaves. The teeth are self-cleaning; as the rake moves, it automatically frees debris. The teeth can be lubricated for ease of movement.

The Quesnelles have been three years in the development and promotion of their rake. Hardware stores are beginning to take an interest in it but in the meantime it can be purchased direct from the factory! Al Quesnelle manufactures them in his welding shop next to the house. They retail for around $40 plus tax.

LAWN STAR RAKE
P.O. Box 270,
Concession 13,
Tiny Township,
Penetanguishene, Ont. L0K 1P0
TEL 705-549-8272

Tundra Swans

One of Ontario's prime wildlife spectacles is the arrival of the tundra swans at the Aylmer Management area just north of the town of Aylmer. These great white birds with brilliant flashing wings arrive late in February. Their numbers build through the month of March, peaking the last week, then sharply diminish during the first few days of April.

A hundred years ago these magnificent birds were rarely seen in eastern Canada. They breed in the far north and tended to migrate along both seaboards where they usually winter.

The migration patterns of the tundra swan have changed for a number of reasons: essentially, the loss of marsh habitats and the increase in corn and winter wheat crops brought them further inland.

The development of the waterfowl habitat at the Aylmer Wildlife Management Site is a prime example of human impact upon migratory flyways. In 1973 no more than 300 swans stopped over at the Aylmer location. In 1977, there were more than 7,500.

Today, roughly 95,000 tundra swans make up the east coast population which winters primarily in the Chesapeake Bay region. Another 68,000 winter along the west coast between British Columbia and California. They stop over in Ontario only on their way to nest in the Mackenzie Delta, close to the Arctic coast, the Old Crow Flats in the northern Yukon, Baffin Island, and the islands of Hudson Bay. The return flight to the coast is non-stop, at altitudes high over Ontario.

AYLMER WILDLIFE MANAGEMENT SITE

DRIVE Highway 401 to Highway 73. Go south on Highway 73 about 16 kilometers (10 miles) to County Road 32 to the first crossroads. Turn left again and drive .4 kilometers (a quarter-mile) to the police college. The Management area is beside the college.

Migrating Monarchs

One of nature's mysteries is the migration of tens of millions of monarch butterflies. Throughout the summer, several generations of monarchs are raised in Ontario. (The adult life cycle is only 30 days.) The last generation to emerge in the lingering days of summer is somehow triggered to migrate south, a journey of some 3,000 kilometers (1,864 miles).

Until 1975, their wintering location was unknown. It was the University of Toronto's Dr. Fred Urquart who first discovered their destination. He traced his tagged monarchs high into the mountains of Central Mexico. Here they hang on trees, dormant until February. This generation mates in early spring, then flies northward, laying eggs along the way. However, most of the adults won't reach Canada. It takes several spring generations to fly to the north. It's still a mystery how those that migrate know where to go.

The monarch's residency in Mexico and Canada is due to the milkweed, the only plant eaten by monarch caterpillars.

The best place to view the fall monarch migration is the tip of Point Pelee National Park because they are funnelled here looking for shorter routes across the Great Lakes.

There are only a few special days in fall, between August and October, that this phenomenon takes place at Point Pelee. It's dependent on weather conditions and the size of the butterfly population. On a warm day, the butterflies go directly across Lake Erie without stopping. In cold temperatures, they roost in trees, waiting for the thermometer to rise and a favorable wind to assist them in their journey across the lake. Observers require binoculars to see roosting monarchs which tend to resemble dead leaves.

Point Pelee gives a daily butterfly report in the fall. They also maintain butterfly counts, provide special programs and exhibits, advocate protection of the milkweed and monarch, and promote the monarch as Canada's national insect.

POINT PELEE NATIONAL PARK
R.R. #1,
Leamington, Ont. N8H 3V4
TEL 519-322-2365
FAX 519-322-1277

POINT PELEE BUTTERFLY HOT LINE
TEL 519-322-2371

Jack Miner Sanctuary

In an age when conservation and the environment are on everyone's agenda — government bodies, volunteer groups, private individuals, and school children — it's easy to forget that such concern began many years ago with just one man, Jack Miner of Kingsville.

Miner is known throughout the world as the "father of conservation" and the "founder of the waterfowl refuge system," pioneered by his sanctuary beginning in 1904. In his day, *Maclean's* magazine considered him to be one of the greatest living Canadians. King George VI awarded him the Order of the British Empire as the greatest conservationist in the Empire. In 1947, the Canadian government proclaimed the week of April 10 (Miner's birthday), as National Wildlife Week.

Miner's life-work shows how one individual can make a difference. This man, who lacked formal education, who couldn't read or write until he was in his thirties, changed the world's understanding of wildlife and their survival. His sanctuary, once the second most popular tourist attraction after Niagara Falls, is still the best place to view Miner's beloved Canada geese.

Jack Miner might happily have continued as one of the most accomplished game-bird hunters of the province. But a tragic accident in which a friend shot and killed Miner's brother changed all that, as did an experience he had with a flock of Canada geese that seemed to recognize him and avoid him as their enemy. He began to study wild geese and realized that they required human interference to ensure their survival.

Miner's sanctuary began as a mud hole, graded into a small pond. He purchased seven wing-clipped geese from a neighbour who had illegally trapped them to use as decoys to attract other birds. For three years no other geese came. A handful joined his flock in 1908. The following year 32 arrived and in 1910, 350.

At first the Miner family fed the geese with corn from their pockets. As the numbers grew the geese were fed by the pail, then from sacks, and eventually by the wagon-load. In 1909 Miner began to band his visitors. Each aluminum tag listed the sanctuary's address and a verse from the Bible. Thus began the scientific tracking of the flight paths of North America's ducks and geese.

To pay for the feed and the banding, Miner gave lectures, sometimes as many as five a day. For 30 years, he spoke from Alaska to Carnegie Hall to spread his knowledge and to encourage others to follow his example. He was admired and sought after by politicians, statesmen, and business people. Richard B. Mellon, once head of the Aluminum Company of America, was so impressed with Miner and his work that his company donated the aluminum for the banding for free and has continued to do so since 1925.

Soon, Miner's campaign on behalf of protecting wildlife took effect. The areas around James Bay were closed to goose hunting; luring waterfowl with artificial bait was abolished; governments and conservationists met on a regular basis; game wardens were trained and were no longer political appointees. Most significantly, Miner demonstrated that humans can alter the flight patterns and affect bird populations and their habitat use.

Today the Jack Miner Sanctuary is operated by the Jack Miner Migratory Bird Foundation, a philanthropic trust that perpetuates his work. It remains on private property and is administered without government funding. There is no charge to visit the grounds, which include a museum, nature stadium, and pond area. Neither is there anything sold on the grounds. It was Jack Miner's wish that "...there be one place on earth where no money changes hands."

The best time to view and feed the birds is in the fall, during the last two weeks of October and all of November, and in the spring, during the last two weeks of March and the first week of April. In the peak season the birds are flushed daily at 4 p.m.

School groups are welcome, but by appointment only.

THE JACK MINER MIGRATORY BIRD FOUNDATION
Kingsville, Ont. N9Y 2E8

OPEN Monday to Saturday
Grounds: 8 a.m. to sundown.
Museum: 9 a.m. to 5 p.m.
CLOSED Sunday

DRIVE Highway 77 to Leamington. Turn west at the Leamington Arena on Concession 3 and follow the signs.

Best Birding

For birders Point Pelee is the best location in North America to observe the spring migration of birds; it's the Warbler Capital of North America; it's Canada's most impressive location for fall migration; and it's an area to sight many rare birds.

The southernmost tip of Canada's mainland, Point Pelee is a sandspit formation that extends 16 kilometers (10 miles)into Lake Erie. (The park itself includes the last 10 kilometers (6 miles), covering approximately 16 square kilometers (10 square miles). Although it's one of Canada's smallest national parks, it's the most diverse. More species of plants and animals are found in this area than in any other part of Canada.

Point Pelee attracts about a half a million people a year. More than half the birders come from outside Canada, especially Great Britain and the USA. Mid-May has become an unplanned birding festival with thousands of visitors arriving to welcome the spring migration. About 350 species of birds have been identified at the park, many of them rare and endangered.

In spring, birds arrive in "waves," a pattern unique to eastern North America. A "wave" occurs as a result of a warm weather front from the south or southeast, meeting a cold weather front from the north or northwest. If the two weather systems meet at ground level or the warm front overrides the cold at the birds' flight levels, the warm, rising air cools forcing the birds to land. Nocturnal, or night-time flyers may find themselves over Lake Erie at sunrise. Exhaustion and cold air force the birds to descend to rest and refuel, rather than fly the extra 32 or 48 kilometers (20 or 30 miles) across the lake.

Point Pelee has become the Warbler Capital of North America because of it's location — far enough north to receive warblers that fly only through Texas and Florida, yet far enough south to attract southern species like the hooded, Kentucky and worm-eating warblers.

Fall migration is just as spectacular although the birds' plumage is duller and their songs are reduced to the occasional call note. Fall migration is less hurried, so rare birds are more likely to be seen. It can begin as early as June and last until late December.

Pre-dawn is the time of greatest activity, when nocturnal migrants, arrive in "waves," looking for a place to rest and feed. Diurnal (day-time) migrants arrive in a different fashion. When they approach the northern shore of Lake Erie, they turn east or west, and follow the shoreline to Point Pelee. This stop- over station shortens the flight across Lake Erie and lets them begin the journey over water with maximum strength.

Many birds are not comfortable flying over water. These include blue jays, bobolinks, and diurnal species like hawks, vultures, falcons, and eagles. These birds follow the shoreline, are eventually funnelled into Point Pelee, and will fly across the base.

The best days to observe fall migration (especially during August), are slightly overcast, with high humidity and a light south wind.

The park sponsors birding programs and hikes with birding guides, and publishes monthly summaries of migratory birds that will be sited at the point.

POINT PELEE NATIONAL PARK
R.R. #1,
Leamington, Ont. N8H 3V4
TEL 519-322-2365
FAX 519-322-1277

OPEN year-round for day use from 4 a.m. to 10 p.m.
ENTRANCE FEE from April 1 to Labour Day

DRIVE Highway 401 to Interchange No. 7. Follow Highway 77 south through Staples, Blytheswood, then Leamington. Follow the Parks Service Beaver Symbol. Highway 77 becomes Erie Street. Continue on Erie Street to the intersection of Seacliff Drive (Highway 18, the 5th set of lights). Turn left at the intersection and follow the Pelee National Park signs to the park gates.

Bald Eagle Capital of North America

The national emblem of the USA, the bald eagle is a familiar image with its distinctive white head and tail feathers, dark body, and yellow curved beak and talons. Yet, although the bird is so completely identified with our southern neighbor, the Bald Eagle Capital of North America is actually the small northwestern Ontario community of Ear Falls, 100 kilometers (60 miles) north of the Trans-Canada Highway 17 on Highway 105.

The bald eagle is native only to North America. It once enjoyed a broad range of habitat that included Alaska, much of Canada, and a good portion of the United States. A decline in the population began with settlement and logging which disturbed nesting sites in tall trees near lakes and rivers where fish was their staple food. Bald eagles were greatly affected by the DDT-type pesticides of the 1950s which contaminated food supplies, resulting in the production of thin-shelled eggs. Of the eggs that did hatch, few eaglets survived.

Northwestern Ontario, a relatively uncontaminated place with less disturbance and loss of habitat, is a major nesting area for the bald eagle. Some birds stay here year-round, although the bald eagle tends to winter along the rivers from South Dakota, Iowa, and Illinois, squth to Texas and the Gulf of Mexico. They return to the nesting areas in February and March to begin nest-building activities and courtship.

Since 1959 these birds have been the subject of research and observation in northwestern Ontario. They are being banded, filmed and observed from blinds to determine their behaviour, population status, and general ecological welfare. Over 700 nests have been found in the region; at least 200 nests are active. Some birds use the existing nest every year or build a new one in the same neighborhood. The structure is hard to miss: a large tangle of sticks placed atop a tall tree or pinnacle of rock within easy flight of a river or lake. The females lay one to three eggs during the month of April and the chicks hatch in May.

The Ministry of Natural Resources appreciates hearing from anyone who sees a nest, and makes the following recommendations for those who go in search of America's national emblem.

- Nests should not be approached closely until after the second week of June. The best time to see the birds near the nests is the last half of June to mid-July.
- Chicks can die from exposure to heat or cold, so don't flush an adult from its nest.
- The best type of weather for viewing is a cool, partly cloudy day with a slight breeze. Mid-morning, after the chicks are fed, and mid-afternoon until an hour or two before sunset is prime time.
- Limit the time near the nest, when within 100 meters (325 feet), to 15 to 20 minutes, only if the bird is not bothered by your presence.
- Never call to a bird that is on the nest or near it, or make excessive noise or motion.
- Never climb the nest tree under any circumstances, for your own safety and that of the birds.
- Never attempt to handle young birds found on the ground or in water. Adults will care for a young eaglet that has fallen from the nest, on the ground. These young birds are also good swimmers and will make it to shore.

EAR FALLS EDO
P.O. Box 788,
Ear Falls, Ont. P0V 1T0
TEL 807-222-2011
FAX 807-222-2471

Owls

Most people have never seen an owl in the wild because these birds of prey are primarily nocturnal. They reside in Canada's tundra and boreal forest where a staple diet of rodents is plentiful. There are, however, 12 species of owls in Ontario, 11 of which breed in the province.

Surprisingly enough, one of the few areas in North America to view these ethereal birds is Amherst and Wolfe islands near Kingston. This is also the place where birders and naturalists gather to observe owls in unprecedented numbers and species, a phenomenon that takes place only two or three times a century.

There are several factors at work to bring this great event about. Owls are stimulated to migrate from their northern habitat at times when their prey diminishes. In Ontario, they are siphoned along the north shore of Lake Ontario to Kingston's off-shore islands, rather than cross open water. It's an area where the combination of agricultural land and woodlots provides abundant rats, voles, and mice.

The numbers and types of owls depend upon the synchronicity of low rodent populations in the north which stimulates owl migration and a surge of rodent populations in the islands, attracting and sustaining large numbers of these predators. Depending on the ratio of the two conditions, the owl population on the islands varies between a handful and dozens of the birds.

The owls usually arrive in mid-December, their numbers peaking in January and February. The dominant species is the snowy owls which wing in from above the Arctic Circle. The massive snowy is easy to observe since it poaches for food by day, an adaption to the Arctic's 24-hour daylight. It perches conspicuously on telephone poles, hay stacks, and barns. Every year the islands attract a handful but in record years there can be a hundred or more.

What owl-watchers hope for is another wintering season like that of 1978-79 when ten owl species were hosted in the area. The great grey owl, rarely seen in its northern habitat, was an even greater rarity at its migratory destination. Unusual too were sightings of the hawk owl, named for its resemblance to and mannerisms of a hawk. Nocturnal hunters, the eastern screech owl and great horned owl, were among the visitors as well as owls of smaller stature, the dove-sized boreal and the saw-whet. The short-eared owls stayed to nest and the most numerous species that season was the long-eared owl. Even a barn owl was spotted, unusual in that it was out of range of its usual habitat.

Pelicans

Pelicans are a familiar sight in California, Florida, or the Caribbean, where they fly in formation along the ocean or sit, statuesque, on fishing piers. They are common to the Prairie lake landscapes of Saskatchewan and Manitoba. But as well, they're a unique inhabitant of two small islands in Ontario's Lake of the Woods, close to the American border.

The white pelican is a striking bird, snow-white except for its jet-black primary and secondary flight feathers, and its orange feet and gular pouch. One of Ontario's "big three" nesting species it has a three-meter (ten-foot) wing span equal to that of the golden and bald eagles. It is also Ontario's longest bird, measuring more than one and a half meters (five feet) from the tip of the tail to the end of its bill. That's a greater measurement than either the tundra swan or great blue heron.

The white pelican no doubt holds the record for soaring in V-formation without flapping, their massive wings stretched to ride the thermals. This aspect of the bird's co-operative behavior identifies the flock immediately. They also flap in unison, each motion deliberate and unhurried, or they flap in succession, the rhythmic ripple of a chorus line that extends to the last bird and is followed by a group glide.

The white pelicans differ from their brown relatives in that they fish in groups to assist each other in catching their prey. When they spot a school of fish from the air, their wings fold and they plummet down quickly, making a set-wing landing, then bob their heads to scoop fish which they swallow immediately. The pouch is not used for storage. The flock stays together, often near shallow water, so they can guide the fish in front of them. Such co-operation is rare among birds.

The pelican is a recent resident in Ontario. Occasionally a handful would be seen migrating in Hamilton Bay or the north shore of Lake Erie. The first record of eight pairs of white pelicans nesting on Dream Island in Lake of the Woods was made in 1938. They were on Canada's endangered species list until 1987. Roughly 50,000 pairs now breed in Canada, the Lake of the Woods colony numbering about 4,000.

Pembroke Swallows

From late July to early August, a dramatic dance is choreographed along the horizon of the Ottawa River, at Pembroke, where the Muskrat River is a tributary. Thousands upon thousands of swallows, all six species of them, fly in to rest and to feed on their migratory route to Central and South America.

Entire legions of birds, as many as 5,000, arrive per minute. Some roll in like clouds, low to the river; others funnel down out of the sky like twisters. They travel in one direction, then suddenly break symmetry, disperse and regroup, and fly off in another direction.

As individual birds dip and dive with the speed and agility that distinguishes swallows from other birds, it's difficult to comprehend what orchestrates entire flocks of birds to move single-mindedly in intersecting directions.

In the mass of swirling birds, it's not easy to identify individual species, with the exception of the barn swallow, with its distinctive forked tail, and the purple martin, which is larger and tends to soar more. All the species are here in numbers relative to the proportions they are found in the province. The tree swallows are the most common, then the bank and barn swallows, followed by the purple martin. The cliff and rough-winged swallows are considerably rarer.

It isn't certain what brings these passerines in such great numbers to the Pembroke area; in fact it's a relatively recent phenomenon. The thickets of willows along the sandbars of the muddy Muskrat have only existed for roughly 50 years, and they seem to be the roosting place of choice. The swallows began arriving in large flocks in 1960, but only since the 1970s have the numbers been excessively large. In 1984 and 1985, the swallow count was an estimated 150,000 birds. This number dropped below 75,000 in 1986, in part due to a cold, wet spring which inhibited nesting. However, the following year the figure rose again to more than 100,000.

Swallows feed on aerial insects, zigging and zagging above the river and travelling as far inland as the city. Come dusk, they fill the air over the willow roost in vast numbers as if for the grand finale of the dance. Suddenly, as if cued, they plummet at breakneck speed, by the thousands, to the willow limbs below. It takes at least 20 minutes for the sky to completely empty and another 15 minutes before the last twitter subsides and the roost is finally quiet for the night.

As successive cold fronts pass through Pembroke, the swallows leave in the same fashion that they arrived, in waves, by the thousands. By September, the branches of the willows are completely empty.

Migrating Waterfowl

In the heart of industrial Canada is an area of some 3,200 hectares (8,000 acres) of marsh and pond, where in spring and fall, ducks, geese, and swans arrive by the thousands to rest and feed during migration. The place is Long Point National Wildlife area, on the longest, wildest, and most complex of the Great Lakes' sandspits.

Long Point, protruding from the north shore of Lake Erie, is a formation of old and new land, created by a cyclical process of wind and wave action and erosion of the sandy lakeshore by currents. The spit started at a point where a glacial moraine intersected with the lake. The Point is thought to be 6,000 years old and has advanced 32 kilometers (20 miles) in that time. Today, it's a complex but fragile habitat with beaches, sand dunes, grass, woodlands, ponds, marshes, and wet meadows. Such diversity supports a variety of flora and fauna, presently about 440 plant species, 60 of which are rare in Ontario, and five of which are the only ones found in Canada.

The property was purchased by the Long Point Company, an exclusive, private sportsmen's association, in 1866. This ended the wholesale slaughtering of birds and the general destruction of this vulnerable ecosystem. In 1979, the company, along with the US Nature Conservancy, donated the area to the people of Canada. Today it's maintained by the Canadian Wildlife Service.

In addition to dabbling ducks, like mallards, pintails, wigeons, and teals, and divers like scaups, mergansers, and buffleheads, the spit is a haven for other migratory birds. The Long Point Bird Observatory, established in 1960 by the Ontario Bird Banding Association, began a banding program that has tagged about one-quarter of a million birds, representing 240 species. Some 300 species of birds, roughly 75 percent of all the birds identified in the province, have been sighted here. Ninety-eight of the species are known to nest on the sandspit.

CANADIAN WILDLIFE SERVICE
152 Newbold Ct.,
London, Ont. N6E 1Z7
TEL 519-681-0486

LONG POINT NWA
TEL 519-586-2703

LONG POINT BIRD OBSERVATORY
P.O. Box 160,
Port Rowan, Ont. N0E IM0

Long Point is located at the southern end of Highway 59, south of Walsingham.

Parrot Farm

In Ontario, a handful of people breed parrots, those birds of colorful plumage and quick chatter associated with the tropical climates of Florida and rainforest habitats. Little is known about these breeders. Some are purposefully secretive and few are open to the public, partly because of the difficulties of breeding parrots in captivity, and partly because the importation of these birds is now more highly government-regulated, soon to be stopped altogether. Some breeders are hoarding some species of birds while others raise parrots strictly for mass markets.

On Highway 56, a short drive from the hamlet of Empire Corners, is the Parrot Farm, owned and operated by Debbie Kinloch. She runs an operation that welcomes visitors. In fact, she is the only breeder who sells parrots directly to the public.

A zoology graduate from the University of Florida, Kinloch has always had a special appreciation for birds, their welfare and the environment. She first worked with raptors before starting her parrot business on the site of her 40-hectare (100-acre) farm in 1986.

The barn has undergone extensive renovations to house her parrot paradise. With drywall and lighting, it's a nice mixture of rustic and modern. There's a showroom of cages where visitors can see a variety of exotic pets up close, and a glass room complete with playpen to view the hand-fed baby parrots.

The breeding room, which holds more species of parrots than the Metro Zoo, is visible through a doorway. Here purchasers of young parrots are seduced by the gaudy plumage amid the chatter of the adult birds — species of Amazon, cockatoo, African grey, lory, poyce-phalus, pionus, eclectus, and gonur — about 130 paired breeders in all, representing about 30 different species.

Some breeders take the eggs from the adult and hatch them like chickens, by means of modern incubation. Others allow the eggs to be hatched and the young reared by the adults. Kinloch finds fault with both methods which often result in parrots with aggressive behaviour. Many of these are the less expensive parrots found in pet stores. Kinloch allows her adults to hatch and raise their babies to the pinfeather stage so they are socialized as birds. She then raises the babies by hand, feeding them to ensure they will be tame and won't bite. This is a labour-intensive job. Hand-feeding is done two to four times a day and it is eight to twelve weeks before the birds are weaned and able to eat on their own. The results are well worth it, making for a better pet and a happier pet owner.

While potential buyers are often captivated by color alone, Kinloch likes to match people with parrots according to the needs of both parties. Some species, for example, are not suitable for families with young children.

For the most part, parrots are gregarious and monogamous. Most pair-bond with a mate for life, unlike many birds in the wild which mate only for a season. The parrot will develop a strong attachment to a human. Potential owners must realize that a pet of this kind, which can live for 30 to 50 years, will be lonely without attention. Kinloch says each parrot has a distinct personality. They are a clever species and most have the potential to mimic words and phrases.

The price of a parrot, depending upon the species, can range from $250 to $1,600. The Parrot Farm is open year-round, by appointment only. Groups are welcome to make a booking and Kinloch often gives educational talks.

PARROT FARM

R.R. #1,
Hwy. #56,
Empire Corners,
York, Ont. N0A IR0
TEL 905-772-3101

- The Carolina parakeet (Cornurus carolinensis), the only parrot indigenous to Ontario at the beginning of the last century, is now extinct.

Loring Deer Yard

Across the province of Ontario deer migrate for great distances to wintering "yards," areas where snow is neither deep nor crusted, and twigs of maple, basswood, aspen, cedar, birch, and dogwood provide a plentiful supply of food. For if deer were to remain in snow that exceeded 50 centimeters (20 inches), or snow that was even partially crusted, a negative energy balance would be created. That is, the deer would expend more energy than was obtained from their food.

The traditional deer yards of Ontario are lowland areas, those with stands of eastern hemlock, white cedar, spruce, and balsam, which hold snow off the ground.

Ontario's largest population of wintering white-tailed deer migrate to the Loring Valley deer yard, south of Lake Nipissing, between Highways 11 and 69.

It's an area of roughly 500 square kilometers (310 square miles) that centers on the villages of Loring, Arnstein, and Golden Valley and runs through six townships. Some deer remain in the yard year-round, but for the most part they arrive as snow begins to accumulate. Depending upon the winter, that can be as early as November or as late as January. They stay between 3 and 4 months, in numbers upwards of 15,000.

The conditions at Loring provide the ideal wintering habitat. It's an area of rolling pastureland, both cultivated and inactive. Stands of balsam, spruce, and tamarack dot the low lying areas, with outcroppings of maple and birch on the hills. The area's southern exposure makes winters less severe.

Deer have been coming to Loring since the late 1800s. It was logging and settlement of the valley that helped create the ideal setting. Habitat management of the yard began in the 1960s. Today feeding hoppers are placed at strategic locations to further assist the deer with supplemental oats and corn. The majority of the land is privately owned so management of the area is a co-operative effort.

LORING DEER YARD

DRIVE Highway 11 to the Trout Creek turn-off. Go left onto Highway 522 to the village of Commanda. Half way between Commanda and the village of Loring, the deer yard begins.

Chapleau Game Preserve and Wildlife Sanctuary

The world's largest game preserve and wildlife sanctuary isn't in Africa, but in Ontario! The Chapleau Game Preserve in northern Ontario encompasses 700,000 hectares (nearly 2 million acres) of land, where the only shooting is done with a camera.

The Ontario government created the preserve in 1925, placing a ban on all hunting and trapping. Even a sling shot is illegal here. As a result, the wildlife populations are considerable and migrate out to replenish areas where hunting and trapping is allowed.

The opportunities for viewing and photographing wildlife, indigenous to the boreal forest region, are exceptional. This is home to furbearing beaver, fisher, fox, lynx, marten, mink, muskrat, otter, and timber wolf. The preserve supports between eight and ten wolf packs. There is a black bear population of roughly 2,000, and approximately 2,500 moose. Elk introduced to the property in 1933 also abound. Wildlife viewing stations situated where the animals are known to congregate, provide shelter and information for the viewers.

Sensitive areas identified in the preserve are the locations of heronries, osprey and eagle nests, waterfowl staging areas, and cold-water fisheries. They are accessible mainly by canoe and on foot, in wilderness where forestry and mining operations can't disturb them.

The Chapleau Game Preserve has a well-preserved historical past from prehistoric pictographs, to Brunswick House, a fur trading post which closed in 1917. Nomadic Ojibwa and Cree, who migrated to the area to hunt and fish, left behind encampment sites and artifacts. The preserve is part of the Canadian Shield, shaped by four ice ages with precambrian rock formations of moraines, kettles, kames, and eskers.

The area offers diverse activities for outdoor recreationalists. Missinaibi Provincial Park has more than 55 camp sites. The preserve is part of a provincial waterway park and several canoe routes. This exceptional fishing area has walleye, northern pike, lake trout, speckled trout, rainbow trout, splake, yellow perch, lake whitefish, and small-mouth bass.

The Chapleau Game Preserve is composed primarily of public land, although there are a handful of private outfitters within the preserve. It is accessible by gravel road, rail, canoe, and plane.

CHAPLEAU GAME PRESERVE

Ministry of Natural Resources
190 Cherry St.,
Chapleau, Ont. P0M IK0
TEL 705-864-1710

LOCATION: The southern tip of the preserve begins at the junction of provincial highways 129 and 101, at the town of Chapleau.

Tyvek Topography

It doubles as a rain hat in a sudden downpour, makes a great table or ground cover for a picnic, and if it gets dirty, you can throw it in with the family wash, then cover it with a towel and iron it, and it's as good as new.

What is this wonderful product that has outdoor enthusiasts and pilots so excited? It's the new series of topographical maps and aeronautical charts printed on Tyvek. Tyvek is a very strong, lightweight, microporous material developed by the Du Pont Company. It looks like paper but feels softer to the touch; yet, it won't rip or tear. It is an alternative material to paper, film, and textiles. It is even used in construction as an insulating material.

The benefit of using Tyvek for maps and charts is longevity. Regardless of wind, rain, snow, or the number of times it is folded, a Tyvek map will survive years of boating, hunting, hiking, fishing, and snowmobiling. Pilots welcome charts that won't rip along the fold line with repeated use and that can sustain cockpit coffee spills. Environmentalists embrace the new product since no trees are cut down to produce new maps and it is recyclable.

Energy, Mines and Resources Canada in Ottawa found a way to print on both sides of Tyvek with standard paper inks. This made the use of the product feasible from a cost point of view. The prototype for the project was the mapping of Algonquin Park.

Maps are usually revised every three to five years; between 200 and 300 revisions are done annually. Photography of an area which precedes the map-making process can only be done in "leaf free" conditions during the spring and fall. Most of the mapping of southern Ontario will be completed within two years.

Tyvek maps come in several scales. The 1:50,000 is ideal for recreational uses from cycling to canoeing, and is also the most popular with government and industry. These maps cover about 1,000 square kilometers (450 square miles); 3 centimeters (1 1/4") is equal to 1.6 kilometers (a mile).

They depict details of hills, valleys, lakes, rivers, streams, trails, and portage areas, as well as major, secondary, and side roads, and man-made features like dams and power lines.

The 1:250,000 scale, considered a reconnaissance-type map, covers a larger area — 11,037 square kilometers (6860 square miles); 2.54 centimeters is equal to 6.4 kilometers (1" is equal to 4 miles). This map is also excellent for road use.

Tyvek maps may be obtained through local dealers listed in the Yellow Pages under "maps and charts." A list of dealers in your area may be obtained from the Canada Map Office and orders may be placed through them.

CANADA MAP OFFICE

130 Bentley Ave.,
Nepean, Ont. K1A 0E9
TEL 613-952-7000
800-465-MAPS

ENERGY, MINES AND RESOURCES CANADA

Products & Services Division,
615 Booth St.,
Ottawa, Ont. K1A 0E9
TEL 613-943-8502
FAX 613-995-6001

Wasaga Beach

Wasaga Beach is the world's longest freshwater beach. This sweeping, 14 kilometer (9 mile) stretch of golden sand along the southern shore of Georgian Bay has been a swimmer's and sunbather's paradise since the early 1900s. On one occasion in 1943 its firm sand served as an airstrip for the first flight by James Ayling and Leonard Reid from mainland Canada to England.

The U-shaped or parabolic sand dunes near the beach are the only ones like them in Ontario. They were created by the receding of glacial Lake Algonquin. The dunes provide an interesting backdrop to hiking, nature study, and bird watching.

Today, this popular beach is a provincial park, divided into eight beach areas that have a range of activities for everyone. The farther west one heads on the beach, the quieter and less crowded it gets.

The shallow, sparkling waters provide safe swimming in summer. Picnicking and barbecuing facilities are situated in each of the designated beach areas.

Docks and launching ramps provide access for motor boats, sail boats, windsurfers, and canoes. Fishing enthusiasts will catch rainbow trout, smallmouth bass, splake, and pickerel at the mouth of the Nottawasaga River and in Nottawasaga Bay, and can compete in fishing derbies in April and October.

Marked bicycle paths follow the shoreline and the Blueberry Plains Trails offer 26 kilometers (16 miles) of marked hiking trails of varying lengths and degrees of difficulty. In winter they are utilized as cross-country ski trails. Courts for volleyball, and tennis and a soccer field are situated in Beach Areas 1 and 2.

In the winter months, a very active Wasaga Beach Snowmobile Club maintains more than 128 kilometers (80 miles) of groomed trails. Competitions are held at the Winterfest celebrations.

WASAGA BEACH PROVINCIAL PARK
P.O. Box 183,
Wasaga Beach, Ont. L0L 2P0
TEL 705-429-2516

WASAGA BEACH CHAMBER OF COMMERCE
35 Dunkerron St.,
P.O. Box 10,
Wasaga Beach, Ont. L0L 2P0
TEL 705-429-2247

Sauble Beach

While Sauble Beach may not be the longest beach in Ontario, it has the best sand — 10 kilometers (6 miles) of clean, white sand. Located on the southeast shore of Lake Huron, Sauble Beach has been called the "Daytona of Canada." Some say it rivals the best beaches in Florida and the Caribbean, for both sand and sunsets.

The sand is kept soft, dry, and free-flowing by its high silicon content. It can even be used to dry flowers! The beach width averages 76 meters (250 feet) from the waters' edge to sand dunes which separate the area from the roadway. It is kept free of cars and vendors but is busy with activities like volleyball, picnicking, and water sports. The shallow, stone-free waters make it ideal for family swimming.

Sauble Beach was first known to Native people and later French explorers, who journeyed down the Sauble River (located at the most northerly end of the beach). The French, impressed with the white sand, named the river "La Riviere au Sable," meaning the river to the sand. The name was corrupted to its present form after 1881. In the early days, the area was well-known for fishing, even of a commercial variety.

Today, anglers will catch smallmouth bass, jumbo perch, rainbow trout and chinook salmon in the area. The boardwalk at Sauble Falls is one of the best places to view the spring and fall run of rainbow trout and chinook salmon.

Sauble Beach is an all-seasons vacation spot. Groomed and marked trails exist for hikers, snowmobilers, and cross-country skiers.

SAUBLE BEACH CHAMBER OF COMMERCE
General Delivery,
Sauble Beach, Ont. N0H 2G0
TEL 519-422-1262

ONTARIO TRIVIA

THUNDER BAY is Canada's western terminus for ocean-going freighters of the St. Lawrence Seaway. It is Canada's third largest port and is the largest grain-handling port in the world.

THUNDER BAY ART GALLERY is the only public gallery in Canada devoted to aboriginal art. It houses one of the largest permanent collections of two- and three-dimensional work by Canada's premier Native artists. It has achieved national and international recognition, and has taken a leadership role in the field of Native art.

THUNDER BAY'S Lakehead University is the first Canadian university to receive a humanities award from the Rockefeller Foundation for the study of Native philosophy. Lakehead has the largest Native population at an Ontario university.

THUNDER BAY is where Terry Fox ended his Marathon of Hope. Having lost one leg to cancer, this courageous Canadian ran halfway across the country to raise money for cancer research. He died on June 28, 1981.
East of the city on Highway 11/17 near the spot where he ended his marathon and overlooking the "Sleeping Giant" is a memorial to Terry Fox. The larger than life statue is made of bronze with a foundation of local amethyst on a 45-ton granite base.

Backus Woods

The best remaining example of a Carolinian forest in Canada is known as the Backus Woods, 260 hectares (640 acres) in the heart of the southern deciduous forest region, not far from the base of Long Point. This is one of the largest forest tracts in southwestern Ontario and is the most densely forested part of the Carolinian zone.

The area is also known as the "Banana Belt," indicative of the relatively warm climate on the north shore of Lake Erie, the shallowest and therefore warmest of the Great Lakes. Erie's influence tempers the climate year-round and as a result, many "southern" species of flora and fauna survive here, some of which are at the northern limit of their range, making their presence significant both provincially and nationally.

At first glance, the Carolinian forest resembles a typical hardwood forest of central Ontario — sugar maple, beech, yellow birch, red maple, and red oak. A trained eye, however, will spot what makes Backus special: the presence of tulip trees, black gum, sweet chestnut, and swamp white oak. Species like white pine, yellow birch and hemlock which are familiar in the Great Lakes–St. Lawrence Forest Region provide a northern influence in the woods.

Both northern and southern species of wildlife co-exist in Backus Woods, including at least 80 species of birds. Northerners like hooded merganser, yellow-bellied sapsucker, and winter wren mingle with southerners like vireo, Louisiana waterthrush, and orchard oriole. The presence of numerous tree hollows attract many cavity-nesting birds like the wood duck, barred owl, and prothonotary warbler.

The small-mammal community is just as interesting with species like the woodland mole and southern flying squirrel. There are six species of bat including the rare eastern pipistrelle and 23 varieties of herptiles (amphibians and reptiles). The 543 plant species here represent 21.3 percent of Ontario's entire floral spectrum.

There are a number of trails of varying lengths, between 3 and 6 kilometers (1.8 and 4 miles). The woods is divided into a northern and southern section by a sand road (Concession 4). Species differ to the north and south of the road.

BACKUS WOODS

Long Point Region Conservation Authority,
R.R. #3,
Simcoe, Ont. N3Y 4K2
TEL 519-428-4623

DRIVE south of Walsingham to Highway 24. Drive east on Highway 24 and watch for signs. Parking available at the beginning of the trails.

Slowest-Growing Trees in the World

Tallest Tree

The oldest forest east of the Rockies is the Old Growth Cedar Forest of the Niagara Escarpment. The eastern white cedar (*Thuja Occidentalis*) are found on the islands of Fathom Five National Marine Park and the Bruce Peninsula National Park, both of which make up Canada's sixth Biosphere Reserve as designated by UNESCO.

These cedars have the slowest growth rate of any plant in the world due to the cooler climate and maritime influence of Georgian Bay. It takes much longer for the trees to reach their upper size limit and those that do reach full size are broken off by winds and ice storms. It's not fully understood why the trunks of these dead cedars don't rot. Some have been dated at 3,400 BC.

The Kirkwood Forest, north of Thessalon, is the home of Ontario's tallest tree: a 350-year-old giant white pine that stands a breathtaking 49.4 meters (162 feet) high. The first branch on the trunk is 24 meters (80 feet) from the ground and at chest height; the trunk diameter is 1.4 meters (4.6 feet). The tree contains enough wood to build a three-bedroom house.

DRIVE to Thessalon on Highway 17. Go north on Highway 129, about 3 kilometers (1.8 miles) and veer left to Little Rapids. The giant white pine is just north of Little Rapids.

PARK TRIVIA

NATIONAL PARKS

- Canada has 35 national parks, 5 of which are in Ontario. They are The Bruce Peninsula National Park, The Georgian Bay Islands National Park, Point Pelee National Park, Pukaskwa National Park, and St. Lawrence Islands National Park. Ontario also has one National Marine Park, Fathom Five.
- Point Pelee National Park is the most southerly of all Canada's national parks.
- The St. Lawrence National Park is Canada's smallest national park, the first to be created east of the Rockies, and the country's fifth oldest park.

PROVINCIAL PARKS

- Ontario has 260 provincial parks covering 6.4 million hectares (15.8 million acres), about 6 percent of the province's land and water base.
- Ontario provincial parks are organized into six categories that delineate their use and how they will be managed. These are nature reserve parks (82), wilderness parks (8), natural environment parks (64), historical parks (4), waterway parks (29), and recreation parks (73).
- Algonquin Provincial Park is Ontario's oldest provincial park.

Algonquin Park

Algonquin Park, Ontario's first and most famous park, celebrated its centenary in 1993. In the hearts and minds of Ontarians, it's one of the best-loved institutions in the province.

The name alone conjures up a wealth of images for every generation of visitors that embraces the vast richness of this natural legacy. This is the place where on a single day in spring, a skilled birder can differentiate the sights and sounds of more than 100 feathered species. Paddlers, canoeing the same waters where Indians harpooned fish as early as 3,000 BC, pause to hear the cry of the loon, a member of the most primitive family of birds in North America. A family, huddled around a campfire beneath a starry, August sky might hear the mournful howl of the wolves.

This is nature at its very best in southern Ontario, a three-hour drive north of Canada's most densely populated region. Nearly three-quarters of a million people visit Algonquin each year to escape the rigours of city life. While the corridor of Highway 60, which runs for 56 kilometers (35 miles) across the southwest corner of the park, has been developed for tourists who prefer the comforts of modern amenities such as campgrounds, picnic sites, self-guided walking trails, and nature programs, the park's interior offers a close encounter with nature for backpackers and canoeists, away from the crowd.

Algonquin is situated on the highest height of land in the province between Georgian Bay and the Ottawa River. Stretching 7,600 square kilometers (2,934 square miles), it is one of the largest parks in Canada. Its west side is noticeably higher than the surrounding areas. Hills around Highway 60 are more than 500 meters (1,630 feet) above sea level, and provide scenic panoramas of the area. In the east, the land dips to 200 meters (652 feet). On the edge of the Canadian Shield, the underlying rocks of metamorphic gneisses and granites are extremely hard, formed some 1.05 billion years ago as part of a mountain-building process. Soil deposits are the result of the last glacier, 10,000 years ago. Algonquin is the transition zone between the northern coniferous and southern deciduous forests, where pine, spruce, hemlock, fir, cedar and tamarack meet stands of sugar maple, yellow birch, American beech and oak. This accounts for the diverse nature of flora and fauna within its boundaries and the need to preserve what hasn't yet been disturbed.

This is a park for all seasons, but prime time is summer. The blackflies are over at the beginning of July and the mosquitoes are gone by the end of the month. Its 2,000 lakes are busy with swimmers, those fishing for smallmouth bass, paddlers crisscrossing 1,500 kilometers (932 miles) of canoe routes, and backpackers traversing one of the thirteen self-guided trails or the more rugged loops into back-country where raspberries and later blueberries come into season.

Spring is the best time to see the carpet of wildflowers on the forest floor, before the buds on the trees come to life and rob them of necessary light. The chorus of mating birds by day (in the range of 246 species) and courting frogs by night is music to the naturalist's ear. May and June also afford the best time to catch a glimpse of the moose, North America's largest land animal. Those who love fishing migrate to the park for some of the country's best trout fishing. More than 230 lakes have native brook trout and 149 have lake trout. Other cold-water fish like burbot and whitefish are also to be found.

In fall, when the crowds are gone, Algonquin is robed in the bold colors of a Tom Thomson canvas which many at first believed were too vivid to be true. Anyone who has witnessed Algonquin's horizon in September and October, entire shorelines ablaze with crimson, orange, yellow, and gold, knows Thompson didn't have to exaggerate. The fall is also one of the most exhilarating times to hike and canoe.

In winter there's a silence and majesty in the frozen white expanse of the park. This is snowshoe country. More than 80 kilometers (50 miles) of groomed trails take cross-country skiers past animal tracks of deer, marten, otter, fox, and wolves, past beaver dams that number in the thousands, amidst the barrel rolls of the raven, and the quick flight of the boreal chickadee.

Algonquin Park is perfect for day visits as well as those who plan a vacation-length stay. There are many access points to the park so it's best to consult a map for the route most convenient for you.

The new Visitor Centre is located at kilometer 43, just east of the Spruce Bog Boardwalk. It succeeds the old Park Museum at kilometer 20 and is nearly ten times larger with 2,600 square meters (25,000 square feet) of space. Three exhibit areas familiarize visitors with the park's topography, the natural history of its five major natural habitats, and the role of people in the park from the days of Native peoples to the present.

The Friends of Algonquin Park was established in 1983 as a non-profit organization. Membership is now close to 2,000 people. The Friends undertake various projects to enhance the interpretive and educational facilities of the park.

ALGONQUIN PROVINCIAL PARK
P.O. Box 219,
Whitney, Ont. K0J 2M0
TEL 705-633-5572 (Information)
TEL 705-633-5538/5725 (Reservations)

THE FRIENDS OF ALGONQUIN PARK
Box 248,
Whitney, Ont. K0J 2M0

Algonquin Daytrippers

For those who fall short in the skills of the great outdoors but have the desire to add Algonquin Park to their personal "to do" list, there is a new service that will initiate the most timid of "wannabe" naturalists. Algonquin Daytrippers takes visitors to the park in the comfort of an air-conditioned bus or van, under the professional tutelage of a nature specialist. This service is ideal for anyone who wants a memorable experience, but is especially designed for first-time adventurers, those wanting to see the park from an "insider's" point of view, and those who don't drive or have access to transportation.

Daytrippers was started by Susan Purves of Baysville. She has worked on contract for the Ministry of Natural Resources since 1979 in programs that included a moose study in Algonquin Park; Crown Land and environmental management positions; and interpretive and teaching jobs in nature settings. The uncertainty of contract work prompted her to start her own business in her particular area of expertise; interpreting nature also happens to be the work that gives her the most satisfaction. She brings 14 years of experience to the position and an attitude that charms repeat customers.

While anyone can drive through the park and see wildlife, Purves and her three naturalist cohorts make it an adventure that's fun and informative. When a moose raises its head from a beaver pond you'll learn that the first time he grew his massive rack of antlers he probably bawled like a baby. It's a painful experience, comparable to a baby cutting teeth. Purves can summon the birds from the trees, make wolves respond to her howl, and spot a maternity ward for bugs in a bog. Customers from Singapore to Saudi Arabia, Holland to Italy, and the USA come away with a whole new feeling and appreciation for Ontario's oldest park, as well as for nature in general.

A typical full-day trip features a nature walk, a tour of the spectacular new Visitor Centre, and introduction to the Logging Museum. Half-day trips tour the Franklin MacDougall Parkway as far as kilometer 47 with a stop at the Visitor Centre.

Algonquin Daytrippers offer full- and half-day trips from Bracebridge and Huntsville. Outings can be tailored to special needs or interests of a group, including French language services. The schedule runs from the end of May to the Canadian Thanksgiving.

ALGONQUIN DAYTRIPPERS
Kelly Rd.,
Baysville, Ont. P0B 1A0
TEL 705-767-3263

Petroglyphs

One of Canada's most intriguing archaeological treasures is located at the Petroglyphs Provincial Park, 55 kilometers (34 miles) northeast of Peterborough. On a flat, 21-meter (68-foot) expanse of bedrock, typical of the southernmost portion of the Canadian Shield, are more than 900 carvings of symbolic shapes and figures. Archaeologists and anthropologists believe these Petroglyphs (petro = rock; glyph = carvings) were likely the work of Algonkian-speaking Aboriginal peoples who lived between 500 and 1,000 years ago. This is the largest single concentration of Native carvings in Canada.

The "teaching rock" as it is known, is revered as a sacred place by members of the Ojibwa Anishinabe Nation. They call it *Kinomagewapkon*, which means "the rocks that teach." They believe the shapes and figures had deep spiritual meaning for those who carved them, and that there are messages here for all nations and people to experience.

The Petroglyphs were discovered in May 1954, in a somewhat hidden, forested area of red and white pine, interspersed with pockets of spruce and mixed hardwood forest, far from any settlement or road at the time. The area surrounding the teaching rock was established as a provincial park in 1976. In 1984, a special building designed with a walkway and glassed light source was built to prevent erosion and deterioration of the drawings while allowing visitors a close view.

The walk from the parking lot to the Petroglyph site is roughly 1 kilometer (.6 of a mile). The park is open for day use only. There are marked hiking trails in the outlying forest, wetlands, and rocky outcrops. The longest trail, 6.5 kilometers (4 miles), past Minnow Lake to High Falls on Eels Creek, takes about 4 hours to complete. There are several picnic sites at the entrance to the park and on both sides of McGinnis Lake.

FRIENDS OF THE TEACHING ROCK
P.O. Box 900,
Woodview, Ont. K0L 3E0

PETROGLYPHS PROVINCIAL PARK
Ministry of Natural Resources,
P.O. Box 500,
Bancroft, Ont. K0L IC0
TEL 613-332-3940
705-877-2552 (Park Office)

Pukaskwa National Park

The park brochure for Pukaskwa (pronounced puck-a-saw) is full of cautionary notes and lists of hazards: warnings about the chilling waters of Lake Superior; the changeability and extremes of weather conditions; the physical challenge of the trails and canoe routes; the presence of black flies, mosquitoes, and black bears throughout the season; and the mandatory, visitor self-registration program. Still people are irresistibly drawn to the park. One reason is that the north shore of Lake Superior is the only remaining coastline of the Great Lakes that is truly wild. In 1983, Pukaskwa National Park was established to preserve a portion of this dramatic coastline, plus 1,878 square kilometers (1,166 square miles) of adjacent Canadian Shield and boreal hinterland.

Any consideration of Pukaskwa, an Ojibway word meaning "something evil," usually begins with Lake Superior and the words of the Reverend George Grant. "Superior is a sea. It breeds storms and rain and fog like the sea....It is wild, masterful and dreaded" (1872).

His words are as applicable today as they were in 1872, and should be taken to heart. Superior has a continental effect on the climate. That means winters are warmer but summers are cooler. The weather along the coast is remarkably unpredictable. Even in summer, sunny skies can cloud over quickly and temperatures plummet. Fog, sudden storms and extended periods of wet, cold weather are common. Hikers prepare a variety of clothing and footwear. Paddlers who venture along Superior's coastline know that even in summer, the waters are frigid. Safety on the lake is often measured by one's distance to shore and knowing areas where the boulder beaches don't inhibit landing. Roughly 11 percent of the park's shoreline is raised, cobblestone beach, 11 percent is sand, and 1 percent is cliff. The remaining 77 percent is rock outcrops.

The dynamic terrain is the legacy of the three-billion-year shaping of the Canadian Shield. The faults, dykes, and floes of rock in the northwest corner of the park near Hattie Cove (the site of the Registration Centre and campgrounds) is the work of age-old volcanic eruptions that have left colors, patterns, and textures etched in the stone. The granites and basalts of the Shield provide an obstinate, rugged contour of broken ridges, cliffs, and rock-rimmed lakes, land buried and exhumed by the advancing and retreating of glaciers.

Remnants of the last ice age exist in the form of Arctic alpine plants, encouraged to survive by the harsh conditions of Lake Superior. Typical of Arctic flora, these plants are small and low to the ground, with small clustered leaves, but have flower heads on high stalks to attract insects for pollination. Bird's-eye primrose, butterwort, encrusted saxifrage, and Alpine bilberry are some of a dozen misplaced species, referred to as relic or disjunct populations. They can be spotted in the coastal areas, but not far inland.

The forests of Pukaskawa are white, cold and silent for five months of the year, accessible only by snowshoe and difficult for cross-country skiing on any but the 6 kilometers (4 miles) of groomed trails.

In summer the coniferous forest, interlaced with stands of birch and popular, are redolent with the thick fragrant earth smells of mosses, lichens, and liverworts.

There are trails into the backcountry, but the main attraction is the Coastal Hiking Trail that winds its way from Hattie Cove, south along the Superior coast for 60 kilometers (37 miles) to North Swallow River. This is an arduous jaunt only to be undertaken with plenty of time, planning, and proper equipment.

The Pukaskwa coastline a 160-kilometer (100-mile) route between Hattie Cove and Michipicoten Harbour as well as the White and Pukaskwa rivers, are a challenge for experienced canoeists and kayakers. The White can be run any time during the ice-free season, but the Pukaskwa is only navigable when the water is high, during spring runoff.

The half-dozen rivers of the park supply a descent catch of trout, speckled trout, yellow pickerel, pike, and rainbow trout.

The animal populations are typically boreal — moose, snowshoe hares, fishers, red fox, mice, and moles. There's also a small band of caribou, numbering no more than 40, the most southerly herd of caribou in Canada.

Anthropology buffs will be fascinated by the Pukaskwa Pits, remnants of an ancient Aboriginal culture. Pits of various depths and sizes, lined with rocks to form a solid structure, have been the subject of speculation by archaeologists since the late 1950s. The use or significance of the pits remains uncertain. These man-made mysteries dot most of the park's cobblestone beach sites and are believed to date back to 4,000 BC.

PUKASKWA NATIONAL PARK

Hwy. 627,
Hattie Cove,
Heron Bay, Ont. P0T IR0
TEL 807-229-0801

ONTARIO TRIVIA

THUNDER BAY has the world's largest, established community of Finnish-speaking people living outside of Finland.

THUNDER BAY is the sports capital of Canada. Here are just some of the reasons why it is the best place to play:

*150 parks

*Canada Games Complex, built for the 1981 Canada Summer Games, with one of North America's largest swimming pools (77 meters long by 21 meters wide (251 feet by 68 feet)), a diving tower, an indoor running track, fitness training facility, etc., all under one roof.

*site of the 1995 Nordic World Ski Championships

*base of the National Team skiers

*Big Thunder is the location of the world's largest ski jump and luge facilities

*Loch Lomond ski area has the highest vertical slope between the Laurentians and the Rocky Mountains

*home of Northwestern Ontario's Sports Hall of Fame

St. Lawrence Islands National Park

Made up of twenty-one island areas along an 80-kilometer (50-mile) stretch of the St. Lawrence River (part of the Thousand Islands), the St. Lawrence Islands National Park is Ontario's oldest national park. It was given official status as a park site in 1904, but had been protected since 1874 when the federal government realized that the islands were being stripped bare of timber and that the Canadian side of the St. Lawrence River might soon be built up with villas, the way the American side had been. Although this is also Canada's smallest national park, it is one of the most interesting from an historical and cultural perspective.

The islands and adjacent mainland are composed mainly of billion-year-old Precambrian rock, shaped by the last ice age some 10,000 years ago. Over time, the barren rock developed lichens, soil, mosses, grasses, shrubs, and eventually forests. Many peoples, from nomads as early as 7,000 years ago to the Iroquois, and later the United Empire Loyalists were attracted to it. From the waters they pulled salmon, sturgeon, and eels. The lands were rich with berries, grapes, acorns, deer, and migrating birds. It was known as *Manitouana*, "Garden of the Great Spirit."

Since 1978, organized archaeological digs have identified artifacts at 44 sites. The period of greatest activity here was between 700 BC (about the time Rome was founded) and AD 1600. Most of the material found was from the Point Peninsula culture, active between AD 500 and 1500. The area was also used by the Laurentian Archaic people, the first people here to use a bow and arrow, and the Woodland people, who made great use of pottery. There's also evidence of the St. Lawrence Iroquois, the first Natives to practice agriculture and live in long houses. The Loyalists farmed and trapped here, and built hotels and even a school.

Today very few of the original buildings exist, but the islands continue to be a microclimate with a remarkable variety of flora and fauna. A short walk across an island encompasses a changing landscape from a northern coniferous forest to a southern hardwood forest.

Among the rarities is the pitch pine, the park's symbol, one of Canada's rarest trees. These scraggly, contorted conifers standing on the edge of granite in dry, open, exposed areas add dramatic beauty to the landscape. The pine cones on the branches are old and the needles may come right out of the trunk — the only eastern pine with this characteristic.

Here in the park and in the Rideau Lakes area, the pitch pine is at its northern limits. It grows here due to the relatively mild climate and acid soil. Although some of the trees are over 200 years old, many seeds fail to take root. More are dying off than are being replaced despite efforts by the park conservationists.

Pitch pines were used by the pioneers for charcoal, tar, turpentine and pitch. Because its wood doesn't decay, Pitch pine made excellent floors for barns (some still in existence 150 years later), and were used to make mine shafts, dock supports, ships' pumps, and water wheels.

Among the more unusual fauna are the Blanding turtle and the black rat snake. The Blanding is a fresh water turtle, immediately recognizable with its black and yellow coloring. A protected species in Ontario, it is considered threatened and endangered in areas of the USA. These turtles are large, averaging around 268 millimeters (10 inches). They are unusual in that they can swallow with their heads above water. The Blanding lives to an average age of 25 to 27 years.

The black rat snake is Canada's largest snake. It grows up to 2.5 meters (8 feet) in length. Despite its size, the black rat is non-poisonous and harmless. It is classified in Canada as a rare species and is found only in the Rideau Lakes and Thousand Island Area, and a few places along Lake Erie. The park carries out an on-going mark and recapture study program in an effort to learn more about this specie's habitat. The chances of actually seeing a black rat snake are as rare as the species itself since they do not frequent the shoreline areas. Besides being large, the black rat snake is shiny black in color with a faint gold pattern on top and cream-colored under-scales.

The islands are accessible mainly by water taxis. For 200 years a vintage tour boat has travelled from Mallorytown Landing to Grenadier Island. There are plenty of camping grounds on the islands, picnicking, and swimming sites and organized nature trails and programs with park interpreters.

ST. LAWRENCE ISLANDS NATIONAL PARK
R.R. #3,
Box 469,
Mallorytown Landing, Ont. K0E IR0
TEL 613-923-5261
FAX 613-923-2229

ONTARIO TRIVIA

TOBERMORY'S M.S. Chi Cheemaun (meaning The Big Canoe) is the largest and most modern ship ever built for ferry service on the Great Lakes. It traverses between Tobermory and Manitoulin Island in two hours. The ferry holds 115 cars and 600 passengers; 230 people can be seated in its cafeteria. It operates from early May to October.

TORONTO'S Harbour is Canada's largest inland port.

TORONTO'S Royal Ontario Museum (ROM) is Canada's largest public museum.

TORONTO'S Art Gallery of Ontario houses the world's largest public collection of Henry Moore's work. His sculpture of the Archer graces the front of City Hall.

TORONTO'S Canadian National Exhibition is the oldest and largest agricultural fair in the world.

Perfect Paddling

WHITE SQUALL

The 30 Thousand Islands along the northeast coast of Georgian Bay rank among the finest paddling areas in Canada, encompassing an entire range of water conditions from the wild, sea-like, open waters of Georgian Bay, to the calm, protected shorelines that power boats cannot reach.

Island hopping provides a number of fascinating landscapes to explore and interpret. Among them are the lonely, outer Limestones; the McCoy and Mink Islands with their gull, heron and tern populations; and the smooth, granite Fox islands dotted with pines and cranberry bogs. Some of the routes follow the paths of the fur trade.

Among the best interpreters of the 30 Thousand Islands are Kathy and Tim Dyer of White Squall. Both teachers, they realized they wanted an outdoor career, saved enough money to purchase a small piece of property on Cole Lake, a 15-minute drive north of Parry Sound, and began a paddling center and wilderness retail shop, specializing in the sport of sea kayaking.

In the early years, before their venture made any money, Kathy, a geography major, and Tim, an environmental studies graduate, continued to teach, recruiting family and friends to help launch the business. Now in its ninth year of operation, White Squall is a full-time occupation for the Dyers and employs ten other people in the paddling season. It has become Ontario's largest company offering sea kayaking trips.

The sea kayak differs from the white-water kayak which is built to turn on a dime and dance across rapids. The sea kayak has a V-shaped hull and a longer, sleeker body. It's a sturdy, stable boat, designed for touring and cutting through any kind of water. It's a surprisingly "user friendly" craft that, with proper instruction, can easily be used by the most novice paddlers.

Sea kayaking is both relaxing and physically challenging. Over a distance, the rhythmic paddle-stroke produces a lulling effect on the paddler who sits snug in the molded seat of the cockpit, just an inch from the bottom of the boat, at the level of the water. At the same time, a proper stroke works the entire body, starting with the balls of the feet, pressed against the foot rests. The knees are taut against the shell, frog-style. The abdominal muscles, the back, and the entire body, as well as the arms, work together to propel the paddle. It feels as if you're wearing the kayak.

White Squall offers day and multi-day trips that explore Georgian Bay's 30 Thousand Islands. The programs are designed for every level and age of paddler and attract about 400 people annually, ranging in age from 12 to 75.

A typical day trip for the beginner or novice paddler begins with morning instruction at the White Squall headquarters on Cole Lake. Paddlers spend several hours learning the ins-and-outs, literally, of the boat, including wet exits. They are instructed in paddling strokes and bracing as well as the proper selection of gear. After the orientation, the White Squall van transports paddlers, boats and equipment to a destination on Georgian Bay.

The eight-hour day provides plenty of opportunity for swimming, exploring, photography, and relaxation, and includes a nutritious shore lunch. There are two qualified staff professionals adept at all paddling skills and water safety with each group of eight paddlers.

The White Squall paddling season runs from May to October. Programs range from one to six-day trips, a paddling distance range of between 8 and 85 kilometers (5 and 50 miles). There is also a Youth Leadership Program aimed at 14- to 17-year-olds, and a one-day Kayak Symposium with seminars and on-water clinics in all aspects of paddling, navigation, water rescue, and ecology.

White Squall is organized, safety-conscious, and ecology-wise. They supply all the necessary equipment, including 2-person, free standing tents, food, maps and marine charts, and a resource library. The staff is willing to accommodate individual requests when possible.

The Wilderness Shop sells canoes and kayaks that can be test-driven off the dock. They stock interesting and often-hard-to-find camping and paddling equipment and provide rental, repair, and shuttle services.

WHITE SQUALL

R.R. #1,
Nobel, Ont. P0G IG0
TEL 705-342-5324

OPEN May to October 9-5:30 daily
9-8:00 Fridays
November to April, by chance or call

DRIVE north of Parry Sound on Highway 69 to Highway 559 west. Go west, about 3 kilometers (1.8 miles) to East Carling Bay Road and turn south about 1.5 kilometers (1 mile).

PUKASKWA NATIONAL PARK

Experienced paddlers are challenged by the spring running of the Pukaskwa River in this national park on the north shore of Lake Superior. A trip begun too soon in May can trap a paddler in craft-crushing rapids that can't be run, too late in June and the river's low flow exposes the boulders of its bedrock.

A nine-day, wilderness sojourn will take the Pukaskwa paddler from the Trans-Canada Highway to Lake Superior, a distance of more than 80 kilometers (50 miles) with 3 kilometers (2 miles) of portages. From the headwaters at Gibson Lake to the river mouth on Superior, the drop is 260 meters (848 feet) through eddies, rapids and pools, replete with trout.

The White River begins 185 km (115 miles) from Superior at Negwazu Lake, just north of Obatanga Provincial Park and can be run any time during the ice-free season. It drops 233 meters (765 feet) through 68 rapids and waterfalls. The frothing waters of the White cut through a gorge roughly 45 meters (150 feet) deep and 21 meters (70 feet) wide, spanned by a narrow, swinging suspension bridge, reminiscent of something out of a Tarzan movie.

Lower reaches of the White are remote and the waters if not bypassed by the portages can be treacherous — people have died on this river. The final leg of the trip, entailing a 6-kilometer (4-mile) paddle on Superior to Hattie Cove, is considered the most dangerous part of the route because of the lake's propensity for bad weather. Paddlers must include extra days in their itinerary to wait for calm waters.

In the bygone days of the fur traders, ten voyageurs in a *canot du maître*, laden with five tons of furs could paddle from the Pic River south along Superior's northern coast to Michipicoten in less than two days. Today, with ideal weather conditions, two men might paddle the same Coastal Canoe Route of Lake Superior in just over four days. However, given the volatility of Lake Superior one can expect to be *dégradé* (windbound) one day out of three. Experienced paddlers allow 10 days to adequately enjoy this 180 kilometer (112 mile) route.

In calm waters, a seaworthy canoe, with spray covers is a must to explore the intricacies of this spectacular rocky coastline with its outcroppings of granite and quartz cliffs that extend deep into the waters of Superior. As the canoe glides over boulders far beneath the surface, the illusion of height can be so apparent that the body stiffens as if to brace for a fall.

The waters of Superior are best negotiated early in the morning or late in the day. Thermal winds can build at midday and wave heights change abruptly, taking the paddler from the heights of exhilaration to the depths of survival paddling in a matter of minutes.

A visitor self-registration program is mandatory.

PUKASKWA NATIONAL PARK

Hwy. 267,
Hattie Cove,
Heron Bay, Ont. P0T IR0
TEL 807-229-0801

Royal Canadian Henley Regatta

Since the summer of 1903, St. Catharines has been home to the Henley Regatta, a name synonymous with the best rowing in North America.

The regatta attracts the finest in men's and women's crews, ranging from 52-kilogram (115-pound) sprites to elite heavyweights and 70-year-old masters. It's the largest regatta of its kind in the western world, with roughly 2,000 participants from 100 rowing clubs and universities from Mexico, Central America, the former Soviet Union, Europe, as well as Canada and the USA. They row in more than 500 heats and finals in pursuit of the prestigious Henley honors. They also come for the camaraderie of regattas past. There's a saying — to compete at Henley is "the mark of an oarsman. Winning at Henley is the proof of a champion."

The Henley course is on the sheltered waters of the Old Welland Canal, known as Martindale Pond. It's a tranquil, 2,000-meter (6,500-foot) stretch of water, the first rowing course in North America to meet international rowing standards.

The organizational standards are impressive and said to be unequalled anywhere in the rowing world. Races begin every 10 minutes from early morning to late evening throughout the five-day competition, with crews entered in 80 categories. It has always had a reputation of being a regatta run for the athletes, with "fairness" the watchword of the week.

On- and off-water facilities are first rate. The Henley course boasts an Albano buoying system, timing pylons and overhead lane markers; adjustable starting gates; a finish tower; and electronic results board. In 1992 a second shellhouse was added on Henley Island with an enlarged workshop and new offices.

Spectators can view the excitement from a number of vantage points, including the grassy banks of Henley Island or the covered grandstand at the finish line.

ROYAL CANADIAN HENLEY REGATTA
P.O. Box 411,
St. Catharines, Ont. L2R 6Y3

WHEN August
WHERE Martindale Pond, St. Catharines

ONTARIO TRIVIA

TORONTO'S Metropolitan Toronto Reference Library is Canada's largest public library with more than 4,000,000 items. It houses the world's best Sherlock Holmes collection.

TORONTO'S Stock Exchange is Canada's largest. It includes a Visitor's Centre.

TORONTO'S George R. Gardiner Museum of Ceramic Art is the only specialized museum of its kind in North America. It includes a collection of 2,000 porcelain and pottery pieces.

TORONTO'S Sir Edward Sabine made the first magnetic survey of the world in 1839 with equipment he designed to record magnetic fields.

Fathom Five National Marine Park

Fathom Five National Marine Park near Tobermory, Canada's first underwater park, takes in 130 square kilometers (80 square miles) of Georgian Bay and Lake Huron. Each year, more than 8,000 scuba divers and snorklers plunge into the deep, clear, cold waters of the lake, attracted not by the prospects of gold, silver, or pirates' booty, but the remains of 20 or more nineteenth-century shipwrecks.

Below the surface of the water on jagged reefs lies a unique record of the early settlements of the area. Europeans arrived here in the 1870s by boat. The soil was poor but timber and commercial fishing allowed commerce to flourish and an important trade and transportation route developed. Over the years June fog and fall storms claimed their share of passing steamers, schooners, and tugs.

There are 23 dive-site locations with something of interest for every level of diving experience, as well as for snorklers. The shipwrecks offer plenty to see and touch. Some wreckage is badly broken and scattered. Splayed hull bottoms, center boards, rudders, and anchors are witness to the violence of the storms which pounded the vessels on rocks. Other ships are more intact with remnants of equipment and machinery still on board. For those who don't dive, several of the shallower wrecks can be appreciated from the comfort of a glass-bottom tour boat.

The park is also a site to observe fish and geological formations. There are interesting glacial scours in the bedrock, pitting, glacial erratics and layered dolomite. East of Fathom Five is a series of underwater caves.

The underwater archipelago is an extension of the Niagara Escarpment, formed over 400 million years ago. This was once an area of warm, tropical seas, with coral reefs much like the Gulf of Mexico. A limestone bedrock emerged as the coral seas retreated. Glacial ice cut into the bedrock and shaped the landforms found here today. The Niagara Escarpment disappears underwater at Tobermory and reappears as islands. Fathom Five National Marine Park and its neighbor, the Bruce Peninsula National Park, were designated by UNESCO as Canada's sixth Biosphere Reserve.

There are nineteen park islands. Flowerpot is the site of picturesque rock formations or "flowerpots," stone towers geologists call "sea stacks." They were formed by wave action working away at cracks in the bedrock at a time when water levels in the area were 10 to 15 meters (33 to 49 feet) higher. The largest flowerpot is 11.5 meters (38 feet) tall and the smallest is 6 meters (20 feet). As well as the flowerpots and caves, the island offers a loop trail for hikers and a light station built in 1896.

Flowerpot Island is accessible by private boat or by tour boat. It's the only park Island with docking facilities, camp sites and fireplaces.

All divers must register at the Diver Registration Centre before going below.

FATHOM FIVE NATIONAL MARINE PARK
P.O. Box 189,
Tobermory, Ont. N0H 2R0
TEL 519-596-2233

Whitewater Rafting

Situated between the sophistication of Canada's capital city, Ottawa, and the wilderness of Algonquin Park is the best whitewater rafting in eastern Canada, along a 14-kilometer (8-mile) stretch of the Madawaska River and on a section of the Ottawa River known as the Fendu. This is shield country, an area carved by a folding mountain range, glacial erosion, and the flooding of ancient seas.

Rapids are classified according to the International Whitewater Difficulty Scale. There rapids range all the way up to Class V, which are "extremely difficult, long and violent rapids with highly congested routes where rescue conditions are hard." Classification of rapids can change depending upon the time of year.

From the beginning of May, when river volume and velocity peaks with spring run-off, to the end of September when river levels are lower, large, rubber raft-loads of people take up the challenge of the white foam.

Some are seasoned veterans. They know the lingo of whitewater rafting and the rapids by name. They thrill to the entrapment of a hydraulic — two opposing walls of water that crash together at a single point. On the Ottawa, "McCoy's Chute" is a warm-up for the "Butcher's Knife," the "Normans," and the Class V monster known as the "Coliseum."

Others who ride the rafts are first-time thrill seekers. The beauty of the sport is that no experience or expertise is necessary, for the twelve passengers who merely supply the paddle power. From a position on the rim at the back, a qualified river guide steers the raft. Guides are experienced in reading and navigating white water, and are also trained in CPR, first aid, rescue, and survival skills.

Each raft is divided into sections with passenger foot stirrups for extra bracing power. Veterans and newcomers alike don helmets, life jackets, wet suits, and rubber-soled shoes. Skilled kayakers trained in first aid and safety are positioned at various points along the river.

Despite all the precautionary measures, whitewater rafting is considered one of the safest sports. There have been no fatalities within eastern Canada. In response to the burgeoning number of whitewater rafting companies, the Eastern Canada River Outfitters Association (ECROA) was established in 1983. The association operates Canada's first whitewater guide school. Its regulations were recommended to the industry in British Columbia after the drowning mishaps there.

RiverRun

Among the founding members of the Eastern Canada River Outfitters Association (ECROA) is RiverRun, near Beachburg, owned and operated by Margaret Horton. She says that whitewater rafting is safer than skiing and is better supervised. Since the formation of ECROA, rafting companies have agreed to limit rafting traffic with a quota system, thus enhancing the rafter's experience.

Margaret Horton is an enthusiastic ambassador of the sport. She founded her company in 1980 after her first run with the competition! Today it's the third-largest rafting company in Canada and has attracted athletes of the corporate world like George Cohon, President of McDonald's, and Neville Kirchmann, President of Coca Cola, as well as athletes of the sporting world, like Eric Lindros.

RiverRun, in the heart of the Ottawa corridor, boasts the shortest bus shuttle ride to the headwaters with a river trip that finishes at their private beachfront. RiverRun guides use both the main (Ontario) and middle (Quebec) channels of the Ottawa River which run all summer long. On a typical excursion, the guides stop before each rapid to assess the river and also break for lunch.

RiverRun is a complete resort facility with a variety of overnight accommodation including hookup for recreational vehicles, wooded campsites, cabanas, and antique log cabins. Activities include volleyball, basketball, body surfing, a canoe and kayaking school for beginners and intermediate paddlers, and saunas. Guided horseback riding along scenic trails is featured, along with mountain biking and the survival game of splat.

After dark entertainment includes dancing in the open air pavilion. Special theme weekends like "Fred's Great Canadian Pig Roast" and "The Molson's Whitewater Challenge" are popular events, so it's advisable to book early.

RiverRun offers a number of packages from one to three-day adventures that include meals. Discounts are available for groups.

RIVERRUN
P.O. Box 179,
Beachburg, Ont. K0J IC0
TEL 613-646-2501 (Information)
FAX 613-646-2958
800-267-RAFT (Reservations)
800-267-8504

FROM TORONTO DRIVE Highway 401 or Highway 7 to Highway 41. Go north on 41 to Eganville. Turn right at the lights, on Highway 60, which becomes County Road No. 8, into Cobden. In Cobden turn right on Highway 17. Go approximately 1 km (half a mile) to County Road 21 to the turn-off for Foresters Falls. Go through Foresters Falls. Approximately l km (half a mile) outside Foresters Falls, turn left at County Road 43, and follow the signs.

FROM OTTAWA DRIVE Highway 17 past Renfrew to Storyland Exit. Turn right and follow to four-corners stop sign. Proceed straight through, approximately 10 km (6 miles) and turn right at RiverRun sign. Continue through stop sign. Proceed straight on County Road 43, over railroad tracks, and follow the signs.

Lucky Strike Bait Works Ltd.

During the Depression, there wasn't a full-length broom handle to be found in the Peterborough neighborhood of Frank Edgar, because he was busy whittling them into wooden fishing plugs, a hobby that grew beyond the neighborhood to become Canada's oldest and largest fishing tackle and landing net manufacturer — Lucky Strike.

In the mid-1920s, Edgar apprenticed as a pattern-maker at his hometown company, DeLaval. With the crash of 1929, he worked only a few days a week for $6. The lay-off gave him plenty of leisure time to pursue his favorite hobbies, carving fishing plugs and fishing. Edgar's success as an angler attracted the attention of fellow fishermen who begged him to sell his plugs. He did, for a dollar a piece.

Sales from Edgar's tackle box expanded when he made up a display board of his best bait for the Charlotte Street shop of his barber, Harold Freeman. As chance would have it, a Toronto traveller for Direct Factory Sales saw the lures while getting his hair cut. He tracked Edgar down at DeLaval and presented him with an order for 10,000 plugs at fifty cents a piece.

With a $75 loan from the Bank of Montreal, Edgar went into business in his garage. He purchased a shipment of cedar and hired two young boys to saw the lumber, turn the plugs on a lathe, and paint them.

With an old punch press and a die he made himself, Edgar added June bug spinners and a variety of spoon lures to his wooden bait line. He offered a prize of a dozen lures to workers at Delaval to suggest a name for the company. Fred Vivash was the winner with "Lucky Strike."

Edgar never stopped improving his lures. He perfected the mouthpiece on the wooden plugs which gave them an action far superior to any product in Canada or the USA. Trips to Great Bear Lake in pursuit of arctic char and lake trout, led to specialized spoon lures for these two species. As business expanded, so did the extension on Edgar's garage.

Son Bill, a tool and die maker, joined the business and together he and his father combined their skills, developing equipment that revolutionized their assembly line production.

Today, the Lucky Strike Bait Works is a sophisticated operation, housed in a modern, 4,880-square-meter (16,000-square-foot) building on the outskirts of Peterborough. Twenty employees make 70 types of landing nets and 1,800 different lures with names like Algonquin Wobblers, Lizard Lures, Tiger Spoons, and Warden Worry.

Methods and materials have greatly improved over the years. Some of the baits are nickel- or gold-plated. Some are painted by a silk screen process or patterned by hand with an airbrush. Swivels are now made with brass which adds weight for casting and sinking.

Lucky Strike has remained a family business since 1929. Bill Edgar refers to himself as semi-retired while son-in-law Kim Rhodes is at the helm.

Lucky Strike products are distributed across Canada and in the USA and may be purchased in stores like Canadian Tire.

LUCKY STRIKE BAIT WORKS LTD.

Whittington Dr.,
R.R. #3,
Peterborough, Ont. K9J 6X4
TEL 705-743-3849
FAX 705-743-4043

Greenwing Fishing Festival

Rain or shine, the Greenwing Fishing Festival for children is held annually towards the end of April (corresponding with the opening of trout season) below the world famous Peterborough Lift Lock. Thousands of youngsters line the banks of the Trent-Severn Waterway to fish for of rainbow trout that are stocked in the canal just prior to the Festival. This is the largest fishing event held for children anywhere in the world. It's also the largest Greenwing event.

A Greenwing is a junior member of Ducks Unlimited, a private, nonprofit conservation organization with chapters throughout Canada and the USA. Ducks Unlimited is dedicated to the perpetuation and increase of North American waterfowl. Some of their activities include the preservation of habitats, the banding of waterfowls and the collection of data. Junior members learn the practices of conservation at an early age, participating in projects like duck banding, retriever trials and nest box programs. Children registered at the Festival become Greenwing members and receive a subscription to their publication.

Greenwings also have a great deal of fun, especially on the day of the Fishing Festival. They have the opportunity to keep the fish they catch, with a three-trout limit. The canal is stocked with 4,000 rainbow trout, ranging in size from 500 grams (one pound) to 7 kilograms (15 pounds). At least that's the size of "Walter," the granddaddy of them all that everyone's out to hook. There are also special prizes, including fishing rods and tackle for anyone who reels in one of the 300 specially tagged fish.

The derby is in its eighth year, and has become a huge success since moving the location to the Lift Lock about three years ago. It attracts 10,000 people, about 3,000 of them children. More than 100 local organizations and their volunteer members, including Ducks Unlimited, the City of Peterborough and the Trent-Severn Waterway make the day a memorable one, registering children and their catches, cooking hot dogs, and handing out prizes.

The Festival is open to all children 15 years of age and under. Those under 10 must be accompanied by an adult. A fishing rod and lifejacket are required.

GREENWING FISHING FESTIVAL
Ducks Unlimited,
427 Pido Rd.,
Peterborough, Ont. K9J 6X7
TEL 705-748-5447

DUCKS UNLIMITED (Canada)
P.O. Box 1160
Oak Hammock Marsh,
Winnipeg, Man. R0C 2Z0

Cruising the Canals

The Canadian Parks Service maintains nine historic canal systems. In Ontario, there are three: the Trent-Severn Waterway, The Rideau Canal, and the single lock at Sault Ste. Marie. All three have National Historic Site designation. Ontario has 869 kilometers (510 miles) of canals and over 100 locks.

TRENT-SEVERN WATERWAY

Trent-Severn Waterway is an inland series of lakes, rivers and manmade canals that meander through the heart of central Ontario, from Trenton on the north shore of Lake Ontario to Port Severn on the eastern shore of Georgian Bay. In effect, one can board a boat in any of the typical Ontario towns along the watercourse and sail to any port in the world.

Just as European canals, once the lifeblood of commercial transportation, now afford twentieth-century tourists a tranquil experience of yesteryears, the 386-kilometer (240-mile) Trent-Severn system, which includes 42 lock stations, allows travellers to reflect upon the historical significance of this watercourse, while taking in a panorama of scenery that varies from Canadian Shield to drumlins of the last ice age, rolling farmland, limestone banks and some of the most valuable wetlands remaining in the province. It has been called "one of the finest interconnected systems of navigation in the world". Modern day voyageurs pass through 87 years of Canadian engineering technology, including hand-hewn stone locks, marine railways, giant modern locks, and lift locks, including the world's largest hydraulic lift lock in Peterborough.

The entire passage only became fully navigable with the construction of locks and dams. This work began in earnest around 1833. The first lock was built in Bobcaygeon; a second followed quickly in Lindsay. By the 1880s, most of the Kawartha Lakes between Lakefield and Coboconk were navigable. The majority of locks were constructed between 1907 and 1914 and it wasn't until 1920 that the entire system could be traversed.

As much as 7,000 years ago, these were the waters that sustained life for the Aboriginal peoples. It was their main source of food, trade, and travel. Not only did they fish these lakes and rivers, but Rice Lake, once covered in wild rice was a prime source of their staple food. Reminiscent of these days is Serpent Mounds, a prehistoric burial ground on the north shore of Rice Lake.

Samuel de Champlain, descended the treacherous current of the Trent by canoe in 1615, guided by the Huron. The lumbermen drove cribs of logs downstream to the planing mills of the waterway communities, where dams provided water power and later hydro-electricity. Despite the unnavigable portions, travel by steamship became popular in the 1880s with outings along Rice Lake, Stoney Lake, and Lake Simcoe. Now the shores of many of the lakes are lined with summer cottages, where fishing, boating, and water sports are the activities of the day.

Throughout the Trent-Severn system, boat rentals and cruises are available. Experienced lock staff will quickly acquaint novice boaters with locking procedures. There are fees for locking based on the length of one's boat. Day and seasonal passes are available. Most of the locks are easily accessible by car and make wonderful picnic destinations.

TRENT-SEVERN WATERWAY

P.O. Box 567,
Peterborough, Ont. K9J 6Z6
TEL 705-742-9267

OPEN mid-May to the Canadian Thanksgiving weekend

PETERBOROUGH LIFT LOCK

One of the true highlights of locking through the Trent-Severn Waterway is Lock 21 in Peterborough. One of only two hydraulic lift locks on the system — the other one being at Kirkfield — the Peterborough Lift Lock is the highest hydraulic lift in the world. It was built to overcome the considerable difference in elevation between Little Lake and Nassau Mills on the Otonabee River, raising and lowering boats a distance of 19.81 metres (65 feet).

First time navigators and visitors to the Lift Lock will be impressed by this cement monolith built into an embankment below Peterborough's largest drumlin, Armour Hill.

Lift locks look very different from regular, gated locks and operate on much different principles. Boats are raised and lowered at the same time, in two waterfilled chambers, an upper and a lower. Each chamber is 42.67 metres (140 feet) long and 10.06 metres (33 feet) wide and, when filled with water, weighs 1,700 tons. The chambers are connected by a hydraulic ram system; any movement of one chamber forces an equal and opposite movement of the other. To raise and lower boats, the upper chamber takes on an extra 30 centimetres (1 foot) of water. The heavier upper chamber travels downward, forcing the lower chamber upward. The chambers have hinged gates at both ends which seal water and boats off from the canal, and

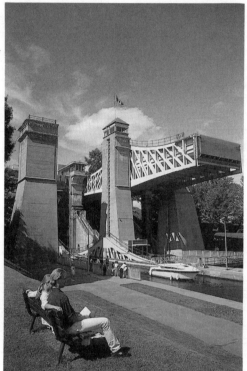

then open to release the boats into the system. The average time it takes to complete a transfer is about 10 minutes. In 1993 4,370 vessels were locked through.

Excavation of the site began in 1896. Men and horses removed clay and boulders down an average of 12.2 metres (40 feet) to limestone bedrock. The debris removed from the site was used to build up the embankments behind the lock. Granite blocks, some weighing more than 10 tonnes, were lowered to the bottom to provide footings for the rams. The concrete work was laborious and intricate. This is a poured, concrete structure without a single piece of reinforcing steel since the method of reinforcing

steel was viewed with scepticism. In all, it took 19,879 cubic metres (26,000 cubic yards) of cement. At the time this was the largest concrete structure in the world.

The Dominion Bridge Company of Montreal did the structural steel work of gates, their mechanisms, the main presses, and rams. It took 744,560 kilograms (1,640,000 pounds) of rolled steel, 224,730 kilograms (495,000 pounds) of cast iron, and 303,726 kilograms (699,000 pounds) of steel castings to complete the job. Most of the original work is in use today. Only zinc refinishing has been applied to the boat chambers and the gates were replaced with aluminum ones in the mid-1960s. The total cost of building the Lift Locks in 1904 was $244,000.

Mr. Walter J. Francis, a civil engineer in the service of the Department of Railways and Canals was in charge of the project. In 1907 he presented a paper to the Canadian Society of Civil Engineers. "Care has been taken throughout to make the general appearance of the work as attractive as possible. All the walls and stairways are protected by suitably designed railings, and the windows and doorways are closed by ornamental grille-work. The lockmaster's cabin on the top of the centre tower is constructed of concrete as high as the window sills. Above the steel frame work is furred with wood, and the whole of the exterior covered with copper. The interior is finished in British Columbia cedar in the natural color."

Care is still taken at the Lift Locks. The setting is one of immaculately groomed lawns where in spring the crabapple trees blossom. A modern Visitor Centre opened by Prince Andrew in 1985, explains the construction and operation of the Lock through films and a working model of the system. Over 50,000 people tour the Centre annually.

The lower canal of the Lock becomes a skating rink in winter. Before the Lock opens in spring, it's stocked with fish for the annual Greenwing Fishing Festival, the largest children's fishathon in the world.

TRENT-SEVERN WATERWAY

P.O. Box 567,
Peterborough, Ont. K9J 6Z6
TEL 705 742-9267
OPEN the Friday before the May long weekend.
CLOSED the Wednesday after the Canadian Thanksgiving.

PETERBOROUGH LIFT LOCK VISITOR CENTRE

TEL 705-745-8389
OPEN May to October.

RIDEAU CANAL

In 1826, the Duke of Wellington was a British hero, the winner of the Battle of Waterloo in 1815, the vanquisher of Napoleon. His attention was focused on Upper Canada where the War of 1812 was a bitter reminder that the threat of American invasion along the St. Lawrence River was always imminent. The British wanted the assurance of an inland waterway to allow British gunboats and supply ships to reach Kingston from Montreal in the event of attack. Wellington proposed a canal to link Kingston and Ottawa. He enticed his former co-campaigner, Colonel John By, out of retirement to get the job done.

Excavation began in 1827 at the Ottawa end. For five years, 2,000 men trenched through malaria-laden swamps, blasted through granite, and hauled limestone blocks for 18 dams and 47 locks, without mechanical assistance. Many of the workers were Québécois; others were Irish immigrants, ill-prepared for backwoods life. Many succumbed to dysentery and malaria. Inaccuracies in the original survey forced constant changes in construction tactics. When the 197-kilometer (122-mile) canal opened in 1832, a marvel of technical engineering for its

time, Colonel By was court-martialled for being over budget.

While the Rideau Canal was never used for its original military purpose, it did serve as an immigration route and a commercial link for all the mill towns founded along the way. It became a recreational highway with the boating boom of the 1950s and 1960s and today it's North America's oldest, continuously operating canal, where most of the locks are still operated by hand.

The tranquillity of the Rideau now defies the sacrifices of the men who built it, and the only evidence of military strategy lies in the powder magazine at Jones Falls and the block houses, still intact at Kingston Mills, Newboro, and Merrickville. The towns and villages that dot the route, span 200 years of architectural diversity, and are a tribute to the United Empire Loyalists who settled the area in the late 1700s, and the English, Scottish and Irish who soon joined them.

Many of the towns have self-guided walking tours. Visitors can stroll the streets lined with beautiful old homes, churches, and public buildings. Georgian-style architecture of the eighteenth-century is recognizable by the quoined corners of brick and stone work, central pediments, and balanced facades; the Roman and Greek Revival of the nineteenth century by its low-pitched roofs, arched doorways, upper storey windows and Doric columns; and the mid-nineteenth-century Gothic Revival, by its steep, pitched roofs, gables, and ornamental gingerbread.

One of the fads of the twentieth-century is antique wooden boating. These mahogany beauties, made by master boat builders in the early 1900s, are very much in evidence along the Rideau. There's an active Antique and Classic Boat Society in the area, with an annual boat show the second week of August.

The Rideau system is also known for sports fishing for muskellunge, walleye, bass, and lake trout. The towns along the way are hosts to fairs, festivals, and regattas.

RIDEAU CANAL NATIONAL HISTORIC SITE

12 Maple Ave. North,

Smith Falls, Ont. K7A 1Z5
TEL 613-283-5170

OPEN mid-May to the Canadian Thanksgiving weekend.

SAULT CANAL NATIONAL HISTORIC SITE

The canal at Sault Ste. Marie was built to provide a Canadian link between Lake Huron and Lake Superior. Canal history in the Sault area began with the construction of a small lock on the north shore of the St. Mary's river in 1797, by the North West Company. This wooden lock was burned by the Americans in 1814 during the war of 1812. The next lock in the area opened in 1855 and was constructed by the Americans on the south shore of the river. But Canada's assurance of using this lock was not always certain. In 1870 for example, the Canadian vessel *Chicora*, bound for the west with military supplies for troops of the Red River Expedition, was denied passage. Flow of Canadian wheat from the west and minerals from the Lake Superior area justified the cost of building the canal, and so construction began in 1887. It would be the last link in an all-Canadian canal system, of more that 1,609 kilometres (1000 miles), stretching from Montreal through the Great Lakes, to the head of Lake Superior.

The canal operated non-stop, 24 hours a day, for 80 years before being retired from the St. Lawrence Seaway system. It was closed to navigation on July 22, 1987, as the result of a structural failure. Today it is managed by Parks Canada as a National Historic Site.

At the time of its construction, the Sault Canal was a marvel of engineering technology. It was built under very difficult working conditions, and took eight years to complete. Stone cutters laboured four years excavating a 1.5 kilometre (one-mile) channel through the red sandstone bedrock of St. Mary's Island, dividing the island in two. The lock chamber was the largest in the world, 270 meters (900 feet) long and 180 meters (60 feet) wide. It was made of limestone from Windsor and Manitoulin Island.

The Sault Canal was the first in the world to be operated entirely by electricity. Its own power-house generated electrical power for lighting the canal, an important feature because it ran night and day. Electricity powered the gates, valves, and the CPR swing bridge. This electrically operated machinery allowed the Sault Canal to operate efficiently in cold weather, whereas other canals, up until then hydraulically operated, would be slowed down considerably or even stopped due to colder temperatures. The Canadian General Electric Company supplied the generators, switches, wiring, and panels of the Powerhouse.

It usually took twenty minutes to lock a vessel through. Water filled and emptied the chamber by a series of supply culverts and discharge drains in the bottom of the lock. This was revolutionary since older canals filled and emptied by means of culverts along the lock chamber walls or openings at each extremity. It took eight minutes, a rate of one million gallons per minute, eight million gallons each time, to fill or empty the chamber.

There are five sets of lock gates. Each one measures one metre (3 feet) thick at the base and the largest ones weigh more than one hundred tons. British Columbia Douglas fir timbers were used to build the gates and they were constructed on site. The original machinery used in their construction remains in the site's Timber Shed today.

If the lock gates ever failed, an unrestrained flow of water would rage through the canal, supplied by the world's largest freshwater lake, Lake Superior, with a surface area of over 48,270 square kilometres (30,000 square miles). The Americans had built an emergency swing dam above their lock for just this purpose. It was calculated to control a head of water 5 meters (16 feet) deep by 33 meters (108 feet) wide in cross section.

A decision was made to construct a similar emergency swing dam, 305 meters (1,000 feet) upstream from the Canadian lock. It was based on the same principles as the American dam, but was unique in several ways. It was constructed entirely of steel and the wickets which would be lowered into place to hold back the water were of a different, original design. The Canadian dam was built to close a channel nearly twice the cross-sectional area of its American counterpart, and would therefore have to sustain considerably greater water pressure.

Like the American dam, this swing dam could only be tested in still water. It remained on stand-by for more than 14 years before tragedy struck. At noon, on June 9, 1909, the *Perry G. Walker*, a freighter loaded with coal, struck the lower gates while a Canadian Pacific passenger steamer, the *Assiniboia*, and an iron ore freighter, the *Crescent City*, were preparing to lock down together. The force of the water drove the *Perry G. Walker* back down the canal and shot the locking vessels downstream in a great torrent of water. Two of the lock's five sets of gates were swept away.

The Sault Canal's Emergency Swing Dam became the only one of its kind ever to be operated under emergency conditions. Within twenty-four hours it was in full operation. It is the only remaining Emergency Swing Dam in the world today.

The site's heritage buildings include the Administrative Building, the Superintendent's Residence, the Canalmen's Shelter, the Powerhouse and the Blacksmith's Shop. All are constructed of Jacobsville red sandstone excavated from the canal during construction. The limestone trimming on the buildings is from Picton, Ontario.

Across the canal gates, on South St. Mary's Island, visitors can walk the Attikamek Trail. The name, meaning "caribou of the waters" is Ojibway for whitefish. The trail skirts the St. Mary's River rapids where the Ojibwa fished as early as 500 BC. An early traveler reported "...the river forms at this place a rapids so teeming with fish...that the Indians could easily catch enough to feed 10,000 men."

The South St. Mary's Island was layered with rocks and debris from the canal construction. The trail is scattered with evidence of those who built, operated and protected the canal, including the remains of World War I and II military encampments. There's a thin layer of soil on the construction rubble with a renewed flora and fauna establishing itself.

South of South St. Mary's Island is Whitefish Island where the Ojibwa settled nearly 2,000 years ago. When the French arrived in the 1600s, they called the natives "Sauteaux", because of the skills they exhibited in negotiating the rapids while fishing ("sault" was the French word for rapid). Thus the settlement on both sides of the river became Sault Ste. Marie. The island has since been returned to the Batchawana First Nations through a land claim settlement and has also been designated a National Historic Site.

SAULT STE. MARIE CANAL

1 Canal Drive,
Sault Ste. Marie, Ont. P6A 6W4
TEL 705 942-6262

Island Hopping

THOUSAND ISLANDS

The Thousand Islands near the mouth of the St. Lawrence River are actually made up of 1,865 islands. All but one are natural and all but 25 are privately owned. Of these, 21 are the property of the Canadian government, operated as park islands, and 4 belong to the American government.

The islands are a by-product of the ice age, sculpted along with the Great Lake Basin. They were first settled by the Iroquois and later explored by Samuel de Champlain in the 1600s. They were on the route of the French coureurs de bois in pursuit of the fur trade. During the Seven Years War between England and France, both nations constructed small fortresses throughout the islands, leaving behind legends of sunken and buried French treasures.

The islands played a role in the American Revolution. Loyalists displaced from the eastern seaboard settled here and assisted the English during the War of 1812. An attack on Gananoque on Christmas Eve in 1814 was settled with the Treaty of Ghent. It forbade warships to enter the St. Lawrence, a provision still enforced today.

The British surveyed the islands and divided them into three groups: the Admiralty Group, the Fleet Group, and the Navy Group. Each island of considerable size was named after a British admiral, battle, or ship. Names like Forsythe, Melville, Tidds, Camelot, and Endymion recall a bygone era.

The summer playground offers fishermen largemouth bass, walleye, northern pike and muskellunge. The world's largest muskie, weighing 31 kilograms 426 grams (69 pounds, 15 ounces) was caught here. Many of the islands are the summer homes of Canadians and Americans who share a common border. Palatial properties were built by American millionaires in the 1900s. Some residences didn't survive the Great Depression, although others have been fully restored.

In fall, the Thousand Islands are brilliant with the changing colors of the leaves.

GANANOQUE BOAT LINE LTD.

The best way to view the Thousand Islands is on the Gananoque Boat Line, the largest and oldest company offering cruises through the islands.

The postman who delivered mail to island residents for many years, often took passengers on board his mail boat to supplement his income. As the mail route expanded so did his tour and eventually his boats became larger. More than 55 years

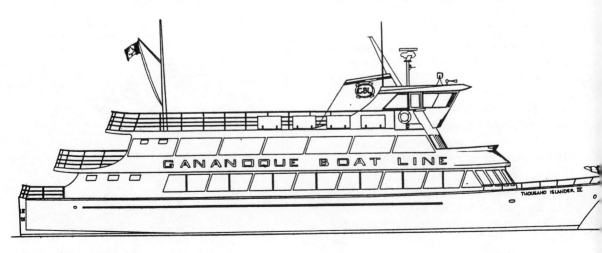

THOUSAND ISLANDER IV

ago, he quit his job as postman and established the Gananoque Boat Line.

The present company operates four ships, two that accommodate 400 passengers and two with a 500-person capacity. They are the only triple decker line with all the amenities: open-air decks, washroom facilities, a liquor license, and snack bar. Padded seats and interior climate control allow for summer and fall comfort. This Canadian Coast Guard approved line winds through all the islands. One-hour and three-hour cruises are offered. The latter stops at one of the area's highlights, Boldt Castle.

This magnificent European-style castle was constructed by George C. Boldt as an expression of undying devotion to his wife. He even had the island shaped in the form of a heart. Tragically, Mrs. Boldt died before the castle was completed. Construction stopped upon her death and it remains a $2.5 million monument to the late Mrs. Boldt.

Among other points of interest is the cruise beneath the Thousand Islands International Bridge, the 12-kilometer (7.5-mile) bridge system that joins Canada and its American neighbor. An area called Millionaire's Row is splendid with grand, turn-of-the-century summer homes. The shortest international bridge in the world connecting the Zavikon Islands spans 10 meters (32 feet). One island is in Canadian waters, the other in American.

Gananoque Boat Lines provides private charters for weddings, reunions, corporate parties, and other occasions. The boats are boarded in Gananoque and operate from May to October.

GANANOQUE BOAT LINE LTD.

P.O. Box 190,
Gananoque, Ont. K7G 2T5
TEL 613-382-2144
FAX 613-382-2148

30,000 ISLANDS

The greatest concentration of islands in the world is the 30,000 Islands in Georgian Bay, that great expanse of water that's almost as large as Lake Ontario and is often called the Sixth Great Lake. In actual fact, there are closer to 100,000 islands in the Bay,

scattered between Killarney and Waubaushene. Most of them along the north and east coasts are privately owned. Fifty-nine islands, or parts thereof — a land area of approximately 12 square kilometers (7.5 square miles) — became the Georgian Bay Islands National Park in 1929. The islands are accessible only by boat in summer and in winter only when ice conditions permit safe crossing by snowmobile, snowshoes, or cross-country skis.

The archipelago on the edge of the Canadian Shield has an interesting mix of northern and southern species of plants and animals. The northern islands, and the northern part of Beausoleil Island, the largest of the park islands, have landscapes typical of a Group of Seven painting. In fact A.Y. Jackson spent the summer of 1913 at a dilapidated bathing hut near Go Home Bay, painting and sketching on into September. Thirty-year-old Jackson had intended to move to the USA but he became so fascinated with Georgian Bay that he decided to remain in Canada. Subsequently, he brought members of the Group, which formed in 1920, to paint scenes of rocky islands swept bare by glaciers and intermittently graced with the outline of pines ravaged by the strength of the west winds. Jackson's "Terre Sauvage," with its heavy clouds, gaudy red maples, and bright green pines, is more typical of the southern islands where rich hardwoods are supported with thicker soil cover.

This is the only home in Canada of the Eastern Massasauga Rattlesnake, (you may notice the rubber boots and peculiar high stepping gait of the local islanders!) now on the endangered species list in this country. Although poisonous, it is a small, timid snake, about 76 centimeters (2.5 feet) long, recognizable by its grey and brown scale pattern and a rattle that sounds like a loud bee. The chances of coming across it are extremely rare. A life-size model is on display at the park's Visitor Centre in Honey Harbour. Boots and long pants are advised for those hiking near swampy areas.

In the heat of summer, Georgian Bay islanders explore the jagged, narrow channels by canoe or kayak, fish, and picnic in the coves, swim in the pristine waters, and enjoy the spectacular sunsets.

One tradition for generations of cottagers, especially in the Pointe au Baril cluster of islands on the eastern shore above Parry Sound, is the shore dinner. Unlike picnics whose fare includes make-ahead sandwiches and potato salad, staples of a shore dinner are bacon, eggs, potatoes, pancake mix, and coffee, all items to accompany the fresh bass fished at the party destination. A shore dinner in progress is recognizable by a flotilla of boats, usually a launch with canoes and rowboats in tow, heading for a sun-warmed rock.

The park islands offer opportunities for hiking, fishing, swimming and snorkelling. Campsites are available on a number of islands, the largest campground being on Beausoleil Island. They are on a first-come, first-served basis.

The waters of Georgian Bay can be treacherous. Those who aren't knowledgeable of the shoals are advised to purchase navigation charts 2202 and 2239. There are no lodge or food facilities on any of the islands and a self-registration program is in effect. Water taxi service is available from Honey Harbour.

GEORGIAN BAY ISLANDS NATIONAL PARK

P.O. Box 28,
Honey Harbour, Ont. POE IEO
TEL 705-765-2417

DRIVE to Honey Harbour on Highway 69, north of Highway 400.

30,000 ISLANDS CRUISE LINE

One of the best ways to view the islands is aboard Canada's largest cruise ship, *The Island Queen*, which each season attracts more than 60,000 passengers from around the world. The cruise line was started By Ron Anderson and his father in 1968 with two small boats purchased from Montreal's Expo '67.

The 40-meter (132-foot) boat follows the route of the old, wooden, side-wheel steamers from Collingwood to Parry Sound in the mid- 1800s. *The Island Queen* departs from Parry Sound several times a day from June to mid-October . This is a three-hour trip on a well-equipped, triple-decker boat that accommodates 550 passengers. It offers a snack bar, a gift shop, heating, and air conditioning and is Canadian Coast Guard approved. An enthusiastic captain details the myths and legends of many of the passages. The last two weeks of September and the first two weeks of October there's a Fall Colour Cruise that's spectacular. There are also sunset cruises and special Festival of Music cruises.

30,000 ISLAND CRUISE LINES INC.

9 Bay St.,
Parry Sound, Ont. P2A IS4
TEL 705-746-2311
FAX 705-746-9696

Errington's Wilderness Islands

Albert Errington and his wife Rose never fit the profile of successful resort operators. Errington had little formal education and was employed for 22 years with the Algoma Steel Corporation. His wife was raised on a southern Ontario farm and had a little experience in retail sales. In 1975 they bought a run-down resort on Wabatongushi Lake, 332 kilometers (206 miles) north of Sault Ste. Marie, accessible only by train or plane. The Erringtons' only assets were three teenage boys and a desire to provide the kind of vacation spot they themselves would enjoy — a wilderness experience with a high degree of comfort in terms of accommodation.

The setting provided the perfect backdrop for the wilderness experience. Picturesque Wabatongushi Lake, a 4,000-hectare (10,000-acre) body of water with more than 70 uninhabited islands, is the natural habitat of walleye, northern pike, jumbo perch, and whitefish. Fed by more than 28 rivers and creeks, the adjacent wet lands are home to abundant loon populations, bald eagles, and osprey. The lake is surrounded by the Chapleau Game Preserve, the world's largest game preserve and wildlife sanctuary. See Chapleau Game Preserve and Wildlife Sanctuary.

Providing guests with all the comforts of home was a top priority for the Erringtons. Over the years they replaced the old cabins with hand-built log cottages which keep the integrity of the landscape while providing the amenities of a first rate hotel. Each self-contained cottage has a secluded view of the lake, complete with private dock and an 5-meter (18-foot) cedarstrip outboard for every two people. The cottages are well appointed with king-size beds, fire places, gas barbecues, and screened-in porches.

In 1987 the existing main lodge was replaced with a rustic, 1,830-square-meter (6,000-square-foot) facility with suites on the lake, a dining room, licensed lounge and recreational area.

In the 1970s and early 1980s, Errington's Wilderness Islands were a well-kept secret, frequented mainly by fishermen from the midwestern USA. Today the place is a paradise, not only for the fishing crowd, but for families and couples eager to explore the Ontario wilderness in comfort and style.

The resort promotes fish conservation. The Erringtons asked the Ministry of Natural Resources to designate one of the best spawning areas as a fish sanctuary. Next they instituted a voluntary slot size. They asked guests to release walleyes between 33 and 36 centimeters (13 and 14 inches). To the surprise of the Ministry of Natural Resources, the average size of the walleyes increased by 5 centimeters (2 inches) over the next four years.

The resort also believes in catch-and-release fishing. They began a catch-and-release contest for any person releasing a walleye over 40 centimeters (16 inches) or northern pike over 50 centimeters (20 inches). Their name is entered into a weekly, random draw for various prizes including a discount on next year's vacation.

Guides are available to enhance the fishing experience and wildlife viewing. Picnic on one of the out islands, walk the nature trails, browse through the nature library, or just enjoy the scenery and relax.

Errington's Wilderness Islands continue to be a family-owned and operated business with Albert Errington Jr. at the helm. He has plans to expand the resort to nearby Heritage Island, and to continue to cater to the environmental tourist.

ERRINGTON'S WILDERNESS ISLANDS
P.O. Box 22057,
44 Great Northern Road,
Sault Ste. Marie, Ont. P6B 6H4
TEL 705-946-2010 (Oct. 1 through May 15)
TEL 705-884-2215 (May 15th through Oct. 1)
TEL 705-884-2020

BY TRAIN board the Algoma Central Railway at Sault Ste. Marie or Hawk Junction to Wabatong. The boat ride to the resort takes 15 minutes.

BY PLANE from Hawk Junction using one of the local air services.

BY CAR to Hawk Junction from Sault Ste. Marie, along the Trans-Canada Highway (Highway 17 north) to Wawa. From Wawa travel 12 miles east on Chapleau Highway 101, then north on Highway 547, 4 miles to Hawk Junction.

ISLAND TRIVIA

- On the Canadian side of the Great Lakes, there are 2,414 "real" islands: Lake Superior (615); Lake Huron (1,720); Lake Erie (29); Lake Ontario (50).
- GEORGIAN BAY'S 30,000 Islands are the largest concentration of islands in the world.
- LAKE OF THE WOODS, Ontario's second-largest inland lake, contains 14,000 islands.
- MANITOULIN ISLAND is the world's largest freshwater island, with nearly 1,600 kilometers (1,000 miles) of coastline.
- WOLFE ISLAND is the largest of the Thousand Islands.

Hiking

THE BRUCE TRAIL

In 1990 the United Nations declared the Bruce Peninsula National Park and Fathom Five National Marine Park on the Niagara Escarpment a UNESCO World Biosphere Reserve. This is the sixth designation in Canada and one of 276 designations in the world. The undisturbed areas are protected because of their significant ecological features and functions. Along with the Galapagos Islands, the Everglades, and the Serengeti, the Niagara Escarpment is recognized as one of the world's unique ecological environments.

Its sedimentary rocks are a record of the past 440 million years. At one time an ancient sea supported reefs and animals now fossilized in the rocks. The sea drained some 250 million years ago, and streams and rivers carved out the Escarpment. The landscape was reshaped by huge glaciers about 2 million years ago.

The Bruce Trail follows the Niagara Escarpment from Queenston to Tobermory — 776 kilometers (482 miles) of diverse, natural beauty.

The trail was the vision of Ray Lowes who first proposed the idea in 1960. On March 13, 1963, the Bruce Trail Association was incorporated. Hundreds of volunteers helped clear and mark the trail which opened in 1967. It's the oldest and longest marked hiking trail in Canada. White blazes on rocks, stiles, trees, and fence posts show the way.

A good deal of the trail runs through one of southern Ontario's largest remaining woodlands. The diversity of the flora is exceptional — orchids in the north, 900-year-old cedars on the cliff face, the unique Carolinian forest to the south.

The hills and valleys, woods, and wetlands are home to more than 300 bird species, 53 mammals, 35 reptiles and amphibians, 90 fish, and a variety of insects. Cliffs, lakes, caves, waterfalls, and channels are there to be discovered.

Over 1.3 million visitors explore the Bruce Trail annually. It's accessible from a number of parks and conservation areas where maps are available. An hour's walk, a full day hike or several days of tripping can be negotiated.

The Bruce Trail Association has more than 8,000 members with 800 active volunteers dedicated to the preservation of the Niagara Escarpment. There are nine regional clubs which maintain a specific section of the trail. The clubs arrange outings and seminars and raise money to secure parts of the trail which cross private property. Their goal is to ensure that the entire trail will always be accessible to the public.

THE BRUCE TRAIL ASSOCIATION,
P.O. Box 857,
Hamilton, Ont. L8N 3N9
TEL 905-529-6821
800-665-HIKE

PUKASKWA NATIONAL PARK

The main attraction at Pukaskwa (pronounced puck-a-saw) National Park on Lake Superior's northern shore is the Coastal Hiking Trail. It begins at the visitor center at Hattie Cove and follows Superior's jagged edge about 60 kilometers (37 miles) to North Swallow River.

This arduous hike requires plenty of time, planning, and proper equipment, including clothing for extremes of temperature and a good possibility of rain, insect repellent, and appropriate footware. All that said, this is a superb excursion.

The scenery runs the gamut from bedrock ridges and boreal forest to wide sandy beaches hemmed in by cliffs. Bridges span most of the rivers. The northern section of the trail, between Hattie Cove and Oiseau Bay, is well marked, while the southern section, Oiseau Bay to North Swallow River, is more rugged and in some areas difficult to follow.

Campsites are half and full days apart, located near some of the best beaches and bays. There are also trails into backcountry. Trail Guides may be purchased in advance or at the Visitor Centre. A self- registration program is mandatory.

PUKASKWA NATIONAL PARK

Hwy. 627,
Hattie Cove,
Heron Bay, Ont. P0T 1R0

ONTARIO TRIVIA

TORONTO is the home of 5-pin bowling, a game established in 1904 by entrepreneur, Tommy Ryan. He reduced the size of the pins and the weight of the ball used in the original 10-pin game, and supplied the customers with balls. His game was less strenuous and attracted women to the sport, and took less time to play so people could have a game on their lunch hours. By the end of World War I there were 32 bowling centres in Toronto. Ryan never patented his invention.

TORONTO is the place where the world's first alternating current tube, invented by Edward Samuel Rogers, allowed for the manufacture of batteryless radios. In 1927 Rogers developed the first batteryless broadcasting station, CFRB, which continues today. The R stands for Rogers and the B for batteryless.

TORONTO doctors Alan Brown, T.G.H. Drake, and F.F. Tisdall of the Hospital for Sick Children, came up with the idea of a pre-cooked cereal for infants in 1930. The invention was Pablum, an instant success. It contained cornmeal, oatmeal, wheatmeal, wheat germ, bone meal, brewer's yeast, and alfalfa.

Snowmobiling

Unless you're an avid snowmobiler, the sport is practically invisible, because it's enjoyed in some of the most secluded, not to mention picturesque, parts of the province where people rarely venture by car or on foot. Ontario has 30,000 kilometers (19,000 miles) of first-class, marked and groomed trails, maintained by a network of clubs, the Ontario Federation of Snowmobile Clubs (OFSC).

The OFSC is one of the largest snowmobile organizations in North America, with 285 local, volunteer clubs. This non-profit organization is dedicated to promoting better snowmobiling in the province. The enthusiasm for the sport and the competency with which the trails are maintained and monitored is unrivalled by any similar organization.

The Federation's Trans-Ontario Provincial (TOP) trail network allows snowmobilers access to travel from Manitoba to the Quebec border without having to back track. TOP raises money through the sale of trail permits and distributes the proceeds among the member clubs for maintenance and equipment. There are 76,000 dues-paying members in the Federation, and 370,000 registered snowmobiles in the province. As North America's fastest growing winter sport, it's big business.

The Ontario government recognizes the significance of snowmobiling to the province's tourism dollar. In an unprecedented move, they entered into a cooperative agreement with the OFSC in 1992. The joint venture is called Sno-Trac and stands for Snowmobile Trail Rehabilitation and Construction. Sno-Trac's investment in the province for 1993 and 1994 is just over 20 million dollars. Three years ago, Ontario's snowmobile trails generated more than 250 million dollars. Since the implementation of Sno-Trac, that figure has jumped to 400 million dollars in 1993.

To ride the OFSC trails in Ontario, sledders must display an official seasonal or visitor's pass, valid on all 30,000 kilometers (19,000 miles) of official trails. The passes are available anywhere there are TOP trails in the province.

TOPS IN TRAILS:

HALIBURTON COUNTY

Ontario's oldest snowmobiling destination, located in the central region of Ontario, north of Peterborough and east of Huntsville, is home to the world's largest snowmobile club with more than 2,800 members.

The Haliburton region led the province more than ten years ago, taking an aggressive approach to developing the ideal scenario for sledders: good, smooth trails, plenty of on-trail services, and easy accessibility from resort and hotel accommodation. Their fine example has become the bench mark for snowmobiling tourism across Ontario.

The Haliburton region has a high ratio of on-site lodging, restaurants, and services, per kilometer of trail. The trails are 2 and 3 meters (6 and 10 feet) wide, and well marked, with more than 8,000 colored arrows and over 250 destination markers.

The terrain is hilly, not mountainous, a county of hundreds of lakes. With the assistance of a local guide, you can ride an endless chain of lakes and portages.

Highlights of the area's 740-kilometer (450-mile) system include the 32-kilometer (20-mile) run between the towns of Kinmount and Haliburton on the abandoned CNR track. From high trestle bridges, sledders view the vistas of the Burnt River.

The Anson Mountain Trail in the southern region is a fine example of stark wilderness. At the northeast corner of the county, on the way to the village of Whitney, is the only legal access by snowmobile through Algonquin Park. This is part of the Trans-Ontario Provincial trail, the major east-west thoroughfare between Georgian Bay and Quebec. The 80-kilometer (50-mile) ride is one of the most exhilarating.

The Haliburton Forest and Wildlife Reserve in the Northern Highlands area is North America's only private snowmobile park. There are 300 kilometers (186 miles) of groomed trails, divided into smooth, dry land, double track trails and picturesque, single track bush trails. The base lodge is well-equipped with food and lodging, snowmobile rentals and services, and plenty of parking. There are five shelter cabins en route.

A separate pass required for these private trails gives sledders a chance to tour Wildcat Lake and examine the gorge.

HALIBURTON FOREST AND WILDLIFE RESERVE

R.R. #1,
Haliburton, Ont. K0M IS0
TEL 705-754-2198
FAX 705-754-1179
800-267-4482

DRIVE County Road 7, north of West Guilford.

HALIBURTON HIGHLANDS CHAMBER OF COMMERCE

P.O. Box 147,
Minden, Ont. K0M 2K0
TEL 705-286-1760
FAX 705-286-6016
800-461-7677

WEST PARRY SOUND

West Parry Sound is the "hot spot" of snowmobiling in the province. The 1,003-kilometer (623-mile) trail system extends from the French River in the north to the Moon River in the south and from the shores of Georgian Bay east to the Magnetawan River. It's been identified as the highest demand area of snowmobiling in Ontario and is an important link in the Trans-Ontario Provincial system.

The region's nine clubs, represented by the West Parry Sound Snowsport Association, maintain these scenic trails whose wilderness beauty is unrivalled anywhere in the province.

The famous Seguin Trail is considered the busiest trail in Ontario. Approximately 61 kilometers

(38 miles) in length, it stretches from Foley Township just west of Highway 69, through Christie and Monteith Townships to the eastern border of McMurrich Township. A 10- to 12-hour run, portions of the trail were once a railway bed of considerable historic significance. In 1889, Sir Wilfrid Laurier declared it the most important railway built to date, next to the CPR. The west terminal at Depot Harbour was the strategic link between Chicago, Milwaukee, Duluth and Thunder Bay and the American and Canadian eastern seaboards.

Evidence of the original rail line are obvious, with small rock cuts along the trail and extensive areas of filling. There are also remnants of bridges at numerous water crossings. The trail varies from flat to rolling. It passes through forested, wetland, and lake topography. Thousands use it on a daily basis.

PARRY SOUND AREA CHAMBER OF COMMERCE

70 Church St.,
Parry Sound, Ont. P2Z IY9
TEL 705-746-4213
FAX 705-746-6537
800-461-4261

ALGOMA COUNTRY

In Algoma Country, the snow arrives early and stays late and the annual snowfall is high, with some areas receiving as much as 5 meters (15 feet) annually. This is the heart of northern Ontario between Sault Ste. Marie and Sudbury. Eleven clubs maintain a network of more than 2,000 kilometers (1200 miles) of breathtaking, marked wilderness. The terrain reaches spectacular heights, overlooking rolling hills and hundreds of remote lakes, excellent for ice-fishing.

The North Shore Trail System is internationally known and attracts sledders from the USA. It's a 400-kilometer (248-mile) corridor along the north shore of Lake Huron, connecting Sault Ste. Marie to Sudbury. The lake provides fast, hard riding and there's plenty of powder snow on a vast network of circular routes.

The ride across frozen Lake Huron to St. Joseph Island, Ontario, or Drummond Island, Michigan, can be an eerie, but exciting ride on the ice. Tree lines connect the North Shore Trail with the Islands. Arrival and departure in American territory is reported to the American customs by telephone. St. Joseph's Island offers a forested playground itself.

The eight-hour ride between Sault Ste. Marie and Wawa is among the most beautiful, a portion of which follows the Montreal River. This is an area of tremendous hills, mountains, and frozen lakes. Much of the landscape is untouched wilderness, so a guide is highly recommended.

ALGOMA KINNIWABI TRAVEL ASSOCIATION

553 Queen St. East,
Suite 1,
Sault Ste. Marie, Ont. P6A 2A3

SAULT STE. MARIE CHAMBER OF COMMERCE

360 Great Northern Rd.,
Sault Ste. Marie, Ont. P6B 4Z7
TEL 705-949-7152
FAX 705-759-8166

ALGOMA COUNTRY SNOWLINE

800-263-ALGOMA (2546)

GREY BRUCE COUNTRY

There are roughly 850 kilometers (528 miles) of double trails and 150 kilometers (93 miles) of single trails groomed by the Grey-Bruce Snowmobile Trails group. The region stretches westward from Thornbury and Meaford to Southampton and runs all the way north to Tobermory. This is a major up-and-coming snowmobile area. Extensive work has been put into the system in the last five or six years.

The trails follow old rail beds and unused road allowances, with challenging cliffs and a changing topography of cedar and hardwood forests, swamps, and farms. The trails do not cross any lakes, but there are well-constructed bridges over a number of rivers and streams.

The 150-kilometer (93-mile) trek from Wiarton to Tobermory and back reflects all the mystique of the Bruce Peninsula.

NORTH WESTERN ONTARIO

The most rapidly developing area of snowmobiling is northwestern Ontario, under the jurisdiction of the North Western Ontario Snowmobiling Trails Association (NWOSTA). Ten clubs groom an area of 2,500 kilometers (1,550 miles), trails which are being expanded thanks to funds from Sno-Trac. There are two regions, one from Shabaqua Corners to the Manitoba border, and the other from Shabaqua Corners to the Manitouwadge and Marathon area.

The NWOSTA trails are the only ones in the system located on the Canadian Shield. Riders experience frozen lakes and spectacular forests without the heavy traffic of other locales.

Among the most unique experiences is the ride from Ft. Francis to the White Otter Castle, built by Ontario pioneer, Jimmy McOuat (pronounced McKewitt), a man of great mystery and legend. The Castle is accessible only by snowmobile, or in the milder months by boat or by plane.

The I-500, the world's largest snowmobile race, begins in Thunder Bay and is completed near Duluth, Minnesota. it's an annual event with more than 300 entrants. Snowmobile manufacturers consider it the most important race of the season.

NWOSTA,

P.O. Box 333,
Fort Frances, Ont. P9A 3M5
TEL 807-854-2273

Stokely Creek Cross-country Skiing

At the eastern end of Lake Superior, on the Goulais River, Stokely Creek is considered the best cross country skiing this side of the Rockies. It has an international reputation as one of the finest cross country ski areas in North America.

The area receives about 508 centimeters (200 inches) of snowfall a year with skiable conditions from November until April. Here, Superior is Mother Nature's perfect snow machine. Prevailing westerlies pick up moisture across Batchawana Bay, and day after day, dump it on the area, under the 153 meter (500 foot) peaks of King Mountain.

Americans Chuck Peterson and his brother Harry began skiing the area in 1965, when the snow conditions were poor in northern Michigan. They first came to the locale with a Native guide, Joe Cadran, who had never seen skis before. The Peterson brothers continued to come to the area, using the Algoma Central Railway as a jumping-off point. The idea of forming a club became a reality in 1977 with principle founders Chuck Peterson, Harriet Black, and Elspeth and Hakon Lien, two Norwegian-Canadians. Chuck Peterson, by then retired, planned and developed the area and Hakon Lien, skilled in laying out trails, became the first president of the Stokely Creek Club.

The trail system is over 120 kilometers (75 miles) long, groomed by state-of-the-art machines, for skating, diagonal stride skiing and back country skiing. Most of it is double-tracked and maintained daily. The trails were built up over the years by volunteer members of the non-profit Stokely Creek Club, whose membership is made up of an equal number of Americans and Canadians.

There is unlimited back country and telemark terrain. This is Algoma territory: rolling hills through dense forest and a spectacular mix of lakes, rivers, ponds, and waterfalls. There are over 610 meters (2,000 feet) of elevation change to challenge every level of ability.

Stokely Creek Lodge was built the same year the area was founded, designed specifically as a cross-country ski resort. The main, Nordic-style lodge, is complete with saunas and fireplaces, built in the middle of a vast, protected hardwood bush known as the Algoma Highlands Conservancy. Chalets for parties of four or more have been added over the years. In all, between 50 and 60 guests can be accommodated. Cars are parked about a third of a mile away and guests usually ski in with their luggage brought in by snow machine.

European cuisine and hardy breakfast buffets are the order of the day with chef Phyliss Burrell-Elyk who has been with the lodge for over 12 years. (She's also written a cookbook that's been popular with the guests). There's bed-and-breakfast facilities year-round and, with the completion of the newest chalet and a dining room addition, Stokely Creek Lodge will be open all year, to service Eco Tours along the picturesque eastern shore of Lake Superior.

The Ski Touring Center is host to a number of races and loppets throughout the ski season, including the Stokely Open which is a USA/Canada Challenge Cup event. None is quite as remarkable or unique as the Wabas Loppet, which attracts between 300 and 400 participants each year. Held since 1979, in the last weekend of March, this is a non-competitive event in the classic tradition, but it requires the skill and endurance of an experienced skier.

By definition, loppet means "long trip" in Norwegian. Skiers of the Wabas board a chartered train of the Algoma Central Rail line out of Sault Ste. Marie and travel an hour north to the original lumbering village of Wabas. From the train they ski a course through woods, over two lakes and several beaver ponds, to a base camp at Shepard Lake, for tea and oranges. From Shepard Lake, the course is on groomed trails and leads to Norm Bourgeois' cabin at Bone Lake. This 27-kilometer (17-mile) run crosses no roads and presents a variety of waxing conditions from corn snow (Klister) to powder (blue wax). Racers finish the course in two hours.

For more leisurely skiers, it will be a 5- to 6-hour trip. Skiers are rewarded at Norm's cabin with refreshments and after a ski back to the lodge, there's a festive barbecue.

STOKELY CREEK LODGE

R.R. #1,
Goulais River, Ont. P0S 1E0
TEL 705-649-3421
FAX 705-649-3429

STOKELY CREEK SKI TOURING CENTER

P.O. Box 507,
Sault Ste. Marie, MI 49783
DRIVE from Sault Ste. Marie on Highway 17 north 32 kilometers (20 miles) to Mahler Road. Turn right; go one block to Pickard Road. Turn left and follow Stokely signs, about 3 kilometers (2 miles) to the parking lot.

Stuffed Pork Chops with Cognac Cream

from *Favorite Recipes from Stokely Creek Lodge*, by Phyliss Burrell-Elyk

INGREDIENTS
6 pork chops (2.54 cm (1") thick, trimmed of fat and a pocket cut in each one to receive the stuffing)
250 ml (1 cup) flour
5 ml (1 tsp) salt
1 ml (1/4 tsp) pepper
175 ml (3/4 cup) oil
STUFFING
125 ml (1/2 cup) onion, finely chopped
250 ml (1 cup) mushrooms, chopped
250 ml (1 cup) bread crumbs
2 ml (1/2 tsp) salt
2 cloves garlic, finely chopped
5 ml (1 tsp) dried marjoram
125 ml (1/2 cup) warm water
50 ml (1/4 cup) oil
125 ml (1/2 cup) cognac
50 ml (1/4 cup) cream

- Make the stuffing by placing 50 ml (1/4 cup) of oil in a skillet over medium heat. Sauté the onion and mushroom for 3 or 4 minutes, add the garlic, 2 ml (1/2 tsp)

salt and bread crumbs. Remove from heat and stir in warm water. Place stuffing into pockets in the chops.

- In a bowl, mix flour, salt, and pepper. Roll the chops in the flour mixture and brown in 175 ml (3/4 cup) oil in a skillet over medium heat. Transfer to a baking pan or casserole dish. Flame the cognac and pour over the chops, along with pan juices. Bake 1 hour at 190 C (375 F). Serve with cream poured over all.

ONTARIO TRIVIA

TORONTONIAN Don Munro Sr. was out of work during the Depression. To entertain his three children, he created the first table hockey game, using common household items. The first set had a 4-man team of wooden figures painted red and green. He patented his invention in 1932 and decided to market it himself. He called on the T. Eaton Co. where the game sold so quickly that his entire family became involved in making the sets: Mrs. Munro crocheted the tiny hockey nets while the children helped wire and paint the sets. Improved versions evolved along with the company, Munro Games Ltd.

TORONTO flew the world's first airmail on board "Jetliner," a locally designed aircraft that flew from Malton Airport to New York in half the usual time which was 2 hours. The flight took place August 10, 1949.

TORONTO'S Norman Breakey invented the paint roller in 1940. He was unable to afford a patent. The idea was made commercially viable by others.

Norm Bourgeois' Cabin

"If you want to meet good people, you meet them in the bush." Norm Bourgeois.

On maps of the Stokely Creek Ski Touring Area, under "land marks and points of interest" the initials "NB" stand for Norm Bourgeois' Cabin. The camp overlooking Bone Lake on an acre of Crown land purchased in 1950, is 10 kilometers (6 miles) from the nearest road. It isn't officially part of Stokely Creek's ski trails, which have only been extended to Bone Lake in the last 7 years, but skiing to Norm's has become an integral part of the Stokely experience, and for many it's the highlight of their cross-country trek.

The sign on the cross-country trail near Norm's encampment says it all: "Welcome." No-one is ever quite prepared for the extent of Norm's hospitality. On a typical winter's day, late in the afternoon, there's standing room only as skiers crowd the part-time premises of the 78-year-old, retired iron worker. They come to dry out their mitts on his woodstove, drink the tea he always has brewing, eat his cookies, sign his guest book which numbers nearly 1,000 names every year, and to talk to Norm.

This gregarious man delights the throng with stories of building his cabin, carrying materials in on his back, including the 100-kilogram (220-pound) woodstove. There are stories of his army days in World War II, how he trained for the CNE's swimming marathon in 1947 by towing a canoe around Bone Lake, and how he came to Sault Ste. Marie on the flip of a coin and helped build the International Bridge.

The cabin is a clutter of bric-a-brac and memorabilia, each one leading to another story. Visitors have stories of their own. Some say that they've visited Norm's 28 times in a year, others comment they've skied everywhere, but there's only one Norm's.

ONTARIO TRIVIA

VERMILION BAY greets visitors with a totem pole carved by Shaman Chief Kitpou of British Columbia. The 15 meter (50 foot) totem pole stands at the junction of Highways 17 and 105.

WAWA's landmark sculpture, the Wawa Goose, is the largest of its kind and known throughout the world. The steel statue of a Canada goose is 9 meters (28 feet) high, 7 meters (22 feet) from tail to beak, with a wingspan of 6 meters (19 feet). It weighs over two tons.

WELLAND is the Rose City of Ontario and hosts a two week Rose Festival in early June.

WHITBY is known as the Home of the Marigold.

Ice Climbing

The cliff faces of Orient Bay Canyon, the Pijitaw-abik Palisades, are a few kilometers from Orient Bay, a southern elongation of Lake Nipigon. In summer, a hundred or more waterfalls cascade over the Palisades where glacial waters once flowed to Lake Superior. In winter, this frozen extravaganza of ice turns into North America's number one ice climbing "hot" (cold) spot.

In Canada, ice climbing is popular in the Rockies, the Laurentians, and the Muskokas. Orient Bay, a thousand miles from any mountain range in the heart of North America, has an almost alpine atmosphere. Not only does it offer the greatest number and variety of climbs, it's easily accessible. While climbers refer to the climbing sites near Nipigon as Orient Bay, there are actually three distinct regions. Orient Bay itself is one kilometer east of Nipigon, Kama Bay is further east, about 22.5 kilometers (14 miles), and Ice Station Superior is on the shores of Lake Superior. Together, they offer about 125 climbs. This is also the locale of Ice Fest, the only ice climbing festival in North America.

Much of it has to do with the efforts and enthusiasm for the sport of just one man, Shaun Parent. The 37-year-old geologist is an experienced mountaineer with a wealth of climbs taken in the Canadian and American Rockies, the Peruvian Andes, Oman, Nepal, Thailand, and India.

Parent began ice climbing in earnest when he and fellow climber, Paul Dedi, "discovered" the Orient Bay Canyon in 1981. Parent published a climber's guide to the area in 1983 which attracted people to the Palisades from southern Ontario,

Manitoba, Minnesota, Michigan, Illinois, and Wisconsin. In 1988 he founded Alpamayo Exploration and Adventure Services which offers instruction in the sport at all levels of experience from non-climbers to advanced. Today people come from all over Canada, Europe, and the USA just to climb with Parent. He's also the organizer of the Ice Fest.

Why does anyone ice climb, given that one of the prerequisites is being outdoors in sub-zero weather that assures the waterfalls stay frozen? This activity appeals to anyone who loves the challenge of ascending even a modest "Grade 1" ice cliff. (There are five grades for rating ice cliffs at Orient Bay, based on the New England Ice rating scheme.) Some are attracted by the ice, its colors and shifting shapes, which change like an ever-evolving sculpture and where no two frozen cascades are the same. Others like the freedom, the ability to go anywhere on ice not obstructed, as rock climbing can be, by trees.

This is a sport for purists. Unlike rock climbing, which has been known to scar rock faces and damage fragile ecosystems, ice climbing isn't a threat to the environment. Come spring, there's no evidence the climber was even there.

This isn't a sport for thrill seekers in that ice climbing is an exercise in safety measures. Even the most inhibited first-time climbers find an overwhelming exhilaration in accomplishing even the shortest of ascents.

Parent starts beginners a few feet above ground, a belay or safety rope extending from their safety harness to an anchor at the top of the climb. The preliminary exercise is a lesson in balance, using leg strength with the assistance of crampons, a set of double rows of spike-like teeth fitted onto the boots. Next the climbers are introduced to the carabiners, ice axes held in each hand that serve as handholds. In an emergency, one carabiner if properly secured in the ice face can support the entire weight of a climber. Amateurs must learn to rely more on their leg strength than to pull up with their arms, or they risk becoming tired very quickly. With carabiners in hand, a climb proceeds up the frozen cliff. Parent adjacent on the ice face, fine tunes even the most awkward technique.

Alpamayo Explorations, named for a mountain Parent climbed in 1988, runs rock and ice climbing courses out of Thunder Bay. There are a number of packages for a full day or a week of climbing and clinics for groups or private lessons. Parent directs climbs in the Agawa Canyon and Montreal River areas in addition to Orient Bay.

Climbers will want to purchase Parent's indispensable handbook, *Orient Bay Ice Climber's Guide*, available from the author. It gives a geological history of the area and the name — yes, each ice face has a name — grade, height, and mile-marker location of each climb.

ALPAMAYO EXPLORATION AND ADVENTURE SERVICES LTD.

P.O. Box 2204,
Thunder Bay, Ont. P7B 5E8
TEL 807-344-9636

DRIVE to Orient Bay from Nipigon, east to Highway 11. Mileage points of climbs begin at Mile "0 marker, a black-on-red sign on a post, 25 kilometers (15 miles) north of the intersection of Highways 11 and 17, on the right (east) side of the road.

ICE FEST

Ice Fest has been held since 1986 and attracts several thousand people to the Orient Bay area during four days in March. There are opportunities to learn to ice climb, swap equipment, compete in climbing competitions, attend seminars and slide presentations, and socialize with other climbers.

TEL 800-667-8386

A

39